Hess

Since 1996, Bloomberg Press has published books for financial professionals, as well as books of general interest in investing, economics, current affairs, and policy affecting investors and business people. Titles are written by well-known practitioners, BLOOMBERG NEWS reporters and columnists, and other leading authorities and journalists. Bloomberg Press books have been translated into more than 20 languages.

For a list of available titles, please visit our Web site at www.wiley.com/go/bloombergpress.

Hess

The Last Oil Baron

Tina Davis
Jessica Resnick-Ault

WILEY | **Bloomberg**
PRESS

Library of Congress Cataloging-in-Publication Data:

Names: Davis, Tina, 1974– | Resnick-Ault, Jessica, 1980–
Title: Hess : the last oil baron / Tina Davis, Jessica Resnick-Ault.
Description: Hoboken, New Jersey : John Wiley & Sons, Inc., [2016] | Series:
    Bloomberg Press | Includes bibliographical references and index.
Identifiers: LCCN 2015031845 | ISBN 978-1-118-92344-3 (cloth);
ISBN 978-1-118-92346-7 (ePDF); ISBN 978-1-118-92345-0 (ePub)
Subjects: LCSH: Hess, Leon, 1914-1999. | Businessmen—United
    States—Biography. | Petroleum industry and trade—United States.
Classification: LCC HD9570.H47 D39 2016 | DDC 338.7/6655092—dc23 LC record
available at http://lccn.loc.gov/2015031845

Printed in the United States of America
10 9 8 7 6 5 4 3 2 1

FSC
www.fsc.org

MIX
Paper from
responsible sources
FSC® C101537

Contents

Preface

A re there any questions?"

The narrow conference room on the first floor of Hess Corporation's 29-story downtown Houston office high-rise was quiet. About 100 people were gathered to see the denouement of a four-month battle between the oil company's board and management and a hedge fund agitating for change.

Chief Executive Officer John B. Hess, son of company founder Leon Hess, was facing shareholders in public for the first time since the fund run by Wall Street activist Paul Singer had announced it had acquired a sizable stake in the company and was seeking to alter its course, demanding it sweep out old board members, sell assets, and refocus its corporate strategy. John, newly stripped of his role as chairman, had agreed hours before to allow the dissident shareholder to appoint three nominees to the board after four months of acrimony capped by negotiations that stretched into the early morning. There were no questions.

Thirty-eight minutes into a shareholder meeting that had been preceded by an increasingly nasty series of letters, battling websites, and name-calling between the hedge fund and the company, it was over.

Faced with the biggest challenge to his family's leadership since the company was founded in 1933, John Hess had blinked.

That May morning in Houston, shareholders rode the escalator into the Hess conference room. The skyscraper, with more than 800,000 square feet of office space, gleams in the heart of Houston's booming energy corridor. Shortly after it opened in 2010, as if in homage to its fossil-fuel–loving largest tenant, wind turbine parts fell off the building. The rooftop wind turbines were quietly removed.

Pieces were falling from the Hess empire, too, and with little fanfare, nine board members were removed to make way for the new nominees and the new chairman. The CEO who took over four years before his father's death had lost some grip on the company whose expansion he had been witnessing firsthand for all of his 59 years.

The company had managed to continue being operated as a family venture through 80 years, large mergers, multiple missteps, and many triumphs. The brand that Leon Hess built from a single delivery truck in the Great Depression to an ubiquitous green-and-white logo along East Coast roadways, was no longer being run exclusively by the family and a board full of friends.

What defined the company without the Hess family in full control? Just like wind turbines that were removed from atop the Houston office one day, would anyone notice the absence of a Hess at Hess?

Chapter 1

Hess Family

Leon Hess's family story is in many ways a well-worn tale of the American dream: an Eastern European Jewish immigrant comes to the United States, followed by other relatives, starts businesses to try to make a living, and leaves much of the old world behind. The family faced hardships and mishaps common from immigration in the early 1900s, including names distorted by officials who didn't speak their language, housing in crowded immigrant neighborhoods, an inability to use skills from the old country, and bankruptcy. In the second generation, though, the story takes a wild departure: filled with a unique mix of Depression-era creativity, World War II logistical knowledge, and inspiration from a powerful mentor, the youngest son would reimagine his father's failed business and establish himself as one of the richest men in the country.

In the first decade of the 1900s, immigrant families—particularly Jewish ones—flooded New York and New Jersey, overflowing available houses, apartments, and tenements from the Lower East Side to the Jersey Shore and beyond. They joined the garment industry or started small businesses as tailors, milliners, and peddlers.

The Hess family's story is in many ways indistinguishable from dozens of others: Mores Hess, a kosher butcher, came from Lithuania with little in 1904—a year that brought more than 1 million people to the United States. Like Mores, three quarters of all immigrants were bound for the New York area, while others disembarked at other large East Coast ports: Boston, Baltimore, and Philadelphia.[1] His ship left Europe from Bremen, a popular departure point on Germany's northern coast, and was called the S.S. *Kaiser Wilhelm der Grosse*, named for the first emperor to rule a united Germany. The other passengers were mostly men, largely ranging in age from 27 to 56. Many were German, but the ship also carried Russians, Hungarians, and people of other nationalities. They were merchants and workers, but also an actor and a jurist. The ship's manifest appears slapdash, with lots of shorthand and empty columns, like many others of its time, a product of the sheer quantity of emigrant paperwork that faced European shipping lines. The manifest suggests that Mores carried over $50, and had never been in the United States before this passage. The exact reasons for his departure were not recorded, but can be imagined as the same ones that propelled many to leave Lithuania: religious freedom, the prospect of education for his children, and economic betterment. The wave of immigration from Lithuania to the United States had many drivers, and began before Mores headed to Bremen. The 1861 abolition of serfdom had increased the number of free people, who were able to leave the country at the same time, and the rising availability of railroads and other transit made it easier for Lithuanians to leave. A depressed farm economy and increased control from Russia also pushed immigrants out.

Two-thirds of the 1904 immigrants were male, like Mores, and 145,000 came from the Russian Empire, which then included Lithuania and Finland. Russia produced the largest group of immigrants behind Austro-Hungary and Italy. Half of those who came in 1904 had less than $50 to their name. Of the more than 18,000 Lithuanian immigrants, Mores was one of the relatively prosperous ones—only 531 carried more than $50. Only 18 of the Lithuanians had ever visited the United States before moving. Three quarters of the 1904 immigrants could read and write, though few spoke English. Together, the 1904 arrivals brought $25 million to the United States, but Jewish immigrants—noted in records of the time as "the Hebrews"—accounted for only $2.6 million of that inflow, whereas they made up far more than 10 percent of the émigrés. Those arriving in the United States were mostly young—under 45—and considered to be in their prime for working and contributing to the economy.[2] They were screened at each point of the journey. Control stations had been set up in Germany's ports, aimed at preventing ill voyagers from bringing diseases like cholera, for which immigrants were blamed for an outbreak in the late 1800s. Steamship companies then reviewed the passengers' health again before boarding. Weeks later, they would be examined upon arrival in the United States, where centers like the immigration checkpoint at Ellis Island had been established to screen them. A handful were turned back for insanity, idiocy, or contagious disease. There was a pervasive skepticism about the potential ill effects of the immigration boom, so people were also turned back for being anarchists, paupers, or entering illegally. Still, the bulk of the immigrants were admitted to the United States, where a booming garment industry and other factories were ready to employ them.

The U.S. government did not expect the influx to boost the economy by much, though, as most immigrants continued to send earnings home. Like many others who arrived, Mores arrived in the United States alone and would have to work for the funds to bring in the family he had left behind in Lithuania. The manifest from the ship doesn't indicate whether he had relatives here with whom he planned to stay, or where he planned to live.

Mores was joined the next year by his wife, Ethel,[3] and toddler son, Henry. The immigration boom was continuing, with 10,000 people a day admitted to New York during a particularly busy season for immigration. Early records of the Hess family after its arrival are sketchy, with different spellings of the family's name and birthdates for Mores[4] on federal census documents suggesting that he could have been anywhere in his 20s or 30s at the time of his move. His family believed he was 34 when he arrived, which is consistent with his ship's manifest.[5]

A couple of years after her arrival, Ethel gave birth to their first daughter, Rebecca, who was born in Pennsylvania in 1907. The family then moved to New Jersey, where Mores started a fruit store in Asbury Park, and a second son, Harry, was born in 1909.

The 1910 census paints a sparse picture of their life: they rented a home on Springwood Avenue, a few doors down from where Mores's fruit store was located. The couple were listed as speaking Russian at home, and Mores could read, while Ethel could not. Ethel stayed at home caring for their three children while Mores worked. The census suggests that Ethel had also lost a child during the year between Rebecca's birth and Henry's, in an era where childbirth was risky for both mother and infant.

But the census document refers to Ethel and Mores as the Mayerowitz family, and calls their next-door neighbors Lewis and Mary Hess—they, too, were Russian grocers, with a daughter called Rebecca. It is possible that the census taker confused the names of the residents of the block. There are other possible explanations: a language barrier may have caused confusion between a census taker and two related families, or Mores may have been known in some circles as Mores Mayerowitz, and had changed his name to Hess to navigate life in the new country more easily, using it on the ship's manifest and his daughter's birth certificate. While the census leaves lots of room for conjecture and interpretation, city directories, photos, and property records make it clear that Mores and Ethel became established as the Hess family of Asbury Park. If Mores chose his family name, it was his fourth child who would go on to make it famous.

On March 14, 1914, Leon was born to Mores and Ethel in Asbury Park. On the day of his birth, 600 girls working in a Newark garment factory narrowly escaped a fire—poor working conditions had been highlighted by a 1911 fire at the Triangle Shirtwaist factory in New York that killed 145 workers. Standard Oil's John Rockefeller was said to plan a $50 million donation with his newfound wealth. The British ocean liner *Lusitania*, one of the largest of the time, worked to set a new record for a speedy crossing of the Atlantic, a year before it would be sunk by the Germans during World War I.

Leon's first few years were spent in Asbury Park on the shore, where his father continued to work as a produce man and, eventually, as a butcher. While many immigrants in the New York area coped with cramped quarters and extended families lived in two-room tenements, Mores was successful in improving the accommodations for his family, buying a house by 1920 and arranging for all of his children to go to school, at a time when many others were forced to work from a young age.

On the eve of World War I, the United States still had an optimistic outlook, with President Woodrow Wilson expecting an economic revival in 1914, easing worries of an early depression.[6] On a more local level, Mores's family likely had a positive outlook, too—10 years after their arrival in the United States, they had their own home and a profitable business.

The family survived traumas both local and international—the Hesses were insulated from a 1917 fire, which started in the swimming center on the boardwalk on Asbury Park's Ocean Avenue and swept through the town, fueled by 60-mile-an-hour sea gales. The damage encompassed a dozen blocks, and major hotels and boardinghouses were flattened, some by the flames and others by dynamite, as firefighters blasted homes to contain the blaze.

A 1918 outbreak of Spanish influenza infected more than a quarter of the U.S. population and killed half a million people, particularly in immigrant neighborhoods where residents were crammed especially close together. Just south of Asbury Park, 3,000 people were diagnosed in the town of Camden in a single 24-hour period in September.

Mores's family may have been infected, but there was no reported mortality from the epidemic. While the family was by no means rich, they had better living conditions—and possibly better luck—than some of their peers. Mores was seen as strong-minded, and thought highly of his own abilities, to a point at which family members said he acted like he knew more than the rabbis of Asbury Park.[7] His confidence was reflected in the many business ventures he would try his hand at after settling in New Jersey.

By 1920, his father, Joseph, a widower who had immigrated around the turn of the century, lived with them and worked as a butcher. But even as they became more involved in Asbury Park, which had a large Jewish population, in the wider world many viewed the family as outsiders: a 1920 census refers to their language merely as "Jewish." One longtime friend said the family spoke Yiddish at home.

Mores became a naturalized citizen along with his wife, father, and eldest son, and registered with the Army as America faced World War I, but remained at home. Amid the hubbub of Asbury Park, Mores began a nondescript coal distribution business along the Jersey Shore, an effort that would be transformed into something incredible by his youngest son. Mores continued to work through the war, opening his first butchery down the street from where his father had worked. His children were taught in the public school system of Asbury Park, with life continuing normally in their increasingly crowded neighborhood, where houses and store fronts were being built up.

The Hesses now resided on Asbury Avenue, which was a haven for immigrants. By 1920, Russian and Swedish were both spoken on the 1100 block, where the Hesses lived. Their stone house, one down from the corner, stood a proud three stories tall with a welcoming porch.

Mores's business expanded as he opened two stores and built another house on Asbury Avenue, delving into real estate. While Mores dabbled in many things but never had great success at any of them, he had strong entrepreneurial energy, trying his hand at produce, then the butchery, real estate, and ultimately coal. By 1926, Mores had moved completely into the coal industry, serving the city's growing needs. Though somewhat erratic, Mores's business endeavors likely set the tone for hard work and self-reliance for his sons and daughter.

Meanwhile, Asbury Park was changing. Cars were becoming popular, bringing the wealthy from the cities to the summertime resort, as the New York and Long Branch railroads continued to cart large crowds from New York City and Philadelphia. The Hess family grew up as the area was in flux, with 13 miles of streets being paved, encompassing most of the city's major intersections. The crowds—which during the summer could reach 200,000 or more—flocked to the beach and to other entertainments, including local carousel rides and amusement parks. Even as they were buoyed by the incoming tourism, residents complained that the growing fleet of vehicles eroded the gravel roads when it rained and brought traffic accidents. Drains were placed around town so that gravel roads could be crossed in heavy rain. Growing traffic also demanded a paid fire department and a police department with a special traffic squad. Just blocks from the Hesses' home, the first "Hertz you-drive-it" opened, the birthplace of the eventual car rental giant and a symbol of the car's growing popularity. By 1928, the stultifying traffic congestion required Monmouth County to begin construction of a new highway to avoid a bottleneck in the center of Asbury Park.[8]

The crowds were not looking only for amusement park rides. On the glamorous beachfront, which had been redeveloped since the damaging 1917 fire, the nine-story Spanish-style residential Hotel Santander was built in 1928, next door to the estate of city founder James Bradley, a manufacturing magnate. Screen actress Myrna Loy took up residence in the penthouse, while Eleanor Roosevelt was rumored to have rented a floor.

The stock market crash of 1929 didn't immediately bring the good times to an end for the beach town. While Wall Street faced panic and a selling off of assets 50 miles to the north, Asbury Park saw itself as a still-prosperous seaside retreat. The town was booming, with three local banks seeing their holdings rise to six times their value by 1931. To some degree, Asbury Park and its residents were initially insulated from the country's economic panic.

"A summer week-end in the city finds upwards of 100,000 motor cars within a square mile, a problem with which other cities much larger than this would not desire to contend," said a guide published in 1931, praising the city's advances. Municipal garbage collection was starting to cut down on dumping in the city, with ten trucks carrying trash to an incinerator plant. Phones were becoming popular, with 4,130 private lines and 7,120 pay stations in the city by 1931. Gas lines were laid beneath the city, with the gas customers rising 61 percent from 1930 to 1931. Despite the city founder's preference for gas lights, the Eastern New Jersey Power Company increased electrical output and built an 11-story office building, the Jersey coast's tallest building.

■ ■ ■

As Asbury Park's tourism boomed, Henry Hess, Mores's oldest son, became a manager at Shore Amusements. Eleven years older than Leon, Henry was the first out of the house as Leon graduated from high school.[9] The Great Depression would eventually reach the family. Leon would discuss going to the shore in the summer during low tide to dig up clams to sell to local restaurants and bars. The boys were lucky to make 50 or 75 cents a day from the digs. But it was another example of the family's work ethic and the hardships they endured. While tourists all around them enjoyed the beach and holiday fun, the Hesses found themselves struggling to make ends meet in the 1930s. As his high school years were drawing to a close, Leon was brought in to help with yet another of his father's fledgling businesses. The family was unable to send the youngest son to college, although the three oldest children had completed school. Mores went bankrupt during the Depression, and Leon hauled coal to families poorer than their own.[10]

8

HESS

· The hard labor at the coal yard helped shape Leon's ethic of working long hours as he made deliveries through the weekends. "I worked for my father in a coal yard delivering coal," Leon recalled in a deposition five decades later. He would later joke in a rare interview that he got into oil because he was "basically lazy" and didn't want to carry around 100-pound bags of coal,[11] which were used for heat and power in the area.

Disheartened by the coal business, where the returns for hauling 100-pound bags were slim, Leon made a critical switch to delivering fuel oil. He saw an opportunity and bet on oil instead of coal as the more economical way to get energy. He would find buyers for the residual oil that refiners didn't want. So, in his own words, he started a "little oil company" in 1933, when he was just 19 years old.

"I bought a secondhand truck, an oil truck, for $350, in Asbury Park, New Jersey, and started a heating oil company and built it up over a period of years," he said, reflecting on his early days in business during a 1986 deposition. Some other accounts peg the truck at even more of a steal—according to some, he bought the truck in North Carolina, for just $24.60. Whether it cost just $25 or more than 10 times that, the truck became the most widely recognized hallmark of his business. He would have a miniature version of it in his office, and it would be the first of the Hess toy trucks that would become ubiquitous in some family households. Ninety years later the truck would be fully restored and polished, and stand as a reminder of the past in the lobby of his multibillion-dollar company's headquarters.

Leon had a vision that New Jersey's steel companies, its manufacturers like Johnson & Johnson, and the state's other prominent businesses could use Number 6 fuel oil, a product much like today's residual oil, that others were just dumping. With just a little boiling or light refining, he found, the oil could fetch a premium price. The seven-year-old 615-gallon truck would be used to collect the fuel—which was also known as black oil—from area refiners and repurpose it as a cleaner alternative to coal.

As New Jersey faced the economic depression, Leon was among millions struggling, trying to launch his fledgling fuel delivery business. With his strategy in place for getting residual oil on the cheap to customers, he was able to turn a profit and buy up more trucks.

By 1938, Leon had amassed about 10 trucks and moved the business to Perth Amboy, New Jersey, where he bought a piece of land on the waterfront, purchased some secondhand oil storage tanks, and started an oil storage terminal on the Raritan River.

The Hess family moved from Asbury Park to nearby Loch Arbour, buying a $16,000 house. His sister, Rebecca, then called Betty, worked as a teacher, and Leon and Harry continued to live at home. Henry, the eldest, had moved to New York City, where he worked as an insurance counselor and lived with his wife, Ada, and son, Robert.

As Leon's business empire expanded in Middlesex County, New Jersey, he met David Wilentz, who was becoming a political heavyweight in the region. Leon respected the man greatly, called him governor[12] (an elected position he toyed with running for but never actually achieved). Leon's connection to Wilentz was critical in helping to shape his success. Wilentz would become his friend, adviser, and, ultimately, father-in-law and help support Leon's transformation from "lazy" coal-hauler to oil baron.

■ ■ ■

Against a backdrop of unemployment and breadlines, voters were incensed by headlines insinuating that the Republican-dominated Middlesex County Board of Freeholders, a local governing body, was corrupt and misspending the taxpayers' hard-earned money.

Behind the headlines in local papers was David Wilentz, a 35-year-old Democrat who had taken over a fairly hapless political organization, the Middlesex County Democratic Party. The son of Latvian immigrants who owned a wholesale tobacco business, David had a passion for making the political system more just. The third of six children, David had grown up in Perth Amboy. After finishing high school, he worked for a local newspaper as a copy boy and sports reporter. Commuting at night to New York University, he studied law and was admitted to the bar. He served in World War I as an Army lieutenant. Upon returning from the war, he immersed himself in the world of New Jersey politics and married Lena Goldman, the daughter of Russian immigrants.

In 1929, Wilentz, who was elected the county's Democratic chairman, ordered an audit of the Republican Board of Freeholders' expenditures, which was then reviewed by a grand jury. The grand jury failed to return indictments of any of the politicians.

Still, the whiff of corruption was strong and roiled the dissatisfied public. Wilentz, who at that time was serving as the city attorney of

Perth Amboy, leveraged this dissatisfaction to his party's advantage in the 1929 election. He seized upon a small detail to paint a picture of a political elite that was out of touch with the populace: the free-holders had been giving away engraved fountain pens with their own names on them—an expense that Wilentz made sure was perceived as frivolous.

The fountain pen scandal led his party to victory in the county. This 1929 success was an early building block of a political machine that would last for 50 years, during which only one Republican, Dwight Eisenhower, ever won an election in Middlesex County,[13] where Wilentz anointed local politicians, governors, and even senators.

As a result of Wilentz's efforts for the party, Hudson County Democratic boss Frank "I am the law" Hague recommended him for appointment as attorney general by Governor A. Harry Moore.[14] Moore appointed Wilentz to succeed William Stevens as attorney general in January 1934. In a political system in which the currency was a few words from the right person, the value of Wilentz's network was rising. He and his wife, Lena, and their three children, Robert, Warren, and Norma, moved to a larger house in Perth Amboy. While David's parents had immigrated, and he was just one generation removed from the experience similar to the one Mores Hess had, Lena's family was more established, and together, the Wilentzes developed a comfortable home life.

Upon his appointment as attorney general of New Jersey, he began immediately to make his mark on the state's political landscape. He wielded wide-ranging power, naming lawyers to boards like the state highway commission, as he became a kingmaker in the party, able to boost or halt political careers. Following an investigation into prose-cutorial failings, Wilentz was also appointed to serve as prosecutor of Monmouth County, replacing Jonas Tumen, who was charged with "misdemeanors and nonfeasance."

Just a year into his tenure as attorney general and months into being Monmouth's prosecutor, he was in the courtroom trying his first capital case—the kidnapping of aviator Charles Lindbergh's 20-month-old son from his home in Hopewell Township. The child had been abducted from Lindbergh's home, and posters of the dimpled baby were highly publicized during a 10-week search for the boy. The family paid a huge ransom—$50,000—in exchange for false information on the child's whereabouts. Ultimately, he was found dead in Hopewell Township. A nation that had celebrated Lindbergh as a hero just a few years before was in shock. Wilentz was tapped to try the case, and he would become a celebrity in the process.

An elaborate case with over 100 witnesses and truckloads of evidence, this was the prosecution that would make Wilentz's career. Bronx housepainter and carpenter Bruno Richard Hauptmann stood accused of the 1932 crime, after he was linked to ransom money that Lindbergh had paid. While Hauptmann repeatedly proclaimed his innocence, Wilentz described him as "Public Enemy No. 1, an animal lower than the lowest form." Lindbergh, who became world-famous in 1927 with his solo flight from Long Island to Paris, brought star power to the trial, which garnered national and even international attention, and was called "the Crime of the Century" (an overused term, to be sure, but this was one of the first trials involving both a horrific act and a celebrity in an era of rapt media attention). In a statement in court that was printed in full, spanning two pages of the *New York Times*, Wilentz called for the death penalty for Hauptmann. "For all these months since October 1934, not during one moment has there been anything that has come to the surface of life that has indicated anything but the guilt of this defendant, Bruno Richard Hauptmann, and no one else. Every avenue of evidence, every little thoroughfare that we traveled along, every one leads to the same door: Bruno Richard Hauptmann."

Wilentz gained notice for his aptitude and zealousness in the courtroom. He ultimately won the conviction that sent Hauptmann to the electric chair in 1936. The case was widely examined by legal scholars in the generation that followed, as Hauptmann's widow continued to insist upon his innocence. But Anna Hauptmann's attempts to overturn the verdict after her husband's death—the last of the cases decided by a federal court in Philadelphia just hours before Wilentz died in 1988—were all unsuccessful in reversing the verdict.

Wilentz and his wife, Lena, were celebrities after the trial, with their photos appearing in newspapers all over the country as they traveled. Speculation arose that Wilentz would run for governor, but he insisted he would prefer to stay behind the scenes. New Jersey, he quipped, was not ready for a Jewish governor.

Instead, he was appointed to a second term as attorney general. Even after he left office to establish his own law firm, many people still referred to him as "general." For his party, he was a commanding officer, pulling people aside and telling them to run for office, and discovering untapped political talent in hidden corners.

Beyond his sharp rhetoric, Wilentz had gotten a reputation during the trial for cutting a conspicuous figure, with cameras outside the courtroom capturing his sassafras-colored felt hat. Wilentz stopped nearly daily for a shave and a shoeshine at Sikes Pharmacy in Perth Amboy[15] and demanded that those around him rise to the occasion in their dress as well. When he backed Richard Hughes for governor, he joked that he could get the former judge elected if he bought a blue suit, black shoes, and white shirt. "I told him he had to throw those damned brown shoes away," Wilentz said.[16]

Funded by David's success, the Wilentz family had hired a live-in maid, and now lived in relative comfort on a street that also housed the head of one of New Jersey's chemical companies. In the summer, the family would go to Deal, near Asbury Park, where they had a summer house and would hobnob with others in New Jersey's upper echelon. The family had membership to the Hollywood Golf Club—which was quickly gaining stature and land as the nearby Deal Golf and Country Club faced financial difficulties and was forced to sell its fourth, fifth, and sixth holes to its neighbor in 1910. The club membership included families from New York who worked for Wall Street firms. In 1938, Wilentz relinquished one of his many roles, giving up the state Democratic party chairmanship, but still maintaining his role as attorney general and serving as a critical cog in the party's machine.

David's sons, Warren and Robert, attended Princeton and the University of Virginia, while his daughter, Norma, went to Wellesley. At the time, Norma Wilentz had a reputation for being a very bright young woman, known for being outgoing at the club. She had a circle of summer friends, and a lifestyle that was focused upon making her an ideal wife for a leading doctor or a lawyer, like her father, while her brothers were trained in the law.

■ ■ ■

Leon had already begun expanding his business beyond trucks when he joined the Army in 1942, one of millions of men who signed on to the war effort after Pearl Harbor. David offered to watch over Leon's terminals in his absence, and make sure that they were well cared for.[17]

Wilentz was widely known for his role in counseling politicians and luminaries across the state. He had gone from being an environmental lawyer to becoming a trusted adviser and caretaker of the business for Leon, who was 20 years his junior. Both men loved spending time at the Monmouth Park racetrack, where Leon would often breakfast while the trainers put the horses through their morning workouts. When Leon took an ownership stake in the racetrack, a room was eventually named after Wilentz.

Both shared an attention to detail in their own and employees' dress, at times pushing their own fastidious need for order onto others (Leon more than once gave his executives new socks after noticing their sagging hosiery). Both balanced long hours with significant time spent with family—for Wilentz, the dedication was shown by being home for nightly dinners. Leon was remembered as an available ear for his children and even grandchildren. Both were able to use their political skills to enrich themselves.

But both shared, perhaps more than anything, the ability to talk with anyone, whether it was a Republican foe, a taxicab driver, or a dictator halfway around the world. Through this candor, they were able to connect with those who ultimately helped them leave striking legacies. Both men created webs of connections across New Jersey and, in Leon's case, around the world, which helped them succeed.

Possibly with Wilentz's help, Leon garnered attention from Chase Manhattan Bank. He gave his underwriting business entirely to the firm, run by David Rockefeller. He was exclusive, he later said, because of the effort they put into the relationship. "They're the only ones who ever paid any attention to me," Leon said later. "The rest never took me seriously."[18] The bank loans from Chase helped back Leon's earliest truck purchases as he expanded.

■ ■ ■

While Leon became far better traveled and connected than his own father ever could have imagined, he retained a deep love for New Jersey.

"While his work took him all over the world, the place he loved best and where he always came back was the Jersey Shore. Asbury Park, where he was born, Loch Arbour, where we would drive from Perth Amboy every Sunday to visit his parents, and in the summers, the house on Roosevelt Avenue in Deal, where he could smoke his cigars and barbecue every Sunday night," his daughter Constance said in a 2011 speech upon his posthumous induction into the New Jersey Hall of Fame.

"Dad is now buried in the shadow of the symbol of what he created, the Hess building in Woodbridge, near his refinery and in New Jersey."

While Leon Hess left a deep legacy in New Jersey—with his name across oil terminals, gas stations, and a refinery, the town he hailed from now stands as a shadow of the way it looked when he was growing up. No longer a vacation getaway for elite New Yorkers, the town shows signs of wear, from the carousel on the shore to the house Leon lived in. If Asbury Park is known now, it's primarily for the Stone Pony bar that helped make Bruce Springsteen a music superstar.

The Santander Hotel and other buildings stand covered in scaffolding now, as an effort is under way to renovate the area, parts of which fell into disrepair in the decades that followed the progress of the seashore town in the 1920s and 1930s. The area still shows signs of damage from Superstorm Sandy.

On Asbury Avenue, where Mores Hess first saw his family and businesses grow, it's hard to imagine the decades of hard-won success he found here. Today, some driveways are filled with old mattresses, discarded couches, and other refuse. Windows are blocked with plywood, the results of Sandy, which tore through the area in 2012, and of neglect.

Two houses have been torn down, recalls Josephine Hammary, whose family moved onto the street in 1957. "White Italians and Jews lived here," but the property values sank over the years and those immigrant groups moved out, ceding their houses to rentals and Section 8 tenants who failed to maintain them, she said.

The Hess family sold their house to one of Hammary's relatives, and moved on.

■ ■ ■

Leon stood next to his son, John, at his wedding to Susan Kessler. It was 1984 and the ceremony was in the family's New York apartment. Leon wasn't only the groom's father, he was also his best man, one sign of the close ties that remained between Leon and his only son—a bond that still showed years after his father's death, with a son who has been known to get his Starbucks coffee order as "Leon." He would leave his father's office untouched for a long time after his passing, a living historical record of Leon's last day in the office.

Leon's brother Henry had served as best man for his own son Robert, when Robert married nearly 25 years earlier. The Hesses were a close-knit family—they spent time together not out of obligation but out of general affinity, and they were fiercely loyal to one another. For Leon, his life's ventures were centered on family, whether it was the family business he created, the fatherly approach he brought to the New York Jets football team, or his actual family, who remain intensely protective of his memory and his legacy.

Leon made sure that all the Hesses gathered at least twice a year without fail: once in the spring for Passover, recognizing their Jewish heritage, and in November at Thanksgiving, celebrating the American traditions of football and turkey. While there were other vacations—in the Bahamas in the winter or on the Jersey Shore for summer months to escape sweltering Manhattan, holidays with the in-laws or trips with grandchildren to London—the major Passover seder and Thanksgiving celebration showed the Hesses as a unified whole, generations assembled together.

Through these gatherings, Leon passed along the lessons he had learned from his father-in-law and father to his children, and eventually, grandchildren. He strove to impart a sense of loyalty, the value of hard work, and humility. While Leon managed a company that was growing into a multibillion-dollar enterprise, making him one of America's richest men, he still found it important to bring his family together. He created a family atmosphere at the company, where it was clear to all who worked there you had to be well dressed and clean-shaven to please the boss. That family approach extended to the football team, where Thanksgiving gatherings after practice eventually expanded to include Jets players and staff along with their families. Leon played the role of patriarch across several platforms.

"He was an extraordinary father and role model," Marlene Hess, his second daughter, remembered in her eulogy for her father. "His standards for himself and for our family were high. He couldn't tolerate 'deadbeats' or liars. He was a man of his word, so we had to be, too. He expected the best of himself and also of all of us. He worked hard—[and] so did we. He cared deeply for his fellow man, and instilled that in us, too." The lessons, daughter Constance Hess remembered, were clear: Treasure a good name. Hold your cards close to your chest. Love is unconditional. If you have to talk to the press, make sure that you aren't the story.

Rarely photographed by the press and not quoted in profile pieces, Leon tried not to call attention to himself or to his family, though he would speak about his business. "He worked hard to keep his personal life private," Constance said in a 2011 speech.

Leon combined his father's entrepreneurial spirit, his father-in-law's political savvy, and his own smarts to succeed in a hardscrabble business at a time when many were failing. But perhaps the role he enjoyed most of all was that of father figure, creating new families beyond just his immediate relations.

■ ■ ■

While it was Mores Hess's financial struggles and failing coal business that opened the door to the oil business for Leon, Mores's earlier efforts starting shops in Asbury Park and trying his hand at real estate showed a willingness to try anything. That sense of daring, that willingness to innovate, the vision to see opportunities others had missed or weren't bold enough to exploit—just the sheer chutzpah of believing in yourself enough to risk your livelihood on what you could dream possible— that was something Leon inherited in spades. While other boys might've looked at the many ways Mores tried his hand at business after business and blanched at the risk, Leon was brave enough to pick up the entrepreneurial torch, striking out on his own even in the depths of the Great Depression. Where did he get such confidence? Some who knew both Leon and his son, John, say that John is less of a risk-taker than Leon, perhaps a natural outcome when you are trying to preserve wealth rather than building it.

But Leon was not only an innovator, he was also extremely focused on details and appearances. "The first thing I look at on a tanker is the engine room bilge," he told a reporter for *BusinessWeek* in 1987. "Clean bilges denote good housekeeping." Right from the start, he made sure his trucks were kept clean, and employees learned early that working at a Hess facility meant painting and repainting to make everything look like new, whether it was huge storage tanks or the white curb on the Hess service stations. Leon realized early on that having the cleanest, safest-seeming gas stations was not only aesthetically pleasing, it could also provide a business advantage. As the family car and car trips were becoming more prevalent, and as women began driving more, it could be an easy choice for those looking for quick service and clean bathrooms, giving him a potential leg up on rivals who did not put as much emphasis on appearances.

Mores also instilled family loyalty in his sons—unlike his brothers, Leon turned down a scholarship to college to work for the family business, bringing it back to profitability after his parents' bankruptcy. In turn, Leon made sure that Mores always had a role in his business—his father was employed by Hess Corp. into the 1950s. Even as his father aged, he still wrote checks for the company—which sometimes had pitfalls. One accountant remembers when an elderly Mores signed all of the week's checks on the wrong side, forcing them to all be redone.

All of Mores and Ethel's children went on to successful careers, some of them in New Jersey, some heading elsewhere to try their luck. Henry Hess, the oldest, had two children and moved to Miami Beach, where he worked as a salesman, and then vice president of an insurance company. His son Robert would attend Yale for his undergraduate and doctoral degrees, and became a scholar, specializing in African studies. Robert would eventually rise to become president of Brooklyn College, a position he held from 1979 to 1992. Robert was brought in to lead the public college after his predecessor was ousted. The prior president had served through a decade of upheaval—the college's enrollment had risen to 35,400 students because of an open admission policy that lasted until 1974, and then crashed to just 17,500 two years later.[19] Robert acknowledged that the college was a mess when he took over in 1979, and led it to a dramatic resurgence, working to smooth racial tensions and improve its academic offerings. Robert died of lymphoma in 1992.

(Beyond his tenure at Brooklyn College, Robert and his wife left the physical gift of The Hess Collection on Ethiopia and the Horn of Africa and the Robert L. Hess Collection on the Continent of Africa, both of which were donated to the school's library after his wife's death in 2015. Robert's own children followed that more academic tradition, with two becoming professors, and one a teacher, while only one pursued business, going into accounting.)

Harry, the next eldest son, remained in New Jersey and had one daughter before eventually retiring to Florida.

The sole girl in the household, Rebecca, known as Betty, lived in Asbury Park and Deal for most of her life. She married Joseph Gilbert, and she became a teacher. Joseph and Betty had one son, Miles.

■ ■ ■

While Leon may have shared many of his father's traits, the role-model who had the most influence over his life and his fortune was David Wilentz. A consummate politician and talker, David had the connections and the ability to show Leon the many ways in which the political system could be used for gain. Leon relied on David as one of his most trusted advisers.

When Leon left for World War II, putting David in charge of his business, David's daughter Norma was newly married to Samuel Feder, a Philadelphia native who had graduated Phi Beta Kappa from Harvard College before attending Harvard Medical School. Samuel served as Chief of Medicine at a station hospital on the Pacific front during the war. While Leon was in his early days of launching his fuel business, Samuel was a pathology fellow and medical and radiology resident at Mount Sinai Hospital in New York City, before doing a fellowship in psychiatry, the field he ultimately chose. The couple had one child, Constance, born in 1944.

Norma's marriage to Samuel failed, and not long after the war David introduced Norma to Leon. He would later tell stories of borrowing the money to pay for a suit for their first date. The daughter of the attorney general, who had grown up with a great deal of privilege, was of a different class from the owner of the fledgling fuel business. But the two quickly bridged the gap, and David had blessed their union. A contemporary of Norma's remembers that at the time she met Leon he was driving an oil truck, but was welcomed by the Wilentzes.

Leon married Norma in 1947, and they maintained a close relationship with her parents, taking vacations together and including them actively in their lives. Leon's respect for David Wilentz was shown in business as well, where the father-in-law was brought on as a board member.

This second marriage for Norma, who was seven years younger than her husband, would be a lasting union. She was known for her intellect and strong support of Leon. New York Jets executive Steven Gutman tells a story about attending a play with Leon and Norma, and Leon becoming particularly animated when he was introduced to one of the comely ladies staring in the production. When he turned back to his wife as the starlet walked away, Norma said simply, with a smile: "I forgive you, Leon."

"If Norma had been born in the era that we're in today, no glass ceiling would've kept her from being whatever she wanted to become," said Gutman, who socialized with the couple outside of his Jets responsibilities. Norma, he recalled, was the most outstanding of David's three children, though her brothers had more celebrated careers.

David's two sons were close to their father and their brother-in-law, Leon, as well. After graduating from Perth Amboy High School, Warren Wilentz, the elder son, attended the University of Virginia, interrupting his college education to fight in World War II, where he served in France and Germany before returning to school and graduating in 1946. He went to Rutgers for law school, and launched a career that resembled his father's—by 1956 he was prosecutor for Middlesex County, New Jersey. Like Leon and David, Warren joined in the singing at family gatherings and was known to serenade the crowd with renditions of "Yea Boo" and "Heart of My Hearts."

While starting to stake out his place in the political machine that his father had run in New Jersey, Warren was known for getting people jobs, occasionally passing them along to Hess Corp. When his cousin, Seymour Miller, approached him, looking to get out of routine accounting work and into something more interesting, Wilentz told him that his brother-in-law Leon was hiring and connected the two—Seymour would stay with Hess for four decades, serving in financial roles at the company. Warren later went into private practice, joining his father's firm at Wilentz, Goldman and Spitzer. In that capacity, he became a trusted adviser to Hess Corp., providing legal guidance as needed.

David's younger son, Robert, attended Princeton, taking two years off for the Navy, and then graduated from Harvard and Columbia Law School. Like his father and brother, he initially pursued politics, before going into law. Robert N. Wilentz was elected to the New Jersey Assembly in 1965 and served until 1969. Like his father, Robert considered running for governor, but opted against it in 1973.

Instead, Governor Brendan Byrne appointed Robert in 1979 to be chief justice of the Supreme Court of New Jersey, despite never having been a judge before. He held the position for nearly two decades, arguing for fairer courts free of gender discrimination. "There's no room for gender bias in our system," Justice Wilentz said. "There's no room for the funny joke and the not-so-funny joke, there's no room for conscious, inadvertent, sophisticated, clumsy, or any other kind of gender bias."[20]

Robert's court was known for its fairness and effectiveness in generating regulations (and getting the political machinery to support his decisions), and also for the consensus he was able to build. Through Robert's smarts and persuasive demeanor, he was often able to achieve unanimous decisions. "Many consensuses were reached during 10-hour discussions in the Chief Justice's chambers, in which he would ply the justices with pickled herring, lox, and coffee cake," the *New York Times* wrote at the time of his death.

Robert's effectiveness as a leader drew on the Wilentz family's tradition of political leadership—Constance quipped that it was inherited, either through genes or cigar smoke. While Leon was never a politician, he also appropriated some of David's leadership style, whether it was attention to sartorial details, a penchant for hard work and long days, or the ability to balance family and an all-encompassing job.

David and Leon continued to share a deep connection until David's death in 1988, when those who remembered him recalled their special bond. "He didn't mind rich people. He liked them, but the ones he really liked started out poor, like his son-in-law Leon, whom he loved,"[21] said Robert Wilentz, speaking in a eulogy for his father.

■ ■ ■

Hess Corp. was fully established as Leon's first child before he met Norma, and he spent long evenings and weekends dedicated to the company's birth and early upbringing. At the time of their marriage, Ethel, Leon's mother, was said to have warned Norma that "All Hess men are strong, so don't let him get away with anything."[22] In their marriage, though, he adopted a more Wilentz-style balance of family and career.

After they wed in 1947, Norma supported his career while prevailing upon him to spend more time with their family, which at first included Constance, Norma's daughter from her previous marriage. Their family then grew with the birth of Marlene in 1948 and John in 1954. All three were treated equally as Leon's own children. "If you were with Marlene and Connie and John, those were his children. The fact Connie was not his biological child didn't matter to him," said Gutman.

Just as David Wilentz had balanced a demanding career with dinner at home each evening, Leon strove to do the same, sometimes returning to his office for long hours at night after spending time with his wife and children. Norma and Leon formed a partnership in which she was his closest, most trusted partner in navigating problems, even in business.[23]

"You knew when you were in their presence that they were a team and that there was a great deal of love and respect between them," Gutman said. "She could count on Leon for being a kind of father and provider and life creator. And he could count on her for making sure she took care of all the family-related obligations and represented them well."

As a young girl in the 1950s, Marlene said she remembered wearing her pajamas, robe, and slippers and returning to Leon's office with him after dinner. This was before the company's headquarters had moved to Woodbridge, and it was still based in trailers in Perth Amboy. He would let her sit at the desk of Bernie Deverin, the company's vice president who shared an office with Leon, and play with the adding machine. Then he would nod at her, and she would get them each a bottle of Coke for a dime out of the building's vending machine, and then they would talk while drinking the cold soda.[24]

The company remained in the background of the family's activities, with Hess corporate values and Hess family values of philanthropy, hard work, and total commitment deeply intertwined.

For his role as a father, the billionaire magnate is remembered for highly ordinary things: taking his children to the office, attending swim meets, and making a legendary fish soup at holiday celebrations—a family secret combo of the freshest catch from the New Jersey docks, for which there is no exact recipe. The family would spend every Sunday afternoon together, either driving to visit the Hesses in Loch Arbour or going to the rides, one of which was operated by Ethel Hess's relatives. The family would also go on vacations, joining David and Lena Wilentz.

Outside of the office, Leon impressed those around him with his ability to be there for his children while still running an increasingly major company—at summer swim meets, he would arrive at the beach club just in time to see John swim, and would then get back into his car, where a driver was waiting to whisk him away. The ability to coordinate timing impeccably in an age before cell phones or text messages was perceived as unique, and created a mystique around Leon as he balanced parenting and corporate life.

Leon had a lighter side at home, too: home from college on vacation, Marlene came in to find her bed shortsheeted (a practice that involves folding the sheets in a way that the unsuspecting sleeper is unable to fully stretch out in bed). She assumed her brother John was responsible for the prank, but didn't complain. The next night, it happened again, and she confronted John, who denied it. The third night, her bed was again shortsheeted, and the lamp from the bedside table was tucked into the sheets. "I started to plead with John to stop the torture, only to realize that the newspaper was shaking in my father's hands and he was laughing hysterically. I couldn't believe it—and always wondered where he learned to shortsheet a bed," Marlene said in her reminiscences about her father.

Despite their relative privilege, his children recall a normal home life, with regular generational struggles. Constance remembers challenging his beliefs in the 1960s. He would get angry, and send his children to their rooms, but later would always come to apologize following one of his favorite lessons: "Turn the page."[25]

On weekends, Leon sometimes made time to go to the Hollywood Country Club in Deal, where he had a standing 10 A.M. Sunday appointment with the pro—the spot was his whether or not he was able to go, and the pro was his main opponent, as he didn't often play golf socially, according to club members. He would occasionally join John for a round of golf, but he never became a regular player.

Leon also made time for religion. "Leon Hess loved coming to the synagogue and participated in a major way in our endeavors. Whenever I called on him, he would say, 'What's on your mind, rabbi?' The truth is, whatever the request, the result was kindness, compassion, and generosity," said Senior Rabbi David H. Lincoln of the Park Avenue synagogue.[26] The synagogue, where Ralph Lauren is a congregant, has a dress code described as "Chanel," and membership dues that can exceed $5,000 a year per family, for those who want access to prime seating at holidays like Rosh Hashanah and Yom Kippur.

Leon was known to be in temple for all of the high holy days on the Jewish calendar. Writer Earl Ganz tells the story of the ribbing he took from a group that included Leon and David Wilentz (who met for coffee at a back booth in the Busy Bee diner) for not knowing what tefillin were. The group ended up walking Earl to a nearby synagogue and solemnly wrapping the straps that held the small leather boxes used for morning prayers around him with a prayer shawl. "With that beard he looks more Jewish than any of us," Leon said.[27]

Leon and Norma would also go to horse races at Monmouth Park, joining her parents, and ultimately bringing their children and grand-children. One report tells of Leon betting $3 or $4 on a race and giving away the tickets. While Leon was a big supporter of the arts, including making large donations to Lincoln Center, his visits to the Metropolitan Opera were punctuated, during football season, with intermissions spent tuning in to the radio to catch sports scores.

The Hesses' social life largely spun around Leon's growing business network, as they entertained bankers and colleagues at home, indoctri-nating their children—especially John—in the corporation's culture and preparing John to run the rapidly expanding business.

It was fitting that for a 1962 costume party, Leon and Norma arrived dressed as Hess terminal employees, complete with starched white uni-forms and hard hats. While the couple was often at the center of social events, Leon wasn't shy about wrapping up evenings singing "Good-night Ladies" to signal guests that it was time to leave, a tradition he had appropriated from David Wilentz.

From an early age, John was brought in as the heir apparent of the company. By the time John was a teenager, Leon was showing him the ropes of the company more actively. On one occasion, Norma called the mother of one of John's friends, inviting him along on a trip to see oilfields and equipment. He joined, and the pair flew across Oklahoma, staying in hotels and going with Leon to review oil wells during the day. As the company grew, John was sent to the Hovensa refinery, where he rotated through various departments at the Caribbean plant.

In college, John studied Arabic and Farsi, preparing for a career leading a multinational oil company, ready to jump into international negotiations and maintain the connections his father had first made, despite his Jewish heritage, in the Arab world. After getting his undergraduate degree at Harvard, John attended business school, striking up connections that would help him guide the company, taking an energy economics class that included energy economist Daniel Yergin, who would later write a seminal history of the oil industry. He also met Andrew Tisch, son of Laurence Tisch, another self-made millionaire. After finishing school, John went directly to Hess, and began working 12-hour days alongside his father. John and his wife, Susan (who, like her mother-in-law, would marry a Hess after a first marriage failed), had three children of their own.

Like Robert Wilentz, Leon valued women's rights even if he wasn't exactly a feminist. He was supportive of Constance's and Marlene's careers, though it was always clear that John would take over the family business. His daughters captured two other values of the Hess and Wilentz families: public service and philanthropy.

Constance graduated from Barnard, and then worked at a stock photography company. She married Sankey Williams, a doctor. She returned to school, earning an MBA at the University of Pennsylvania, and then waited for her daughters to graduate from high school before diving into politics.

She ran successfully for a seat in the Pennsylvania House of Representatives in 1997. She served one term, and was elected to the Pennsylvania Senate four years later.

While in the House, Constance was seen as a champion of children's causes and an advocate for education spending. Like Leon, Constance was connected in political circles, serving as the Pennsylvania co-chair of Bill Bradley's 2000 presidential campaign. Also like her father, she was known as a moderate, and although she was a Democrat by party affiliation, she got Republican support and campaign endorsements because of her bipartisan record.

When taking the oath of office for the senate, she was joined by family members, including Wilentz and Hess cousins, as well as Norma, Marlene, and John Hess, who was CEO of Amerada Hess at the time, but still attended his sister's swearing-in. His presence was more evidence of the family's extended commitment to one another.

Marlene went to Mills College in California, and then joined Cannon Properties, a company that developed screenplays for motion-picture producer Cannon Group. She had a son and daughter before divorcing her husband. Marlene became a vice president of corporate communications and the manager of public services marketing at the Chase Manhattan Bank in New York. During her time as a single mother, she credits Leon with special support. She married James Zirin, a lawyer, in 1990. Marlene became director of not-for-profit relations at Chase and then managing director of global philanthropic services at JPMorgan.

At the bank that had first extended a hand to her father, she became the face of charitable giving, forming partnerships with the nonprofit sector, working with the Children's Defense Fund and New York City Department of Health to found a child vaccination program. Her personal philanthropic endeavors are extensive and range from membership on the boards of the Museum of Modern Art, Sesame Street Workshop, and organizations her father also supported like Rockefeller University, Lincoln Center Theater, and the Metropolitan Opera.

■ ■ ■

Leon worked to instill commitments to philanthropy and public service in his grandchildren, as well—the group includes a teacher and several who are trying their hand in real estate or finance. But this generation has come of age in a world far from Leon's own Depression-era New Jersey. And while John faced a smooth path to ascension at Hess, the path at the company for his son Michael is more complex.

"Grandpa did more than just hold you up. If he loved you, he included you in his day-to-day life," remembered Marlene's son, Peter Hess Friedland. Peter recalled a grandfather who encouraged close familial ties, and cultivated a genuine friendship with his grandson, watching sports broadcasts over deli pickles and pastrami, either in New York, Deal, or even on annual trips to the Bahamas.

While the grandchildren's world was far removed from his own tough childhood, he managed to connect with them, becoming known as a genial jokester at brunches, football games, and through letters that he signed with a smiley face. Each was left a substantial inheritance: a million dollars in cash as well as other gifts controlled in trusts in both Leon's and Norma's will.

Peter, the oldest grandson, has tried his hand at a real estate venture and has begun to raise his own family.

John's son, Michael, followed in his own father's footsteps and is being groomed to take over the family business, which had grown by the time he was born to an enormous enterprise stretching through more than 20 countries and multiple U.S. states.

Michael and his two younger brothers went to Deerfield Academy, an elite boarding school in western Massachusetts. Once there, all three Hesses played an active role in the school—John's youngest son, William, was made "Captain Deerfield" for his school spirit and recalled being attracted to the intense sense of community. One of his brothers, he said, had a computer background of himself painted green, being driven around by the school's headmaster.[28]

After Deerfield, Michael and William went to Harvard while David attended Brown University. At Harvard, Michael attracted attention when he invited Paris Hilton to be the first woman of the year for the Harvard Lampoon's initial spoof of the traditional Hasty Pudding Woman of the Year event. The hotel heiress said at the time that Michael was a friend. He served as treasurer of the Lampoon, a semi-secret society that previously published a humor magazine.[29]

Michael then attended Harvard Business School, graduating in 2013, just as the school came under scrutiny in the *New York Times* for rifts between the haves and the have-nots. Michael's social media feeds, which included photos of lavish trips around the world, photographs of singer Mick Jagger close-up in concert, and courtside seats at a Knicks game, were among the evidence that some students used to prove a growing class divide at the school. Michael, whose father was particularly active in fundraising for Harvard Business School, became a target in these discussions about class differences, and others suspected he was a member of Section X, an elite group of students who took particularly lavish vacations and threw storied parties.

Still, those who know Michael say that many of the trips were related to efforts to prepare him for leadership at Hess. Like his father, he is being schooled alongside other young scions of fortune—he is often pictured with the son of Goldman Sachs CEO Lloyd Blankfein (Goldman has been the main bank for Hess under John's tenure). Beyond his graduation coinciding with class concerns at Harvard, it also came as Hess was reorganizing under pressure from investors like Elliott Management. These factors might have influenced the decision to have Michael seek employment elsewhere, rather than going straight to Hess after business school, as his father did.

John would buy a $5.6 million three-bedroom apartment for Michael to use for a time in Tribeca. John himself resides at 778 Park Avenue, where residents have included Brooke Astor and William F. Buckley. The address is not far from his father's last Manhattan apartment, at 625 Park Avenue, which sold for upward of $17 million after Leon and Norma died.

Michael spent time working as an associate at private equity firm KKR & Co. in New York (his father serves on their board), and holding junior positions at Goldman Sachs. Michael has also joined the board of a private school in the Kingdom of Jordan. "Michael is a young gentleman with an amazing personality and a great network whom we believe will add a youthful perspective to our board," Kings Academy Chairman of the Board of Trustees Karim Kawar said in the announcement of Michael's promotion to the body. Michael was also recognized for his knowledge of Jordan, finance, and Arab culture.

While succession plans for after John retires remain in question, many at Hess still think Michael will be a viable candidate to succeed his father.

Chapter 2

Hess at War

Leon Hess joined the U.S. Army on November 12, 1942, 11 months after the Japanese attacked Pearl Harbor and the United States declared war. At that point, the draft was in place and men Leon's age (he was then 28) were being drawn into the fight, with 10 million eventually called to serve. Hess's military records are scant—a 1973 fire in Missouri destroyed a large portion of Army personnel materials from 1912 to 1959.

Leon left his burgeoning business in the hands of David Wilentz, a well-connected lawyer who would later become his father-in-law and had given him environmental advice and become a mentor of sorts.

"My father proudly served as head of transportation logistics in Europe under General Patton, and was decorated a lieutenant colonel," John Hess remembered in his eulogy for Leon. "Throughout his life he was very proud of serving his country. He was indeed a true American patriot."

While he definitely served some role in the Transportation Corps, Leon was not, in fact a lieutenant colonel, and there is little evidence that he was the head of logistics for the group, since his name doesn't appear in any of the official military histories of the era. Some newspaper reports said Leon had been shot in the cheek during the war. Some said he was eligible for the Bronze Star. Neither of those things can be proven. Leon would tell New York Jets player Dennis Byrd a story about being in battle during the war and seeing a soldier to his left shot in the head and another one on his right killed by a piece of shrapnel from an exploding bomb.

"The point he was making to me was there was no way to explain why a man on each side of him died like that while he was spared," Byrd, then lying in a hospital bed after an on-field injury, wrote in his autobiography.[1]

Hess returned to the United States in December 1945, almost seven months after victory was declared in Europe. At the port of embarkation in Brooklyn, Hess was processed as having reached the rank of major in the Transportation Corps. He was unmarried and gave as his address as a house in Loch Arbour, New Jersey, a town just north of Asbury Park, where his parents were living. The Army gave him $273.90 for his last three weeks of work and expenses and sent him on his way.

He was eligible to receive the World War II Victory medal and the Honorable Service lapel button for World War II, both standard for soldiers.

Hess would tell relatives that he served in the most famous logistical enterprise the U.S. Army Transportation Corps ever knew—the Red Ball Express—helping to supply fuel for troop movements and honing his experience in a way that would serve the company he would eventually build into the thirteenth-largest oil company in the country. While he didn't often discuss his time in the war, it would forever change him and it would change the nature of the world's relationship with oil.

■ ■ ■

On September 27, 1944, as the U.S. Third Army continued its pursuit of German troops across Europe, General George S. Patton sent a commendation to the chiefs of all supply and administrative sections. "It is regrettable that your work gets little of the public acclaim it so richly deserves," Patton wrote. "Without the countless hours of vitally important duty performed in dust and rain, in scorching sunshine and clammy darkness, the gas, the rations, the ammunition, and the other stores would not have arrived, and the Army could not have conquered."

A month earlier, as the Allied forces broke through the German lines quicker than expected in the wake of the D-Day landing in Normandy, leaders scrambled to get supplies, fuel, and troops to the front line that was beginning to stretch farther and farther away from the stockpiles near the beach. Initially proposed as a few days' worth of a concerted supply push, the Red Ball Express was under way.

A fleeing enemy and damage done to French rail networks by re-sistance saboteurs and Allied bombings meant to hinder German troops on the coast before the D-Day landings "created a demand for large movements to support the First and Third Armies."[2] With reduced rail capacity, that demand could be met mainly through trucks—lots and lots of trucks (Figures 2.1 and 2.2).

Figure 2.1   U.S. Army truck used in World War II.
SOURCE: Photograph by Tina Davis.

In seeking a name for the new operation, organizers used railway parlance for fast "through freights," and called it Red Ball Express. Red Ball road markers were easy for truck drivers to follow, especially at night when the markers and a direction arrow pointing the way could be readily distinguished. The concept of the operation was to give driv-ers exclusive use of a one-way loop highway, drafting all available motor

Figure 2.2   A World War II–era sign at the U.S. Army Transportation Museum summarizes how much the U.S. military relied on trucks to haul thousands of tons per day.
SOURCE: Photograph by Tina Davis.

transport to operate around-the-clock with temporary supply and maintenance areas set up along the route.

"The Allied Armies' advance to the Siegfried Line by September 1944 upset the planning for phased operations on the Continent, and placed a severe strain on motor transport and railway lines of communication facilities," according to a historical account written by the Army Transportation Corps and published a year after the war. "Indeed, the lack of transportation facilities was a principal factor in bringing the advance to a halt."[3]

The movement was so fast (troops covered ground in three months that planners had expected would require at least 10 months) that by the end of July, convoys that had previously had taken only a few hours to complete their trips needed three to five days to reach the First and Third Armies, find their unloading points, and return to the coast for new loads.

Instead of lasting a few days, the operation went on for 81 days, from August 25 until November 13, by which time more ports had opened on the coast and railroads had returned with enough capacity to move supplies. A total of 412,193 long tons of cargo was moved by the Red Ball Express.

The initial push for Red Ball came about when the need arose to move 100,000 tons of supplies from Normandy to Army dumps inland by September 1. Available rail facilities could only move 25,000 tons. On its first day, the operation consisted of 67 truck companies that moved 4,482 long tons. Four days later, the capacity to transport supplies had almost tripled, with trucks moving 12,342 tons. While it fell short of the initial 75,000-ton target for the first day of September, by September 5, it reached 89,000 tons.[4]

"The Express faced a number of organizational and operational problems. Strict rules were set for operations, but enforcement was spotty. There were never enough MPs to police the routes. . . . Convoy discipline left much to be desired, because many drivers had little or no training. Low productivity resulted from slow loading and unloading, and underutilization of vehicle capacity," according to a U.S. military history of the Transportation Corps.

"Much of the early confusion was due to the hasty organization of the project, inexperience at all operating levels, and a command structure that invited jurisdictional problems." Plus, there'd been little opportunity to actually see if the whole thing would work in real life. "Prior to the invasion, planners attempted to organize and test a truck express system, but equipment and manpower weren't available, so it had to be activated without a test."

The rush of men and materials would eventually end with the demise of Nazi Germany. But transporting the equipment and personnel from the D-Day beaches in France to the ever-changing combat lines wasn't considered a heroic duty, even though supply companies were shot at by snipers and faced strafing from German planes.

"I arrived here 7 September, with the 104th (Timber Wolf) Division," a frustrated Terry Allen wrote in a September 29, 1944, letter to Patton. "We hoped for an early combat assignment, but conditions apparently made that impossible. This division has been required to organize numerous provisional truck companies in order to relieve the supply situation and to maintain a regiment of infantry and one or more infantry battalions on the Line of Communications, for security purposes, train guards, etc. We hope that by handling these necessary SOS 'chores' with the utmost efficiency, we may be released for an early combat assignment; at least that is the attitude of our units."

A month prior, on August 21, Patton had written that the pace of movement was so furious that "This Headquarters has moved on the average of once every three days since we have started. Last night, we camped in a woods. . . ."

The general was determined to push forward and press his advantage as the army gobbled up territory once held by Germany. "When you get the enemy on the run, keep him there," he wrote earlier that year.

When things did get bogged down, Patton was quick to acknowledge both his own impatience and that of the outside world. "I presume right now that since I am not advancing sixty miles a day, I am considered a failure," he wrote to General Robert Howe Fletcher on October 4. "But, as a matter of fact, I have killed more Germans lately than I did during the whole of the fast advance."

A few weeks later, he wrote to Major General Guy V. Henry a reason for his slowed progression: "Of course, I regret that we did not continue our advance as it would have been possible had we not outrun our supplies."

■ ■ ■

Red Ball truck drivers, who were routinely called on for shifts lasting more than 24 hours, were mainly African American soldiers who had been kept back from combat duty in the segregated Army. The Express, which inspired a movie, a short-lived television series, and a Broadway show tune, is largely forgotten outside of military circles, but at its prime, it was a marvel of logistics and, by some measures, helped ensure the Germans (who were still heavily reliant on horses) crumpled under the onslaught of a quick-moving opposition. In its 81 days, it created a blueprint for how to move much-need supplies across the field of war.

The need for speed in the dispatch of supplies and troops across the battlefield wasn't a new approach to winning a conflict. Union General William T. Sherman's "war of movement" across the South is credited with helping bring the Civil War to a faster end. Military leaders weren't interested in repeating the war of attrition that bogged down troops battling for yards at a time during World War I. With the advent of planes and trucks replacing horse-drawn transport, the means to give serious chase and gain substantial territory were available.

After the Allied landings in Normandy, troops moved across Europe at a speed even the generals hadn't anticipated. "With the Germans in full retreat, the American Army was transformed, despite its logistical problems. What had formerly been a tentative force became a roaring menace that made full use of mechanization," journalist David P. Colley wrote.[5]

Trucks, which had first been used in combat by the United States Army against Pancho Villa and again in small numbers during World War I, became crucial in that mechanization that by some measures made the difference once Allied forces came ashore in Europe, leading to the end of the war there.

"[R]apid, sweeping massed movement of forces deep into the enemy's heartland was the best way to destroy an enemy army," General Omar Bradley wrote.

The United States produced more than 800,000 2½-ton trucks, known as Jimmies, for the war effort. The workhorse vehicles were used and abused as the Army required swift transit across the Continent. One company, the I Company, put 259,009 miles on its trucks in a month.

The Germans, the nation that had perfected the "blitzkrieg" style of striking quickly and moving through territory, meanwhile continued to move the bulk of their army by foot and their supplies by horse and wagon.

"On the entire Brittany front, the German Army is faced with a definitive shortage or complete lack of supplies," according to an August 11 memo to headquarters on the Third Army's interview of captured German Major General Karl Spang. "Ammunition and food are short. Gasoline is almost non-existent. This accounts for the almost complete absence of air support."

The German officer was impressed by his captors' logistical operations: "While en route from Headquarters Third U.S. Army to Headquarters Twelfth U.S. Army Group, the General expressed his utter amazement at the mass of motor vehicles encountered. He stated that it was a shortcoming among the German generals that they were quite ignorant of the capabilities of the American supply lines."

Moving thousands of troops hundreds of miles came with logistical problems—namely, keeping the men fed and provisioned while they were racing after the enemy. That meant shipments of ammunition, rations, gasoline, and equipment for river crossings, among other items. At times, the distance between supply depots and the front line stretched as much as 250 miles.

Among the participants in the Red Ball Express was Platoon Sergeant John Houston, father of singer Whitney Houston, who said the crews never got enough credit for what they did. "I always felt the Army would never have won without us," he told Colley.

Fuel and other petroleum products to move troops, supplies, and tanks made up a quarter of the material being moved (a Sherman tank got gas mileage of one to two miles per gallon). Fuel was becoming the most necessary commodity in the battle for Europe. General Patton told General Bradley, "If I could only steal some gas, I could win this war." And stealing—sometimes dressed up as "requisitioning"— did take place, even among troops of the same army. Patton's men, who captured a million gallons of German fuel, still had to resort to commandeering jerricans of gasoline (a five-gallon container with a design stolen from the German "Jerrys") that were headed to supply other U.S. troops. While officially frowning on gasoline theft from other troops, Patton wrote about word of his soldiers passing themselves off as belonging to another unit to get access to a gasoline dump:

"To reverse the statement made about the Light Brigade, this is not war but is magnificent."

The thirst for fuel eclipsed anything Army logisticians had foreseen, with the First Army alone burning 782,000 gallons a day, five times the height of demand during World War I's Meuse-Argonne offensive. Lack of gasoline on the German side, meanwhile, "led to ammunition shortages and more failures and deficiencies all the way down the line," according to Colley.

Representative Clarence Lea, chairman of the House Committee on Interstate and Foreign Commerce (which looked into petroleum's role in World War II in a series of hearings in 1946), said, "The activities of the petroleum industry of our country was one of the important, if not a dominating feature, that led to the early victory in the war."[6]

■ ■ ■

By the spring of 1946, the Petroleum Administration for War was rapidly disbanding. The government group, made of industry experts, was formed to ensure the United States had the necessary supplies to last through the war. Demand and production ramped up rapidly in the United States during World War II. Since the dawn of the twentieth century, production had climbed from 174,300 barrels a day to more than 4.6 million barrels by 1945. That year, total world demand, excluding Russia and the Axis states, reached more than 7 million barrels. At the time, the United States was producing about twice as much as the rest of the world combined. But that was about to change.

Starting with the attack at Pearl Harbor, the United States produced about 75 percent of the Allies' oil during the war, and its refineries accounted for 82 percent of the gasoline and 85 percent of the airplane fuel consumed, the Petroleum Administration for War said.

At the congressional hearing in April 1946, members of the subcommittee were told that the largest oil producer outside of the United States, the Axis allies, and Russia, was Venezuela, with more than 1 million barrels a day of output. Also in that group of suppliers were Mexico, Canada, and Argentina.

There was another large source of oil, one that up to that point was largely untapped. Howard Page, director of the Petroleum Administration for War (or PAW) division of production, flagged the possibilities of oil from the Persian Gulf area: Iran, Iraq, and Saudi Arabia. Even at 400,000 barrels a day, the region was "nowhere near the production that can eventually be developed with the reserves that are there." The problem was only how to get the oil out, with so little infrastructure in place. "The limitation is not upon the number of wells that can be drilled or the productive possibilities, but on the transportation facilities?" Congressman John Hinshaw asked.

"Yes," Page replied. "[G]iven time and money, the amount of production that can be developed in that area is, you might say, unlimited, with the high reserves that are available there, proven reserves."

While some in the industry were skeptical of the Middle East's capabilities as a major oil producer, Page had just shone a spotlight on a change in the industry that would have major effects on oil companies and geopolitics for the rest of that century and probably most of the next.

■ ■ ■

When Leon was mustered out of the Army, the energy business had changed considerably. U.S. oil production had increased by about 1 million barrels a day in just the three years from 1942 to 1945 (the equivalent of all U.S. production at the close of World War I). Even with that leap, there were the first signs that things were changing—"Evidence points to the imminence of a shift from a condition in which this country has surplus oil for export to one in which the nation will become a net importer of oil," the Petroleum Administration for War's Foreign Operations Committee wrote in a report. That shift would have a profound impact not just on the industry but on national and international politics.

The refining of crude oil had shifted considerably since the industry's earliest days. Instead of most of the crude being processed into kerosene for lamps, it was now being used primarily for gasoline (41.7 percent of refinery output) and fuel oil (42.3 percent). New methods of "cracking" crude yielded more gasoline, helping to create the modern car culture in America. During the war, "all of the refineries of the country were operated as if they were component parts of one huge refinery,"[7] with substances transported between them. Coordination of resources meant that there were only two completely new refineries built during the war.

Fuel oil, the waste substance from refining that Leon had found buyers for in New Jersey, was now suffering shortages because of the high demand for its use in cargo ships. The use of oil and gas for heat and power went from 8 percent in 1900 to almost 44 percent in 1940.[8]

The war also highlighted the transportation problems of moving so much product from the U.S. Gulf Coast to the major demand centers on the East Coast—especially when German submarines lurking offshore could take out a tanker. To obviate that threat, the U.S. government ended up building two major pipelines, known as Big Inch and Little Inch, that would bring 550,000 barrels a day to New York and Philadelphia. One of the pipeline segments, stretching from Texas to Illinois, was completed and placed into service in five months. That evolution in transportation would last for generations, as the majority of petroleum and its products switched to move by pipeline instead of tankers or rail.

While producers, transportation, and refineries benefited during the war, the last part of the energy food chain had much less fortune. Only about one fourth of the 425,000 gas stations that existed before World War II were still there by 1946. The war effort cut off supplies and usurped workforce for the stations. Some would reopen after the war, and some never would. Rationing was uneven in an effort to be targeted. Stations visited by hospital staff would get gas to ensure that doctors could get to work. Farmers got gas. The military, obviously, was a priority.

The government wasn't only coordinating U.S. output, it was also helping other nations produce—sending equipment to Venezuela and Russia and laying pipelines in Saudi Arabia while the British sent equipment to Iran through the Anglo-Iranian Oil Co. Major oil-consuming nations were realizing they needed to stake their claim to foreign oil, as colonial powers felt the need to grab for resource-rich territory in the prior century.

While oil prices were low in the 1950s and 1960s, this arrangement between the oil industry and the U.S. government to encourage supplies from all corners of the globe was tolerated. But in the 1970s, the toppling of one major oil producer's regime, coupled with falling U.S. output, would combine to drive prices to new records before an embargo forced gasoline rationing, making the American public question the formerly friendly relationship between oil companies and lawmakers.

Chapter 3

After the War

I think you know once the Arabian producing states manage to get together and then discover the tremendous dividends that would come from a united action, their attitude toward the whole of the Western World will change.
— Senator Frank Church[1]

After the war, Leon returned home to New Jersey, ready to put to work all that he'd learned about logistics in the Army's scramble to supply one of the quickest-moving groups of soldiers the world had ever seen. As the war concluded, demand for fuel oil surged to unprecedented levels as its use for power generation and in shipping expanded.

The industry also grew to serve a burgeoning U.S. middle class that wanted—needed—to drive more, and Hess metamorphosed from a small dealer into one of the largest gasoline retailers on the East Coast and a force to be reckoned with in an industry that was becoming one of the nation's most important.

Not content with just delivering fuel, Leon would extend his reach into refineries in the 1950s and then take the leap into the exploration and production business in the 1960s, giving the company that had started with a single truck a piece of the entire fuel cycle from drill bit to gas tank.

In the process, he would use his considerable political and negotiating skills to give him a unique advantage in the Virgin Islands and to take the opposite end of the table from foreign despots.

But first, he needed money. He'd handed control of the fuel oil company he'd established before the war to David Wilentz. He returned to New Jersey with less than $300 in his pocket. According to the *Washington Post*,[2] a friend allowed Leon to buy a barge-load of heating oil on credit, from which he was able to make enough to buy another and start to build a fortune that would put him among the richest men in America.

There was an odd romance for Leon in fuel oil, the heaviest of the substances that are separated out in the refinery process. The fuel has the consistency of molasses—oilmen have called it "the bottom of the barrel" because it was the heaviest of refined products. Refiners would often dump it, but Leon saw the value where others saw waste, feeding what would become a growing thirst for the fuel among utilities that used it to generate electricity. To do so required quick action and a mastery of logistics since the stuff had to be kept warm to stay liquid. Leon told one story about getting a truckload of residual oil to an Asbury Park hotel and finding it had cooled and hardened. To get it off the truck, he took the rather risky maneuver of using a blowtorch on the drainpipe, and spent a day getting the oil out.

He offered to buy the oil from a subsidiary of Royal Dutch Shell if the company would build storage for it; from that start he would build one of the largest oil delivery and storage businesses on the East Coast, with a large share of the heating oil and fuel oil market. Having a huge network of his own distribution assets would come in handy as competitors fought to find ways to bring their oil to market. In one case, he was accused of using those assets for ill-gotten gains—three Hess workers would testify that they siphoned oil out of tanks it was leasing to another oil company (the court case would be settled for $440,000 in 1968). He was so obsessed with the details of delivery at budget meetings that he would quiz the head of the company's trucking division on the amount of life left in the tires (the same sort of attention to detail and sense of thrift would lead him to use a dime to tighten a loose screw in a chair at a shareholders' meeting).

The company called fuel oil "the workhorse fuel of industrial America" for its uses in utility boilers, driving factory machinery, and heating large buildings. "[F]or Amerada Hess, residual fuel oil is the mainstay of the business.[3]" The company is "one of the East Coast's leaders in that indispensable source of energy." That leadership came in part from the world's largest refinery, which Leon built in the U.S. Virgin Islands and which benefited from political maneuvers that allowed it to be both a U.S. refinery and not a U.S. refinery, enjoying advantages his rivals didn't have. In 1969, the company noted that fuel oil sales to utilities had more than doubled.

But the Arab oil embargo and shortages that surrounded it would help to kill use of fuel oil by power plants as the 1970s wound down. Today, fuel oil accounts for less than half of 1 percent of the U.S. electricity supply, according to the Energy Information Administration.

Hess would make some futile efforts to keep demand for fuel oil alive, calling in 1976 for the government to prohibit the use of natural gas (a rival fossil fuel used to generate power) for anything other than home heating and chemical purposes. To be fair, there was a long line of skeptics who worried about the use of gas as a power-plant fuel before the shale revolution unlocked huge reserves in North America. Samuel Bodman, U.S. Secretary of Energy under George W. Bush, likened burning natural gas to make electricity to washing your dishes with scotch. At the time, natural gas was running at more than $12 per million British thermal units, before it would fall off a cliff to below $2 just a few years later after shale supplies kicked in.

While the company had a soft spot for the residual oil that others threw away, Leon was also smart enough to diversify. With the same attention to detail that drove him to paint his oil trucks on a Saturday so they would look good on Monday, he strove for perfection in his gasoline stations. The first station opened in 1960 in New Jersey; by the end of the decade the company had operations in 16 states.

The Hess logo became ubiquitous to drivers from Maine to Florida. The stations were known for the painted white curbs that made them clean and welcoming. Unlike the usual practice, Hess station attendants didn't change your oil, they didn't carry batteries, tires, or windshield wipers, or have car mechanics on-site, and for a long time they didn't take credit cards, something that Leon felt slowed the process down. By moving more customers through and offering them clean restrooms, the company could focus on revenue.

In 1962, Hess merged with Cletrac Corp., a Cleveland-based farm equipment maker that had formerly been known as Cleveland Tractor. Cletrac had sold off most of its equipment business the year before to White Motors. What Leon was getting with the purchase was a seat on the New York Stock Exchange—Hess would finally become a publicly traded company. Becoming publicly traded opened new sources of financing to Leon. It also came with tremendous risks for a venture that had been run principally by one man since its founding. Bringing in shareholders could invite trouble, especially if they clashed with management or fought his plan to hand off the company to his son, John. To protect against this risk, the family held a majority of the shares (that number has since been whittled back to closer to 12 percent). And Leon surrounded himself with board members who were not eager to challenge his management plans.

Having allies on the board ensured his role and his vision (and eventually the role of his son as CEO and chairman) weren't challenged. In a 1986 court case, Leon said that while he served on the board of Capital Cities Communications, which then owned the ABC television network, he never asked to see contracts as part of his oversight role of management (Alan Greenspan also served on the board).

"No. Never see any contracts," Leon said. "When you are on a board of directors, you support management or you get off the board."

That was a belief system he wanted in place at his own company. Those who served on the Hess board included former senators and governors, roles that were often intertwined with jobs on Leon's philanthropic venture, the Hess Foundation. Some of the same men served as executors on Leon's will. Even from the grave, he was still ensuring his friends had steady paychecks.

In another bit of guidance for business leaders, Leon told a court in 1986 he did "not believe in making any notes."

"Why is that, sir?" he was asked.

"It just keeps you out of trouble."

"And you haven't produced any in connection with this litigation, have you?"

"Absolutely not."[4] You can almost hear the pride in his voice at hindering the plaintiffs' attorney.

■ ■ ■

When World War II began, oil producers were dealing with the lingering aftermath of the Great Depression and oversupply that led to crude being sold for as little as 10 cents a barrel. While the war boosted demand for fuel, companies still faced price controls (the average price at the beginning of the war was $1.16 a barrel), scarce supplies of equipment, and a lack of manpower because the draft and the heightened need for skilled workers drove up labor costs. Producers found themselves unable to make the numbers work, and many independent companies faced losses in the crunch between higher costs and capped government pricing. According to U.S. Treasury records, 436 fewer oil production companies had taxable income in 1943 compared with 1942.[5] Most of the smaller companies sold their output to majors, who had the pipelines and processing facilities to turn the petroleum into usable products like gasoline and kerosene.

Independent producers, sometimes called "wildcatters," were, and still are, a key part of oil output in the United States, responsible for discovering some of the biggest fields. It was independent companies that figured out in the early part of the twenty-first century how to crack shale and get access to huge reserves of oil and natural gas in hard rock formations previously known to hold hydrocarbons but considered too costly to develop. In the early part of the twentieth century, it was an independent company—Amerada Petroleum Corp.—that would develop the reflection seismograph, a key tool in helping geologists "see" underground to figure out where oil may lie. Amerada head Alfred Jacobsen called it "the most important instrument, the one that has found the greatest number of oil fields."[6]

With seismic information, the number of dry holes went down. By 1944, more than 91 percent of exploratory wells were using some sort of scientific assessment to avoid what had become an increasing cost of failure. The search for oil had begun to go deeper and into new areas than before, as the easy oil that used to be found by spotting natural crude seeps that bubbled up to the surface was gone.

The independents were also more likely to snap up older fields and find ways to extract the leftovers that major oil producers didn't find worthy of their efforts. These were companies that had to be optimistic about finding oil, since that was often all they had to sell to their investors—a belief that the big find was close at hand.

". . . I think it can be fairly said that in spite of the declining rate of new discoveries in evidence during the last few years, we need have no fear of an oil famine or even an oil shortage in the foreseeable future provided the domestic producer receives a proper price for his oil," Amerada's Jacobsen said in 1946. "Even if the declining rate of discovery should continue, a very substantial volume of new oil will be discovered each year, and in the meantime continuing advances in the technology of finding, producing, and refining oil will enable us to utilize to greater advantage the supplies we do have."

Interestingly, one of the biggest domestic threats independent producers like Amerada saw in 1946 was farmers. The oil companies complained to Congress that farm cooperatives were taking over oil production. The co-ops, which enjoyed tax advantages and could borrow money from the government, were snapping up the smaller producers as well as pipelines and refineries suffering from price controls that were slow to rise after the war ended. Cooperatives handled "10.6 percent of all gasoline, kerosene, and other light refined oils brought into Minnesota in 1939."[7]

"The conclusion is that perhaps the cooperatives will eventually be competing with the majors," Chairman Joseph O'Mahoney, a Wyoming Democrat, said at a Senate hearing in March 1946. This fear was overblown—while co-ops did rise from supplying 14 to 41 percent of farmers' needs,[8] they never threatened major oil producers. They did, however, create some notable energy investments, including the Seaway pipeline connecting Oklahoma and Texas (the reversal of which would be key to helping ease some of the glut years later of shale oil sitting at a storage hub in Cushing, Oklahoma) and the Texas City refinery, where an explosion in 2005 killed 15 workers at the then–BP-owned facility.

The bigger threat to the oil producers after World War II wasn't farmers, of course. It was OPEC (the Organization of the Petroleum Exporting Countries).

■ ■ ■

In 1959, President Dwight D. Eisenhower announced an import control program for crude oil and related products. The proclamation "confirms his determination to ensure, in the interest of national security, a stable, dynamic industry in the United States capable of exploring for and developing new oil resources within our borders."[9] Wartime thirst for fuel had proved to Eisenhower the importance of petroleum, and keeping the domestic producers alive was key to ensuring adequate supplies. At the time, producers in the United States were subject to state limits on output, a way for governments to make sure oil prices didn't get too low or too high.

Eisenhower couldn't have known that in less than a generation there would be a profound reversal in the relationship between producing and consuming nations. His proclamation came one year before OPEC was formed, a reaction to price drops that came in an era flush with new oil production from global wells. It would be another decade before OPEC would be able to flex its political might, making clear that consumers were no longer able to control their appetite for fuel.

Amerada Hess would bump up against these restrictions before they were eliminated after the Arab oil embargo. In 1971, it gave notice that the government was asking it to "substantiate its compliance" with a 15,000-barrel-a-day import limit on fuel oil and other products from its Virgin Islands refinery.[10]

A year later, the company declared that "the era of abundant, low-cost energy is behind us" as prices soared. Leon reassumed the role of CEO in late 1972, taking back the job that Amerada's head had acquired in a 1969 merger. In early 1973, restrictions on imported heating oil were lifted as a bitterly cold winter caused supplies to dwindle. The shortage had started, and that was even before the embargo, which was imposed later in the year. A sinking dollar value was causing the price of crude to rise, as producing nations demanded bigger price increases and a bigger stake in operating profits amid threats of asset seizure.

Arab nations banded together after the Yom Kippur War between Egypt, Syria, and Israel in 1973 to use what energy historian Daniel Yergin has called the "oil weapon."[11] After rejecting calls to nationalize U.S. assets in their countries, they agreed to cut output by 5 percent each month and to explicitly ban shipments to the United States to punish the country for its support of Israel in the conflict. Iran was one of the suppliers who boosted output to make up for the lost oil, but it wasn't enough.

"Amerada Hess made every possible effort during 1973 to meet customer needs for fuel oil and gasoline supplies," the company said in its annual report. It temporarily suspended construction of new gasoline stations, as supply rationing led to stations receiving only 85 percent of their historical volume by the end of 1973. Sales of gasoline rose to 232,000 barrels a day from 203,000, while residual fuel oil rose to 615,000 barrels from 575,000.

A year later, the company was giving another wrap of the tumultuous business environment: "During 1974, prices for imported crude oil increased to approximately twice that of domestic crude oil. In competing with many companies that utilized domestic crude as their major supply, your Corporation was forced to reduce its profit margin to remain competitive and maintain its share of the market." Amerada acknowledged the fact that it was particularly vulnerable to the swings "because of its strong dependence on imported crude oil."

Revenues almost doubled as the price of gasoline rose, but the company's profit fell on a per-share basis in 1974.

Net production from Libya plummeted to 38,663 barrels a day from 92,730 the prior year (a pittance from the time when Amerada was getting as much as 280,000). Worse, the prices the Libyans were setting were still too high, so the company struggled to find buyers—"For the last half of 1974, Amerada Hess was unable to market Libyan crude profitably because of its high cost and the reduction in worldwide demand." The Libyan government lifted its embargo on U.S. shipments in January 1975. "However, the price of Libyan crude continues to be above competitive prices in both the European and United States markets."[12]

Sales of both gasoline and fuel oil fell in 1975 as supplies dwindled, conservation measures kicked in, and economic activity slowed. Even so, Hess finished up expansion of its St. Croix refinery, bringing output to as much as 700,000 barrels a day, a long-term bet that demand would pick up again. In a nod to the changing climate, the company was adding the capacity to make gasoline instead of so much fuel oil.

On the production side, the company was heralding efforts to get oil at home as production from abroad became increasingly complicated from a political perspective. Hess won its first lease to explore in the Gulf of Mexico, an area that would (despite the former Amerada CEO's forecasts) become a major source of crude, eventually supplying about 11 percent of the company's total U.S. output. Returning its focus to the United States after so many disruptions from abroad, the company included a special section in its 1975 annual report devoted to the Bakken formation in the northern plains states:

"Under the sweeping plains of the Dakotas lie the sediments deposited by a huge inland sea. But it was not until 1912 that a fossil coral discovery suggested the presence of a major oil reserve there. And although serious attempts to find it began in 1923, it was not until 1951 that an Amerada Hess well established oil production in this large geological province, now called Williston Basin. The extreme cold and blizzards of the Dakota winters plus the remoteness of the location made exploration costly and difficult. But the effort has proved worthwhile. Today Amerada Hess operates 450 producing wells in the Williston Basin."

The Williston Basin would become more famous 30 years on as the home of the Bakken, when companies finally figured out how to unlock the oil and natural gas trapped in hard rock formations that they had formerly drilled past to get to easier-to-access reserves.

Hess would have less success trying to drill for oil off the mid-Atlantic coast (some testing off the coast of New Jersey was met with a lawsuit and the Interior Department eventually removed the area from leasing). It also made little headway getting oil out of Alaska, a process that began in 1969 as Libya's government was being toppled and the industry was showing intense interest in promising prospects from "Seward's Folly" (one lease sale a decade later in the North Slope would yield $1 billion, a ringing endorsement by the industry of the prospects for getting oil out of the state). Amerada Hess bought 18 oil and natural gas leases on Alaska's North Slope in 1969 and took a 3 percent stake in the Trans-Alaska Pipeline System, a massive and oft-delayed project to bring what the industry knew was a large supply of hydrocarbons to ports on the state's southern coast. Hess would drill unsuccessfully for oil at a place called Beechey Point. By 1972, it was not planning further drilling. Where other companies, including BP, would help make that state an oil powerhouse in the 1970s and 1980s, Hess would end up quietly exiting Alaska without much luck, getting production to the meager level of 5,700 barrels a day in a state that would eventually churn out more than a million barrels a day from the North Slope at its peak.

One area that would pay off for the company would be its investment in the North Sea off the coasts of the United Kingdom and Norway. One field was estimated to be worth $1 billion in 1991. The company often used unorthodox techniques to tap into the vast reserves of oil and gas in the region, a place it entered like a startup, with no support network or history, just a chance to drill in one of the best offshore areas. By 1994, its holdings in the North Sea represented 50 percent of the company's proven reserves.

■ ■ ■

After World War II, Leon busied himself with the logistics of buying and selling and storing fuels. He expanded an oil terminal in Perth Amboy, New Jersey, and bought a 10,000-ton tanker to ship fuel by sea (he would later name one of the company's tankers the *David T. Wilentz*, in honor of his father-in-law).

Seeing demand for fuels ramping up after World War II, Leon responded by building a refinery in Port Reading, New Jersey, which began operating in 1958. The company would no longer be a middleman between refiners and their customers; it could now make its own product at its own facility. As more oil began to flow from holdings in Libya, Leon was planning an even more ambitious project—what would become the largest refinery in the Western Hemisphere. Another refining facility, in Purvis, Mississippi, was purchased from Gulf Oil in 1972.

"Anyone who has ever seen a refinery knows that it is an immensely complicated facility, a wondrous maze of purposive pipework, strange tall towers and cylindrical storage tanks," the company said in 1976,[13] using language that sounds like it was lifted out of *Charlie and the Chocolate Factory*.

Refining was, and is, a tricky business. The company's annual reports are littered with references to unplanned outages and strikes at the refineries it owned. (The plant in St. Croix would be struck less than five years after it was built and both it and the facility in Mississippi would have union action in the same tumultuous year.)

The 1960s were a time of intense building of refineries and petrochemical facilities by the industry, as they saw U.S. production declining and overseas markets increasing. Offshore refineries grew popular because of continuing tariffs on oil imports, an anachronism that dated from a time when U.S. producers feared the flood of cheaper crude from foreign markets. The Caribbean became one destination for refiners that wanted access to the bounty of oil coming from South America and still have a quick trip to reach the demand-hungry eastern U.S. markets. It also offered tax advantages.

The industry, led by Edward Carey, the brother of New York Governor Hugh Carey, successfully fought in Congress to lift a quota system that prevented it from importing unlimited amounts of residual fuel oil (Carey would build his refinery in the Bahamas). That would help spur a bonanza in utility use of the substance for power—a validation of Leon's first business plan. Eventually, the Caribbean refineries would produce 80 percent of the heating oil used on the East Coast. In 1969, Amerada Hess would double sales of fuel oil, as the Federal Power Commission reported a 40 percent increase in utilities using it to generate electricity. By 1976, price limits and quotas on fuel oil and heating oil were removed after a particularly bad winter put them in short supply.

■ ■ ■

As a manager, Leon has been described as tough but fair. He had an exacting eye for detail but he imposed the same standards on himself as he did on others—work hard, know everything you could about your business, and if you made a mistake, learn from it and move on. That instilled great loyalty from his employees, who felt they were working for a man, not just an anonymous multinational corporation. He is often described as fatherly, and no one at the company or the Jets wanted to disappoint him. He wasn't prone to emotional outbursts, but you would know when you'd failed him, according to people who worked for him. He was an engaged and engaging people person who enjoyed getting to know those around him. While he's often described as a man of few words, that meant that when he did speak people listened closely. He also came from a school in which a handshake was sufficient for a deal.

He could also be a fierce competitor—during a Teamsters strike in the 1960s he sold off the majority of his truck fleet instead of yielding to union demands, *Business Week* reported.

Many of the men who worked for him describe him in fatherly terms, as a mentor.

T. Boone Pickens is considered an éminence grise in energy circles these days, routinely asked for his thoughts on oil prices and the best companies to invest in, but he was once a rabblerousing upstart and corporate raider who wasn't afraid to take on big incumbents (*Time* magazine described him in 1985 as the real-life J. R. Ewing). The Oklahoma native started his career as a wildcatter, founding Mesa Petroleum with $2,500. With his aggressive acquisition of Hugoton Production Co.— many times larger than Mesa—Pickens's company had been transformed into one of the largest oil producers. With Hugoton under his belt, he tried to buy a series of other companies. One of his boldest moves was for Gulf Oil Corp.

Pickens had quietly amassed an 11 percent stake in Gulf by November 1983, and the company was trying to keep him off its board. To keep him at bay, they planned to transfer the company's domicile to Delaware from Pennsylvania, where regulations made it more difficult for minority shareholders to get elected to boards.[14] The company was successful in that initially defensive move, but Pickens kept pushing. In a preview of an approach that would be repeated at Hess years later, he argued that at least half of Gulf's domestic oil and gas reserves should be spun off, and made into a trust, separate from its other assets.

In the middle of the heated battle for Gulf, Pickens met Leon at an American Petroleum Institute meeting in 1984. Curious about Pickens's plans, Leon invited the younger oilman to have lunch or dinner with him the next time he was in New York City. "We had never talked, and he said 'I'd like to know what in the hell you're doing,'" Pickens recalled. Pickens immediately made plans to travel to New York.

Over a pleasant lunch at the Amerada Hess offices, the junior and senior oilmen talked.

"I never called him Leon," Pickens says in his southern drawl. "I said 'Mr. Hess, these companies are poorly managed. Gulf is one of the worst, assets are worth vastly more than the market is willing to recognize.' And I said I'm going to try to get involved as a large shareholder and make something happen. And I think just in case I end up running one of these companies, I'll do better than the management they presently have."

Leon asked Pickens some questions about his strategy and approach to companies. After the lunch, the two men walked to the elevator. Leon slung his arm around Pickens, like a father would, and said, "Young man, you have brass balls."

It would not be the last time the two men crossed paths. Pickens would acquire stakes in Amerada Hess periodically, buying in 1987 and 2011. Pickens's protégé, David Batchelder, would go on to found Relational, where he would be one of the hedge fund executives who voiced support for Elliott Management's challenge to John Hess.

■ ■ ■

While he was schooled in the sometimes boring world of logistics by the rapid need for fuel movement during the weeks after the D-Day landing in Europe, Leon was always a gambler at heart. Not only at the racetrack, Leon also liked to take chances in business. He wasn't frightened of risk and liked to do things that sometimes flaunted the conventional wisdom. One of the attractions of joining the business when Leon ran it was that it had the ambition of a major oil company with the mind-set of a startup.

Being in the storage business gave him his first chance to bet on the spread between supply and future demand. Being able to hold the stuff in huge tanks meant you could also buy when you thought the price was low and sell when it was high. Naturally, there were times when those guesses were wrong—in the mid-1980s, when oil prices bounced against new lows on a regular basis, Leon was caught with way too much crude in his tanks. Oil that he'd bought for $30 a barrel was now worth about $12.

"I hated to face up to reality every morning," Hess told *Business Week* in a 1987 interview (his first, according to the magazine). The company reported a $222 million loss in 1985 after writing down the value in ships it had built to move fuel (there was less need for the ships since it was producing less from its refinery in the Virgin Islands—which was struggling to switch over to serving gasoline demand instead of fuel oil).

It stopped paying a dividend as oil prices cut revenues from crude sales by more than half. Its Libyan assets had to be sold after U.S. sanctions made it impossible to do business in the country anymore. Leon had reassumed (for the second time) the role of CEO at the company in 1986, but to most everyone familiar with the company, he never really ceded control. Shares in the company were down by half, an aggressive investor (T. Boone Pickens) took a big stake, and there were calls for the company to split up, an early but less successful effort that would be echoed almost 20 years later. Like his son would years later, Leon went to the largest institutional investors to assure them that the company was worth more as a whole than it would be if split into pieces. One analyst predicted in 1987 that "most of its history" was behind the company, but Leon fought through the tough times to right the corporate ship, mostly by cutting costs as he waited for oil prices to rise again (1986 capital spending was less than half that of 1985 and the company reduced its headcount by more than 10 percent).

Five years later, Leon's big bet on oil would pay off handsomely in the wake of Saddam Hussein's invasion of Kuwait. Prices swung mightily in response, going from $15.06 a barrel in June to $41.15 in October. Leon had made a huge wager in June, buying crude oil futures after OPEC set a target price of $21 a barrel. "The Corporation's purchases were intended to protect its refining and marketing operations against the expectation of higher crude oil prices later in the year," it explained in its annual report. Instead of just protecting the company, the bet led to a $214 million gain in the third quarter. Still, Leon in public railed against the futures markets for their volatility and suggested more stringent trading measures to limit who could use the practice.

■ ■ ■

By the time Leon fully surrendered control of the company in 1995, at the age of 81, Hess Corp. was worth $4.9 billion. On sales of $7.3 billion that year, the company reported a $394 million loss as petroleum product prices increased more slowly than oil prices. The company also took a $416 million charge for its Port Reading facility, for writing down the value of its ships and certain oil producing properties. A year earlier, Hess had begun accepting credit cards at its gasoline stations and by 1995 it had introduced its own branded card. John, 41, was taking over as the company was adapting again to its changing environment.

Ten years later, the company John led was worth twice as much and profit was a record $1.19 billion amid a surge in refining demand. But the good times were not good enough for some investors, and John would face the biggest challenge of his career.

Chapter 4

Amerada

In December 1968, Hess announced an agreement to merge with Amerada in what was the biggest deal in its history. It was a pairing that would take Hess in a new direction—the company that began as a small-time distributor of residual fuel oil was now looking more like a miniature version of Exxon, expanding from just refining and selling fuel into a company that found and produced millions of barrels of crude oil. The deal would make Hess, which would be known for the next 38 years as Amerada Hess, into a vertically integrated energy company with its hands in every stage of oil's journey from discovery to gas tank.

Amerada Petroleum Corp. was an oil producer facing the prospect of dwindling reserves. This was only a decade after the company was heralded for its incredible prowess at finding oil, and particularly at opening up the Williston Basin in North Dakota to oil production, drilling the state's first successful well after scores of others had tried and failed.

In 1952, Amerada CEO Alfred T. Jacobsen appeared on the cover of *Time* magazine, in a glowing profile that proclaimed him "The Great Hunter" (he was also apparently nicknamed "The Oil Garbo" for his reluctance to say much).

Amerada was "the most famed independent oil hunter in the oil industry," *Time* wrote. The company was also the seventh-highest priced common stock on the New York Stock Exchange at the time (its shares traded at $185 apiece—about $1,340 in 2015 dollars) and "the No. 1 favorite of the investment trusts."

The reason Amerada was so hot at the time was its position in North Dakota, which in 1951 became the twenty-seventh U.S. state to produce oil. Amerada owned 1.5 million acres in North Dakota by 1952, when it had attracted plenty of competitors in the state.

Time magazine breathlessly described the oil rush that Amerada had spurred in North Dakota, language that sounded eerily similar to news reports of the 2010s, as that state once again experienced the joys and pains of being awash in men and companies seeking quick fortunes from oil production.

"The land that had been a dust bowl only 20 years ago was now an El Dorado to farmers who had been on relief or working for WPA [the Depression-era government work program]. Overnight, they had become wealthy," *Time* wrote.

Amerada found oil where other major energy producers had failed, in part because of technological advantages.

Jacobsen was a taciturn Dane who was quoted saying he didn't have personal friends because "I don't go in for that sort of thing." He had been a part of wartime negotiations between the British and U.S. governments in what became the Anglo-American Petroleum Agreement to try to ensure adequate supplies of petroleum. Fears it would actually swamp the United States with foreign oil helped to kill the deal. Jacobsen had taken over the job at Amerada from Everette DeGolyer, a geologist who rose to fame for practically inventing the practice of using seismic equipment to find oil.

The industry had long suspected there was oil on the state's plains beneath the gently sloping rock formations that are often the sign of an underground bunker housing oil. Using blasts of dynamite to generate sound waves that would indicate where underground salt domes were likely, and armed with the theory that the domes often occurred near oil deposits, geologists began to take some of the guesswork out of drilling.

■ ■ ■

In fact, Amerada was largely set up to allow DeGolyer to test his theories that use of seismic information—some of it from equipment used to find artillery batteries in World War I—would help reduce the number of "dry holes" that were drilled. The company was formed by Sir Weetman Pearson (later Lord Cowdray) in 1919 to search for oil and was named for where it would do business—America and Canada. The venture was created (with DeGolyer as vice president and general manager) a few years after the geologist was abruptly forced to leave Mexico in a hurry after a coup ended the 30-year reign of Porfirio Diaz, a general and close friend of Pearson's. In 1911, Mexico accounted for one quarter of the world's oil output, so naturally the change in leadership drew attention world powers and the oil companies jockeying for the lion's share of the nation's resource wealth.

Backlash from the appearance of U.S. Marines at Veracruz led Pearson to establish an all-British management team for his assets in Mexico, necessitating the departure of Kansas-born DeGolyer.

The oil business was something of an anomaly in the wide-ranging career and business interests of Weetman Pearson. His firm S. Pearson & Company had gone from a small Yorkshire enterprise to one of the premier engineering companies of its time. Pearson found his way to Mexico as part of his convalescence after becoming partly paralyzed from an injury at a digging project to build a tunnel under the Hudson River connecting Jersey City, New Jersey, with Manhattan. Compressed air used to keep the water and silt from collapsing the tunnel could also cause "the bends" in workers when they returned to regular atmospheric conditions (the condition is now more generally associated with scuba diving). Never one to hang back, Pearson's time alongside the diggers in the tunnel led him to experience the problem firsthand, prompting his wife to encourage a Mexican sojourn for recovery.

The ever-resourceful Pearson agreed to the trip, in part because he was already eyeing several large engineering projects in Mexico, including a canal to drain excess water in Mexico City, a workable port at the city of Veracruz, and a transcontinental railroad. Pearson's entry into the oil business was almost accidental—he missed a train connection in Laredo, Texas, and was forced to stay in the city for nine hours. At the time, Laredo was full of oilmen talking about the massive find at Spindletop, in Texas. Remembering a story an employee had told him about evidence of oil near San Cristobal, Mexico, Pearson sent a telegram directing the employee to buy up land.

"The oil business is not all beer and skittles," Pearson wrote to his son in a March 1908 letter. "I entered into it lightly, not realizing its many problems but only feeling that oil meant a fortune and that hard work and application would bring satisfactory results."[1]

Following the traditional practice of drilling wherever oil was found seeping from the ground, several companies had had limited success in Mexico, including Rockefeller's Standard Oil. Pearson had begun investing in the country's infrastructure, building terminals and buying tank ships to move more oil than he was yet producing. A few months after DeGolyer joined Pearson's Mexican company, the Brit had lost 50,000 British pounds bringing foreign oil in to supply the nation's demand as he tried to take over the lion's share of its crude market. He had wound up in a furious price war with Henry Clay Pierce, head of the Standard Oil–backed Waters, Pierce Oil Co., which had ruled Mexico's oil industry. And he was losing money trying to win the battle by using the traditional Standard Oil tactic of lowering prices to starve competitors of funding.

"In a mild way I am going to be ruthless," Pearson said at the time. Standard Oil had never had a real fight before, he said. They would, he rightly predicted, "tire first."

On December 10, 1910, DeGolyer's instinct for drilling paid off, when a well in the Potrero De Llano field came in big. "The greatest oil well yet discovered in the world, it has remained the champion of all time in productive yield, reaching to more than a hundred million barrels before playing itself out, eight years later," according to DeGolyer's biographer. The field's output has since been surpassed, but it set the high-water mark in the industry for a very long time.

Amerada would be focused on the United States after the Mexican coup. DeGolyer, a heralded engineer in the industry, would leave Amerada in the 1930s and form several more companies, including DeGolyer & MacNaughton, an oil consulting company that became the industry standard for independent reserve estimates and would, some 30 years later, deliver a damning report on Amerada's oil reserves. It's the firm Hess uses to this day to certify its reserves.

"I am tired of working for bankers, and I want to work for myself," DeGolyer wrote to friends, explaining his decision to leave.[2] Years later, the 5'6" self-made millionaire, suffering from declining health, would shoot himself in the head at his office desk at the age of 70. He had made a good living working for himself.

■ ■ ■

By the mid-1960s, Amerada's luck at finding oil had run out. The rest of the industry was using seismic, which had become (and still remains) the standard for finding oil. The company was no longer replacing the amount of oil it was producing with sufficient new reserves, meaning it was starting to burn through its inventory of crude. For any oil company, the need to continually add reserves is, according to oil analyst Thomas Petrie, akin to walking up a down escalator—you must make sure that you are still growing your potential even as you produce what you've already found. Jacobsen pondered liquidating the company's assets or finding a buyer.

"Jacobsen had told me at our first long conversation about this that he figured that in 15 or 16 years Amerada was apt to be out of business, out of assets," Frederic Brandi, chairman of investment bank Dillon Read & Co., testified in a court case that arose from the Hess merger. Brandi also said he thought Jacobsen was getting ready to retire and "wanted to wind up his stewardship of this great corporation."

Dillon Read (which was acquired in 1997 and eventually became part of Switzerland's UBS bank) had been associated with Amerada, which operated without debt and thus had little use for bankers, since the company sold the first shares of Amerada in the United States in 1926. The share sale was required after some U.S. lawmakers began to raise questions about foreign-owned companies taking over U.S. oil fields, without allowing U.S. companies reciprocal rights to drill abroad. Lord Cowdray died a year after his family surrendered its majority stake in Amerada. His larger company, now known as Pearson Plc, continues to this day as a publishing and educational venture. Its most notable holding was the *Financial Times*, as well as a minority stake in *The Economist* magazine, both of which were sold in 2015.

In 1962, Jacobsen would tell the *New York Times* that he was "getting sicker and sicker of all these unfounded rumors" about a sale of Amerada.[3] At that time, there was speculation that Royal Dutch Shell and British Petroleum might be planning a joint bid for the company. The newspaper described the 72-year-old chairman as "crusty" as he rejected talk his company would be bought. But early in the 1960s, Jacobsen began seriously considering a plan to break Amerada into pieces and sell them.

That plan was problematic because Amerada couldn't convey to a new owner concessions it had to produce oil in Libya. Amerada held talks with several companies as it struggled to find a way forward.

Dillon Read suggested Amerada talk to the big industrial companies, including Dow Chemical, Union Carbide, and International Nickel Co., since they were big consumers of oil and gas (Union Carbide would later build its own oil and gas unit and then sell all properties when the business proved harder to profit from than expected). In one of the most misguided theories an oil CEO could have, Jacobsen told Brandi that "he had a feeling that the future of the value of crude oil would lie very largely in its chemical applications, rather than as a fuel."

(In another prognostication that seems woefully off-base in today's world, Jacobsen told a Senate committee—while discussing the oil prospects that everyone agreed lay in the deep waters of the U.S. Gulf of Mexico—that "it is most likely that it will be far cheaper to produce oil by conversion from coal than to drill at any great depth of water in the open sea."[4] Billions of barrels of oil would prove him horribly wrong. But to be fair, the historic path of the industry is littered with many failed forecasts about where it was heading.)

There were other hunters sniffing around Amerada: two brokerages, Lazard Freres and Loeb Rhoades, which considered plans to buy it and sell off the pieces. The prospect angered Jacobsen so much that he closed his accounts with Chase Bank after learning they were involved in potentially financing the hostile takeover.

By 1966, Jacobsen was set on selling to an oil company. Brandi and his investment bank suggested oil producers that might buy, including Sinclair, Standard Oil of Ohio (known as Sohio), and Ashland Oil & Refining. The major oil companies were to be avoided, it was thought, because of potential antitrust issues (the industry was on edge about this after Superior Oil's attempted deal with Texaco was scuttled by the Justice Department). The most logical suitor, Standard Oil Co. of Indiana, was ruled out because the company got almost all the crude for its refineries from Amerada, making an antitrust review impossible.

Jacobsen liked the idea of selling to Sohio, because it was a Standard Oil company, a legacy of the huge trusts that John D. Rockefeller had built to control all aspects of the oil business in the first part of the twentieth century. But those negotiations ended without a deal.

In the fall of 1966, Amerada began talks with Ashland Oil. Appro-
priately enough, on Valentine's Day in 1967, the company announced
an agreement with Ashland. But the relationship would not be consummated. As part of finalizing the deal, both companies did due diligence
on each other, a sometimes delicate dance in which books are laid open
and an entity's current and future prospects are judged. As part of that,
Ashland requested a third-party opinion on how much Amerada had in
oil reserves (the company had never had an independent appraisal done).
In May, the consultant DeGolyer & MacNaughton, the firm formed
by former Amerada president Everette DeGolyer, issued its appraisal of
Amerada's proven reserves. The news was not good—Amerada's reserves
had declined by 25 million barrels between 1967 and 1969, showing that
the company was eating its future output to feed current demand. The
number was also about 100 million barrels less than the company itself
believed it had. A day after receiving the report, Ashland called off the deal.

The report "showed a reserve considerably smaller than what they
had anticipated, and also they had received indications that the cost of
operations in the United States were substantially higher than they had
anticipated and that, of the total earnings of Amerada, an amount somewhere around $25 to $27 million had come from Libya, a fact which
they had not appreciated prior to that time," Brandi said in a deposition.

Libya was an especially thorny issue for anyone interested in Amerada. The company had been in the country for more than a decade at
that point. By 1957, it had a one-third interest in about 62 million acres
in Libya (an area about the size of Wyoming). Two years later, Amerada
was telling investors it saw oil "in very widely separated areas and in a
number of geological horizons" in Libya—in other words: the stuff was
just everywhere. The company quintupled its rig count in the nation
from two to 10.

Production from Libya rose from 38 percent of Amerada's total output in 1963 to 68 percent by 1968.

Mindful that oil prices at the time didn't support more expensive
projects, Amerada said in its 1959 annual report that "while Libya production will be coming into a world market already fully supplied with
oil, it will . . . be in an advantageous position with respect to cost of
transportation to the principal European and North American markets."
The company sold oil at an average price of $2.84 a barrel that year.

Doing business in Libya was never easy, to say the least. The company had to surrender about one quarter of its holdings in 1960, and organized a new company, Oasis Petroleum, with partners including Marathon, to handle the concessions. Ashland's decision to shy away from the Libyan holdings was prescient. The company's holdings in the nation would be subject to substantial fluctuations until it exited altogether after Moammar Qaddafi took power in 1969.

As DeGolyer once wrote (having learned about government interference in oil assets during Mexico's coup): "[A]ny foreign operation is in constant danger in a small country where it represents the most important and the dominant factor in the economic life of the country." Many oil companies have learned this lesson the hard way.

Years later, investment banker Brandi would call what happened with the Libyan assets a "fiasco." The company would continue to struggle with Libyan output and a volatile political situation. The Arab oil embargo of the 1970s meant Hess couldn't send the oil to its own refinery in the U.S. Virgin Islands. And the company had to surrender 51 percent of its Libyan holdings "under threat of nationalization" in 1973 before U.S. sanctions in 1986 forced it to sell the holdings altogether. The company announced its return to Libya in 2005, after Hess and its partners paid the bargain price of $1.3 billion to the Libyan National Oil Corp.

When Ashland balked at a merger, Brandi suggested they restructure the deal, but Jacobsen, who only ever entered negotiations with one company at a time, said the agreement was for better or worse. And so it died. Despite being "badly bruised" by the very public rejection of Ashland, "Mr. Jacobsen was still as determined as he was before that a deal should be made," Brandi said.

After toying with a few other oil companies, Amerada approached Hess. According to Brandi, before Jacobsen died "he had developed a very high regard for Mr. Hess, [for] his success in his own business." That differs starkly from other characterizations of their relationship—Milton Gould, a lawyer representing clients who sued in the aftermath of the merger, said in his opening statement in court that Jacobsen "didn't want to deal with Hess. Hess was a raider, a bandit, all kinds of things, and he didn't want to do anything with it. Then providentially that gentleman died and his successor did not have the same feeling of revulsion toward Mr. Hess because we find in not a very long time they are dealing together, Mr. Hess becomes a member of the board, a member of that inner council, and all that was acrimony becomes friendliness between two companies."

To be sure, a defense lawyer responded to the opening statement that "there is not a scintilla of evidence in this case that that view was ever taken of Mr. Hess by anyone" at Amerada. We may never know if Jacobsen went to his grave admiring or reviling Leon Hess. Selling to a company that had no real production but was refining and selling the fuel was a turnaround for a man who said in 1946 that he had been integral in keeping Amerada from doing things other than finding and producing oil, despite having "had plenty of opportunity to become integrated by merger and otherwise." In advice that might echo through the years for John Hess as he battled an activist shareholder, Jacobsen said the best business to be in was production. "[T]here is not necessarily any particular advantage in being an 'integrated' company. Many smaller concerns engaged in only one branch of the business do relatively better than larger companies engaged in all branches."[5]

In any event, Leon was already very familiar with Amerada, having joined the board 11 months before the merger was announced. That director seat came after Hess made a big investment in the producer two years earlier, in 1966. Hess spent $100 million to buy 1.243 million shares (a 9.7 percent stake) in the company and became one of its largest shareholders, snapping up an interest that had been held by the Bank of England.

When Hess bought the huge position in Amerada, paying about $20 a share over market price, Leon had called Jacobsen to tell him he was buying as an investment because the shares were undervalued. Jacobsen was apparently annoyed that the Bank of England had sold without telling him first, so the company could've had the opportunity of buying back its own shares.

The bank, for its part, was looking to wind down its equity investments and shore up the value of its currency after buying up shares in American companies from British citizens during the economic mobilization that led up to World War II. Hess "was told that the British government needed $100 million, and they were willing to sell Amerada for $100 million," Brandi said.

Amerada had reported several years of uneven earnings before Hess signed on, but the trajectory was generally upward for a company that had paid a regular dividend since 1922 and had the highest profit margin (27 percent) of any industrial company on the Fortune 500 in 1965. Profit had almost doubled, from $29.948 million in 1957 to $58.461 million in 1967, a year when the company announced record U.S. crude output and told investors it saw the presence of "very large gas reserves" in the U.K.'s North Sea (a premonition that would be borne out in coming years). The increased production didn't tell the whole story, however.

"Beginning in the late 1950s, independent producers of crude oil and natural gas, including Amerada, encountered long-run economic problems seriously threatening their competitive position in the oil industry," according to a trial memorandum by attorneys supporting Hess's position. "The average annual increase in the price of crude during the five-year period from 1958 to 1963 was .1 percent and during the 10-year period from 1959 to 1968, the price actually declined at an average annual rate of .25 percent."

The boom and bust cycles that had been particularly vicious in the oil industry came with each new field causing wild fluctuations in supplies and, thus, prices. A discovery in Oklahoma City caused the price of oil to drop from $1.10 a barrel to 10 cents in six months as the Great Depression sank demand. Without the bigger resources of a major company (and the ability to capitalize on the other end from refining a cheaper fuel), smaller producers folded.

In fact, such huge swings in pricing were one of the things that led Rockefeller to create his trusts, in an effort to stop overproduction and transportation failures from constantly ruining the industry.

By the 1960s, "It was becoming more difficult to find reserves to replace those being produced, and a number of companies were looking into the proposition of merging or disposing of assets at that time," said Thurl Jacobson, who took over as president of Amerada after Alfred Jacobsen died in December 1967. A month after Jacobsen's death, Leon Hess was on the board of Amerada.

Leon was "somewhat cool to the idea" of a merger with Amerada when first approached, according to Brandi. Preliminary talks with Hess began in June 1968, with negotiations becoming more serious in the fall. Leon was the only person representing his company at the start of negotiations.

The agreement offered Amerada shareholders preferred stock, which was convertible after one year into 2.2 shares in the new company.

The ratio valued the Amerada stock at about $108.50 a share. Investors were also promised higher dividends (a benefit Leon had fought but eventually acceded to). Amerada had a market value at the time of $1.38 billion and Hess was worth $649 million. But Hess's sales figures were higher, almost twice what Amerada pulled in for 1967. In essence, Amerada shareholders were trading one third of their debt-free balance sheet for two thirds of the earnings and assets of Hess. Amerada reaped bigger profits, but without a drastic change, it was going to eat its own children soon.

Hess, for its part, had become a huge buyer of oil after expanding its refining assets. Before the merger, it was Shell's biggest single customer. The company didn't want to be held captive to producers anymore.

"Hess was an oil refining and marketing company with no significant production facilities. Amerada was an oil producing company with no refining or marketing facilities at all. The purpose of joining these two companies into one was to create a full integrated oil company and thus to achieve for both of them the advantages that would flow from such union," according to a trial memorandum from the companies.

In fact, Hess had a small oil and gas production business, but it was in no way capable of feeding the company's immense appetite. In 1968, Hess refineries handled an average of 253,000 barrels of crude a day, of which only 1 percent came from its negligible production. On the other hand, Amerada produced an average of 291,978 barrels a day that year.

"No oil company can long remain in business unless it has refineries, and Amerada didn't have them; Hess did," Brandi said at the shareholder meeting to vote on the merger, according to one Amerada shareholder who opposed the deal.

Months after negotiations grew serious with Hess, executives from Phillips Co. showed up and wanted to talk about buying Amerada.

The new Amerada president rejected the Phillips offer, even though it valued the shares at a higher price and would've brought bigger dividends.

"The Hess deal was a very real bird in the hand, whereas the Phillips proposal was no more than a very tentative bird in the bush," according to a trial memorandum from the Hess defendants. Furthermore, "[the] past history of Hess showed a huge growth potential, whereas the past history of Phillips showed none."

To be specific: Phillips's earnings had climbed 3 percent in the previous five years, whereas Hess's had increased 181 percent. There were also
potential antitrust concerns in joining with Phillips.

Hess, meanwhile, had experienced several years of quick growth, but
it was having to get oil from more far-flung places as easily accessible
crude became harder to find in the United States. "They were fairly
unique in the oil industry in that a very high proportion of their sales
were fuel oil," Bryan H. Lawrence of Dillon Read testified in court.
"Almost all of the oil that was refined in their refineries were from
international—were from countries overseas."

According to Brandi, Phillips made the offer without knowing that a
binding agreement had been signed with Hess (the companies had only
publicly acknowledged they were in talks to merge).

Five days after Phillips submitted its proposal to the Amerada board,
in March 1969, Leon Hess offered to release Amerada from the merger
agreement signed the preceding week. Instead, the board chose to stick
with the Hess offer.

To strengthen his hand, Hess proposed buying $240 million in
Amerada stock. The tender offer was at $125 a share, well above the $110
price the stock was trading at, and would give Hess an 18 percent stake in
Amerada. Doubling its holdings would ensure more yes votes at the May
shareholder meeting. But the share acquisition needed Amerada's signoff,
since the agreement the companies had signed prevented either from
doing any business that would boost debt in the run-up to the merger's
completion. This tender offer would become another bone of contention
for those suing the companies, as investors complained the $240 million
cost was just saddled onto the previously debt-free Amerada. Hess was
basically borrowing money from the shareholders of the company he was
trying to acquire.

But the board unanimously approved a waiver, allowing Hess to go
forward with the share purchase. The merger agreement required investors to hold onto a "convertible share" that could be cashed in two years
after the deal. The tender offer, the board decided, was a good option
for shareholders seeking to cash out without the burden of holding the
preferred stock.

In the end, Hess didn't appear to need the extra votes, as the shareholders voted to approve the deal by 10,957,330 to 281,109 in May 1969.

According to one eyewitness at the May shareholder meeting, the vote was "absolutely irregular."

"There was a motion on the floor to postpone the meeting for a minimum of two weeks," John Weisner testified. "Suddenly, a big up-roar and there was pandemonium, that's all I can tell you. People were screaming at everyone, and all of a sudden they said it was passed, the merger is completed, which is absolutely irregular because there was a motion on the floor which should be handled first preceding whatever happened before the other motion, so, therefore, I say to you in all fair-ness that what occurred on that date was the most irregular, flagrant violation of law."

■ ■ ■

Less than four months after the final deal was announced, a Brooklyn resident named Aldo Del Noce met with an attorney. Six months later, a complaint was filed against a Hess holding company called Jomarco, named for the first letters in each of the Hess children's names (John, Marlene, and Connie).

The suit eventually targeted Leon Hess, several entities that held Hess stock, and some of the executives who were involved in the merger, alleging a "conspiracy of the Hess defendants (originated in 1966) to take over the control and ownership of Amerada and its assets. . . ."

The merger grossly undervalued Amerada's reserves, including the oil in the ground in Libya, and went forward despite an offer from Phil-lips that had better terms but didn't guarantee tenure to any Amerada board members (thus explaining the board's preference for the lower offer from Hess), according to the plaintiff's attorneys.

The court case finally went to oral arguments in June 1975. For five days, the lawyers battled over whether Hess had stolen Amerada for a price well below its true value. Representing Del Noce (who'd bought 10 shares of Amerada in 1967 for his daughter, Denise), were a team of lawyers including Milton S. Gould, a partner in Shea & Gould (the other namesake partner, William Shea, is perhaps more famous for hav-ing had the Mets team stadium named after him in honor of his efforts to bring baseball back to New York when the Dodgers left). Shea & Gould, which was dissolved in 1994, had had some high-profile clients, including Aristotle Onassis.

The arguments before the judge got testy, sometimes devolving into name calling. At one point, a defense lawyer objected, saying, "This is absurd." According to the court transcript, Gould took umbrage:

MR GOULD: It is what, it is absurd? I don't think it is absurd and I don't think counsel should characterize it that way. I think *he* is absurd. [emphasis added]

The judge calmed the lawyers down, noting he was their only audience: "Please, gentlemen. It is a non-jury case. There is no use having raised voices."

A year after oral arguments and seven years after the merger was completed, the judge ruled that the company had violated securities law in failing to disclose in the proxy statement sent to investors that the comparative assets of the companies played no role in determining the conversion ratio for the merger. It was a small technical win for the plaintiff and his lawyers, who had alleged fraud by Leon and other board members.

"Messrs Jacobson, Brandi, and [William] Moses admitted that neither Dillon, Read nor Amerada's management ever considered the real value of Amerada's assets in negotiating the merger terms. . . . Misrepresenting to stockholders that assets were considered is a serious misstatement in any merger," the court ruled.

More important for Leon, the court said: "Hess and the Hess defendants did not violate provisions of the act . . . and that, from the time the merger negotiations commenced, Hess acted properly and in good faith in his capacities as Director of Amerada and Chief Executive Officer of Hess Oil."

The Hess family, which at that time controlled 57.15 percent of the company's shares, was not liable for any wrongdoing in the merger.

To settle the violation, Amerada Hess agreed to pay $4 million to shareholders, about 38.5 cents a share. The company ended up paying out $2.2 million of that to stockholders who came forward to claim their share. As late as 1981 (13 years after the merger was announced), shareholders were still trying to claim their money.

After the deal was completed, Leon took the position of chairman of the new Amerada Hess. In the early 1970s, with Libya demanding more concessions for producing oil on its soil and strikes affecting two of the company's refineries, Leon (then aged 58) reassumed day-to-day control of the company, pushing aside the Amerada CEO, A.T. Jacobson, who was five years his junior and had been president of the new entity for just three years. He resigned and became a consultant to the company. Leon became chairman and CEO of the combined company on September 1, 1972.

The biggest corporate merger in Leon Hess's life was done and his control over his company's business was complete as it spread into all facets of the oil and gas industry. Just as Rockefeller's Standard Oil had, Hess moved from handling the "downstream" (refining and sale) of oil into the very start of the process. It was now a mini-Exxon, ready to compete with much larger vertically integrated energy companies.

Chapter 5

Hess Abroad

On April 7, 1976, Leon Hess sent a letter to shareholders (Figure 5.1).

"You have read in recent months of disclosures by many corporations of political contributions and foreign payments. With that in mind I would like each of you to have the following information," he began. "In the hope of obtaining a benefit for our corporation, I made a series of payments, substantial in the aggregate, to a foreign government official." Leon declined to identify the official or the country, saying only it was "a significant source of supply for the corporation."

The bribery was unsuccessful, he told shareholders. "The payments were made in the hope of promoting a project which never materialized, and the company received nothing as a result of the payments," which had ceased about two-and-a-half years before. The bribery money was his, it didn't come from the company's coffers, and he hadn't sought any reimbursement and no deductions were taken from the payments.

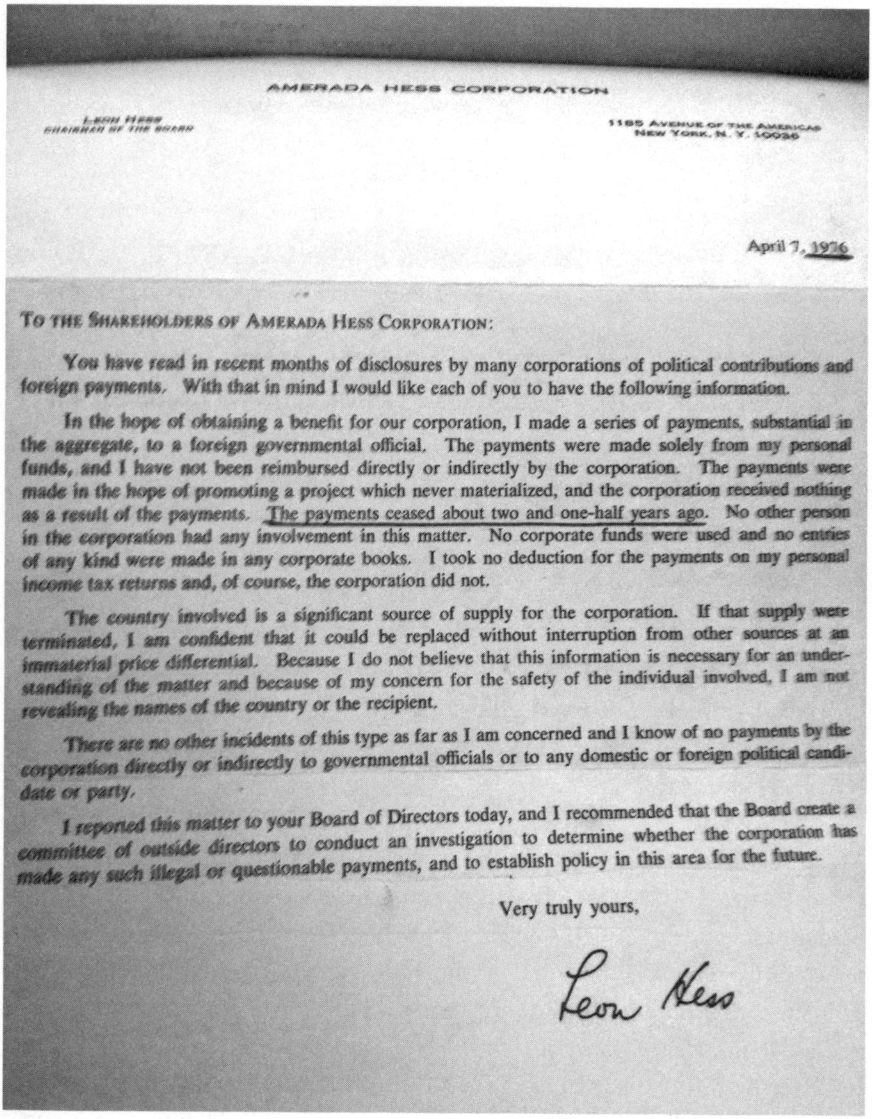

Figure 5.1 Leon Hess's letter to Amerada Hess shareholders.
SOURCE: Photograph by Tina Davis.

In less than a year, the payments Leon Hess was writing about would be illegal, as Congress enacted the Foreign Corrupt Practices Act to make overseas bribery and political contributions a crime in the United States. A practice as old as cross-border trade itself was now under scrutiny.

■ ■ ■

Hess was far from alone in confessing the payments. Evidence of U.S. companies bribing foreign officials and making contributions to overseas political parties first came up as part of the work of the Office of the Watergate Special Prosecutor, with follow-up from the Securities and Exchange Commission. In the process of looking over the books for illegal political donations, "The staff discovered falsifications of corporate financial records, designed to disguise or conceal the source and application of corporate funds misused for illegal purposes, as well as the existence of secret 'slush funds' distributed outside the normal financial accountability system. These secret funds were used for a number of purposes, including in some instances, questionable or illegal foreign payments."[1]

Bribing foreign officials wasn't illegal—the SEC said it was reviewing the payments to determine if they should have been disclosed to investors. With sunshine as its disinfectant, the agency could publicly shame companies engaged in the practice. In May 1975, Senator Frank Church, an Iowa Democrat who would challenge Jimmy Carter for the presidential nomination, started holding hearings on the overseas bribes.

". . . While bribes and kickbacks may bolster sales in the short run, the open participation of American firms in such practices can, in the long run, only serve to discredit them and the United States," Church said. The problem was not only in public perception of America abroad, it also posed foreign policy challenges if companies were propping up governments that weren't democratic. The State Department should set the nation's foreign policy, not the CEOs of the largest multinationals. "The Communist bloc chortles with glee at the sign of corrupt capitalism," Church said.

Among the companies the hearings looked at were Gulf Oil (a company founded by Pennsylvania's Mellon family, which would later combine with one of the original "seven sisters" from the breakup of Rockefeller's trusts to form Chevron Corp.) and Mobil Oil, later to merge into ExxonMobil Corp. Gulf had been contributing to political campaigns in South Korea, Italy, Bolivia, and other countries. Mobil had been giving money to Italian political parties. A smaller company, Ashland Oil, had been paying the president of Gabon.

In a post-Watergate world, Congress was eager to be seen as cracking down on corporate malfeasance, especially any real or perceived
interference in political processes at home or abroad. While some lawmakers derided the push for stricter rules on foreign payments, saying
U.S. companies were far from the only ones engaging in the practice, the
lingering outrage from President Nixon's scandal necessitated a response
from a Democratic-led Congress.

The chairman of Gulf Oil during one hearing asked Congress to
enact legislation that would outlaw foreign contributions by U.S. companies, saying it would ease pressure that was being brought to bear and
had long been the price of doing business in some areas.

Robert Dorsey would be forced out of his position as chairman in
1976, amid the aftermath of revelations that Gulf Oil had used a $12
million slush fund based in the Bahamas for all sorts of payments. The
company admitted to $100,000 in illegal donations to Nixon's 1972
reelection fund, according to news reports at the time.

■ ■ ■

In the 1970s, Hess was doing business in several nations, not all of them
free of the kind of corruption that would involve substantial payments
to "promote a project." Certainly, Leon was far from the first oil executive to try to buy his way into a country's good graces. But the bribery
admission was an unusual one from a man who would be lauded by his
company after his death as having had "the very highest standards of
ethical conduct."[2]

Leon traveled a lot for his job, and he encouraged those who worked
for him to travel as well to find new opportunities. As an entrepreneur, Leon
had the opposite mind-set of some of the major oil companies that let opportunities find them. He was always hungry for new prospects, according
to people who worked for him, and he was never averse to taking risks.

Was the foreign official Leon Hess had been paying from Libya? It's
possible—the country accounted for a major portion of Hess's output at
the time. Hess inherited the Libyan holdings when it bought Amerada,
an oil producer that had bet big on the nation as it emerged from being
administered by the Western Allies after World War II.

Amerada announced in 1957 that it had added to its holdings in
the United Kingdom of Libya, and had a one-third interest in about

62 million acres[3]—an area equivalent to more than twice the size of the state of New York. The announcement came the same year that Esso, part of Standard Oil of New Jersey, struck oil in the North African country.

Libya had become an independent sovereign nation just eight years earlier. The country, which had been colonized by the Italians, emerged as a whole unit after the French and British separately administered its three provinces during World War II.

Only two years after the war ended, the British military kicked a three-man survey team sent by Standard Oil of New Jersey out of the country. The jockeying for resources in Libya was already under way.

Libya moved quickly to exploit its oil, with production beginning a scant 10 years after the nation was formed in 1951. Output soared to 3.5 million barrels a day by 1969–1970. Because the country and the regime essentially owed their existence to the Western Allies, Libya was extremely friendly to foreign oil companies. That close relationship went so far as having the government bring in a former Royal Dutch Shell executive and an adviser to the British government to help draft petroleum laws that opened the nation to exploration, a move that caused U.S. oil companies to cry foul for fear their British counterparts had an unfair advantage.

The eventual terms under which companies could participate in Libyan oil were "a foretaste of paradise for the oil companies," with low buy-in costs, taxes, and royalties, Frank C. Waddams wrote in a history of the nation's oil industry.[4] Of course, that paradise was eventually lost—within two years of the nation's petroleum law being enacted, Libya was seeking to change terms the government belatedly realized were inordinately generous.

But in the meantime, "The open-door policy of the Libyan Government allowed both major internationals and new-comers equal opportunity to participate. The majors were anxious to the point of obsession to obtain secure additions to their future supplies. Independents [like Amerada] took the opportunity to embark on new ventures in the context of a great burgeoning of transnational activities of U.S. companies," according to Waddams. Libya, for its part, was keen to play the major oil companies and independents (that is, companies that focused on production and didn't own the full suite of oil refineries and transit assets) off one another, to help ensure the highest levels of production.

Eventually, 70 percent of Libya's land mass was offered for drilling. Esso (another Rockefeller legacy company) and Texas oilman Nelson Bunker Hunt received the first two concessions that allowed foreigners to drill in Libya. "[D]rilling in Libya by our group as well as by others has shown the existence of oil in very widely separated areas and in a number of geological horizons," Amerada said in its 1959 annual report. The number of drilling rigs was expanded, a signal of how enthusiastic the company was despite depressed oil prices.

In 1960, Amerada pooled its concessions with two other independent oil companies—Marathon and Continental—to create Oasis Petroleum. The three companies, which were relative newcomers to overseas oil production, were about to become the largest operators in Libya, surpassing Esso's output four years after the first crude began flowing from their fields in 1962.

In 1966, Shell bought half of Amerada's stake in Oasis, giving the organization another buyer for its output (which had previously all been sold to Continental—the company that would later become Conoco). By that time, Amerada was getting 188,000 barrels a day of production from Libya, more than twice what it was producing in the United States. Libya accounted for almost two thirds of the company's total acreage.

■ ■ ■

Three years later, Libya underwent a revolution that would give prominence to a man called Moammar Qaddafi. Unlike his predecessors, Qaddafi didn't view foreign oil companies as essential to the nation's prosperity.

"The Libyan people, who have lived for 5,000 years without petroleum, are able to live again without it," he told oil company heads in January 1970. Libya wasn't happy with the price it was getting for the oil, and producers that had flooded the country and helped pump the output of its crude during the past decade would have to reach a new deal. The presence of so many smaller oil companies meant the government was in a good bargaining position—it could lean heavily on the companies that didn't have much production elsewhere to pay higher prices for the oil, unlike the majors that might've otherwise been able to withstand the pressure.

What happened in Libya would have ripple effects in Saudi Arabia and the rest of the oil-producing world, as nations began to demand a higher price and bigger percentage of royalties from the oil that foreign companies were pumping.

Libya began ordering companies to reduce production, a move it said was being done to save the viability of its fields from the kind of rushed output that would deplete a field too quickly, leaving less recoverable crude. The producers saw it as a pressuring tactic to force them to raise prices. One of the companies that bore the brunt of the negotiations was Occidental Petroleum (often called Oxy), which depended on Libya for a big chunk of its output. "The Libyan accusation was that Oxy was producing, Occidental was producing, at a very high rate in order to get the oil in the country very, very rapidly, write off its investment and then the hell with everything else and the hell with Libya," Ambassador James Akins, who was head of the State Department's Office of Fuels and Energy, testified at a hearing in 1973.[5]

Oasis, the producing group that included Amerada Hess, was forced to cut output by 12 percent—a mild reduction compared with others (Occidental's production was cut almost in half).

The Libyans were seeking a 40-cent hike in per-barrel oil prices. The major producers set posted prices at given hubs in the Middle East. Those prices were used to calculate oil taxes and "bore no relation to market prices," according to an executive with the Bunker Hunt Oil Co.[6] The U.S. State Department thought such an increase was reasonable, given the lower costs to get Libyan oil to Europe (especially with the Suez Canal shut down) and the lower-sulfur content of the oil, which made it easier to process into fuel. The oil companies, however, were only willing to increase the price (and thus the benefit to the home nation) by five cents a barrel. In the midst of this, Shell and Phillips saw their assets in Algeria seized. "A top official of a major oil company seriously urged the American Government to dare the Libyans to nationalize" the oil assets, Akins wrote in *Foreign Affairs*.[7] Akins declined to identify the official to a Senate subcommittee.

Eventually, Occidental reached a deal to raise the price by 30 cents, plus a series of future increases and other items. Most important, the agreement raised the tax rate to 58 percent, exceeding the traditional 50/50 split that other nations had received. Ten days after Libya had a deal with Occidental—and one day after Libyan producers had met in New York to discuss the possibility that the deal might be forced on others—the government reached out to Oasis. It wanted a price hike.

Leon would later tell a story about negotiating with a representative of Qaddafi who put a gun on the table between them. It hardened him to future talks—not much more can seem scary in business once you've done a deal over a (presumably) loaded firearm.

Leon loved negotiating, and by many accounts he was great at it. He was always slightly unpredictable in talks, which he used to his advantage. He would take a lot of trouble to get to know his counterparties and their families and he built some very strong relationships with people he was buying crude oil from. Those relationships weren't limited to the CEO or the minister level—he was quite happy sitting down with the midlevel technocrat if that's where he thought the decisions were going to be made.

But even Leon would struggle to get a good deal out of Libya. Oasis became the second producer to capitulate to the Qaddafi regime. Three of the owners agreed to raise the posted price of oil retroactively and for the future, and pay an additional 4 percent tax rate. Shell balked at the demands and was refused permission to move oil out of Libya. The company, which like Amerada Hess held a 16.5 percent stake in Oasis, gave up its holdings to the government.

Other oil-producing nations watched Libya's aggressive actions with interest.

"As a result of the revolution in Libya, it was no longer going to be possible to keep politics out of oil negotiations," George Henry Mayer Schuler of Bunker Hunt Oil Co. told a Senate subcommittee.[8]

After Libya succeeded in changing the rules of the game, the Organization of the Petroleum Exporting Countries (OPEC) met in Venezuela and changed their tax rates to better match what Libya was getting. Eager to avoid a constant ratcheting up of demands, the oil companies banded together in what was called the London Policy Group, getting a U.S. government waiver of antitrust provisions so that they could negotiate with all the OPEC countries in a single round of talks. (It was a much less complicated dance for their European counterparts, which were mostly state-owned.) For U.S. participants, the London Policy Group would ultimately report back to a group of CEOs in New York, a group that included Leon Hess. The U.S. CEOs would gather at the University Club, Mobil's offices, or in conference rooms at Chase Manhattan Bank to guide the industry negotiations, usually talking by speaker phone with representatives in London. The deal they reached amounted to about $10 billion in added payments, and would be known as the Tehran agreement. It was supposed to offer five years of stable pricing. But as Senator Church said, it was more like the time Neville Chamberlain bought in Munich. After the Arab oil embargo, it was clear to all observers that the oil-producing nations could and would withhold supply to hike prices. The United States was no longer driving the world's production; it could exert pressure only from the sidelines.

Far from ending the arms race between producers for a bigger slice of production, the Tehran agreement prompted Libya to go even further, requesting not just a stake in the companies but a majority share. Some backed down and some exited or saw their assets seized. Bunker Hunt's properties were nationalized in 1973, according to Qaddafi: "The nationalization of the American company is only a warning to the oil companies to respond to the demands of the Libyan Arab Republic . . . [and] a warning to the United States to end its recklessness and hostility to the Arab nation." Under threat of nationalization, the group of companies that formed Oasis gave in, agreeing to hand over a 51 percent stake to the Libyan government for $18 million, in a complicated arrangement that also forced them to buy output from the nation.

Phillips Corp., another independent, surrendered its unprofitable field rather than give majority control to Libya. In December 1971, BP's assets in the nation (which were being operated in a joint venture with Bunker Hunt) were taken over in "retaliation for Britain's failure to act to prevent Iran's seizure of the Tunb Islands in the Arabian Gulf," the Libyan government said.

An agreement among the oil-producing companies that they would step in with supplies if anyone was nationalized quickly proved worthless. Exxon, Texaco, BP, and Standard Oil of California provided oil. Amerada, Continental, Marathon, and Occidental didn't live up to the agreement. Basically, the companies that had extra oil ponied up and those that were still heavily Libya-dependent gave nothing.

Even getting the oil out of Libya after nationalization became a legal wrangle—one supplier to utilities, the New England Petroleum Corp., was told that it shouldn't take delivery of crude from Libya's national oil company because of Standard Oil of California's claims to it. The company informed the State Department that the U.S. president alone could make that call—its customers needed fuel oil to keep the lights on, and only Richard Nixon's word could halt crude deliveries that might cause a blackout in New York City.

The once close relationship the Libyan government had with foreign oil companies was over. The gentleman's agreements that had defined the way corporations had done business with governments that were largely put in place by the Allies after World War II were done. In 1973, Libya banned oil shipments to the United States as part of the Arab oil embargo.

Oil from Libya, which had been going to Amerada Hess's St. Croix refinery, was now being sent to other countries not subject to the embargo. The price of Libyan oil increased from $8.925 a barrel on October 19, 1973, to $15.768 on January 1, 1974 (just after the 1969 revolution, it was $1.50). Amerada's share of the production from Libya kept declining, falling to 92,730 barrels a day in 1973, from more than twice that amount a few years earlier. So the company was getting half the oil and paying 10 times as much for it.

The company would be given special dispensation (along with four other oil companies) to continue operating in Libya for a while after the Libyan government was found to have supported the 1986 bombing of a German nightclub that killed two U.S. soldiers. Operations would be suspended entirely later that year. By all accounts, Leon was sorry to have to leave Libya, which had been such a huge source of oil for the company. The Oasis group would announce plans to re-enter the country 20 years later, but the unrest that has followed the Arab Spring has continued to put the vast quantities of Libyan oil just beyond the reach of hungry producers.

■ ■ ■

By 1965, the industry was investing more in foreign oil and natural gas production than it was in the United States. (By 1971, it spent almost double the amount overseas that was spent at home.)[9] While the promise

of Alaskan oil was still in its infancy and the United States was just moving to claim its rights to drill in the Outer Continental Shelf of the Gulf
of Mexico, producers were largely turning their attention to foreign oil.

Like Libya, Iran was a place that promised a lot of rich oil deposits as
U.S. producers, no longer having access to easy oil in their home nation,
turned overseas for crude. Iran, home to the first oil well in the Middle
East, was a powerhouse of production in the 1970s, rising to 6 million
barrels a day from a third of that amount just a decade earlier.

Working in the Middle East meant Leon would have to learn to get
along with despots who didn't always like him, even before they knew him.
According to one account,[10] the Shah of Iran initially balked at the idea of
doing business with Hess because Leon was Jewish. An adviser pointed out
that Israelis were partners in a company that serviced the nation's military
aircraft. The Shah yielded, as Leon and John awaited word in the Tehran
Hilton. (Years later, Hess would be the conduit to send heating oil and
kerosene to Iran at a time when it had petitioned the United States for the
refined products—and then said it didn't need the supplies after all.)

Leon had stronger relationships in the Arab region than many companies that were not owned by Jewish men. That was due in part to his
sheer longevity. He'd been around for a long time, and had seen a lot of
what went on. Crown princes and oil ministers knew that the major oil
companies they dealt with had a revolving door of executives—the person you made a deal with today might be gone tomorrow. But Leon was
always there. He was a tireless traveler who was always seeing new opportunities (going to London when he was no longer allowed to travel
to Iran). And he would be there next year. It was his name on the side
of the storage tanks. His counterparts also came to know that he would
be as good as his word, even as the era when a handshake could seal a
deal was starting to fade. He was a man who believed in making lasting
connections, which served him well at a time when information wasn't
as readily available as it is now. And he had great connections, part of his
effort to know everyone he worked with (one former Hess executive
says that Leon knew the name of the guy who fixed the air-conditioning
in his office).

He had both an exacting attention to detail and the type of outgoing, engaging personality that made him stop executives and industry
acquaintances who were too eager to get into business talk at the start of

a phone call. Instead, he wanted to hear about their wives, their children, their lives outside of the office. Getting to know everyone well and being someone who could retain considerable information about suppliers, logistics, and figures were two qualities that made him a formidable opponent across a negotiating table.

The company announced an agreement in 1971 with the National Iranian Oil Co. to explore a modest area—about 1,400 square miles—in the Persian Gulf. Making deals with the Shah was never a sure thing, though, especially at a time when Libyan demands were spurring others to leapfrog over one another requiring higher taxes or bigger stakes from producers. Communiques between members of the London Policy Group noted that the Shah was furious at the deals Libya was making with producers, which were sweeter than his own arrangements.

The company would expand its holdings in Iran until 1978, when the nation's output accounted for almost half (46 percent) of the crude Amerada was running through its refineries. All that stopped when the Shah was toppled. The new government no longer sold oil to Westerners, which helped to alleviate some of the oversupply in the world but also complicated the company's ability to operate the refining business. Hess began stockpiling the fuel at its refineries in the latter half of 1978, worried that its supply would run out once the new government was in place. The worry was well placed—Iran cut off supplies in December of that year.

Eventually, the deposed Shah, who had questioned doing business with a Jew, would become close with Leon—the Shah's twin sister would buy the penthouse in the same Park Avenue building that Leon and Norma lived in (it would be reported that he stayed in Leon's pad when he was in the city for medical treatment after he was deposed, but it's more likely he was rooming in the palatial triplex spread upstairs that his sister would eventually sell to private-equity billionaire Henry Kravis, who is also Jewish).

■ ■ ■

When he took over the company, John Hess continued to expand its oil production business into exotic locales. With the acquisition of Triton Energy in August 2001, Hess was pulled into nascent oil plays in areas that it hadn't trod before. Triton, like many small explorers, focused on identifying new plays and ultimately turning them over to skilled operators like Hess, Exxon, BP, or other major players.

The smaller company operated in Africa, Asia, and South America, with a majority stake in the Ceiba field in Equatorial Guinea, an interest in three contract areas in Colombia, and a stake in a joint venture in the Gulf of Thailand. In buying Triton, Hess entered Equatorial Guinea, a country just larger than the state of Maryland, nestled between Cameroon and Gabon. The nation has been run since a 1979 coup by President Teodoro Obiang Nguema Mbasogo.

In 1995, the nation hit its first oil riches with the discovery of the Zafiro field. The Ceiba and Okume fields followed, and the Aseng field opened up after that. As with Libya, Equatorial Guinea experienced a huge ramp-up of oil output, becoming sub-Saharan Africa's third-largest exporter in the past decade, according to the CIA.[11]

The gross domestic product of Equatorial Guinea tripled in the early years of its drilling boom, and American companies like Exxon, Mobil, Chevron, Texaco, and Marathon Oil all jockeyed for a place at a the table, investing over $5 billion in the country. That investment was most often made by buying the assets of smaller independent companies that had done the hard work of getting leases and testing the areas for economically recoverable oil. The bigger oil companies may not have asked enough questions about how the leases were secured. When the big boys entered the market, it drew attention from lawmakers and others in a nation where corrupt practices might otherwise have continued largely unremarked upon by the world.

Despite having the forty-second-largest oil reserves in the world, the country suffered from poverty. The United States shuttered its embassy there in 1995 in protest of the country's poor human rights record (early in the next decade, it was quietly reopened).

As oil production increased, GDP grew by an average real annual rate of 26.2 percent during Hess's first four years in the country, according to the World Bank. Production of oil, condensate, and natural gas is the basis of the country's economy. According to the International Monetary Fund's latest data published in 2012, the hydrocarbon sector represented over 90 percent of government revenue and about 98 percent of export earnings.

Hess was responsible for a great deal of oil infrastructure development in the country, operating two major offshore projects—the Ceiba field, 22 miles offshore, and the adjacent Okume Complex—with partners Tullow Oil and GEPetrol. The blocks Hess operates there span 1.3 million acres. Beyond the Ceiba field are the Okume, Oveng, Ebano, Elon, Akom, and Abang fields.

After the acquisition of Triton, Hess was optimistic: the company planned to more than triple oil production from the Ceiba field between 2001 and 2002, to consider developing additional discoveries in the country, and to actively seek new discoveries.

The upbeat tone made sense for the company—its proven reserves had risen by 189 million barrels in the year with the acquisition of Triton and its own discoveries, and it was becoming increasingly global, with only 20 percent of its reserves in the United States.

While an additional 40 percent of the reserves were in more stable regions of the world, like sections of the North Sea controlled by the United Kingdom, Norway, and Denmark, Hess was charting new territory in areas that were complicated to operate in, like Algeria, Azerbaijan, Colombia, Gabon, and, of course, Equatorial Guinea.

Positive developments followed in Equatorial Guinea as an appraisal well drilled in early 2003 confirmed an earlier discovery well in 2002. But the upbeat tone around production growth cloaked the complexities of operating in Equatorial Guinea.

Triton, it was revealed, leased property from the fourteen-year-old son of the president, who was represented by his mother. Under the lease, Hess and Triton paid nearly half a million dollars to members of Obiang's family. Triton had also leased a tract of land to operate as a heliport from a military officer, paying $300,000 for the parcel.

Hess was forced to use security services provided by a company called Sonavi, owned by the president's brother, with non-negotiable rates set by law. Hess and ExxonMobil, two of the largest operators there, contended with this problem, while four other oil companies said they were able to get security services elsewhere.

While Amerada Hess had a written policy preventing violations of the Foreign Corrupt Practices Act, the company told a Congressional subcommittee that it was very common for government officials in Equatorial Guinea to have shares in private companies, so there may be instances of such payments of which the company was unaware.

Even in trying to raise the level of education in a country with widespread illiteracy, there were sometimes complications—between 2001 and 2003, Hess paid nearly $2 million to fund education abroad for students from Equatorial Guinea. Five other U.S. oil companies that were operating there also made payments for students studying in the United States and Canada. However, most of the children who benefited from the programs were the children or relatives of government officials, according to a U.S. Senate subcommittee that looked at banking in Equatorial Guinea. It was unclear whether the oil companies were aware of the students' status, the investigation found. A Hess representative told Congress that the company just funded the programs; it had no control over which students were selected.

In 2004, the company was named as one of several oil producers being investigated by the U.S. Securities and Exchange Commission for bribery in Equatorial Guinea, after the government was found to have held about $700 million in cash and investments at Riggs Bank in Washington. A Senate subcommittee that reviewed the operations of Riggs Bank found the bank was "dysfunctional" in its implementation of anti–money laundering obligations.[12] Riggs was found to have held amounts ranging from $4 million to $8 million of Chilean ex-dictator Augusto Pinochet's funds from 1994 to 2002. It also found 60 accounts associated with Equatorial Guinea (the bank had prided itself on its business servicing embassies in Washington). In those accounts were between $400 million and $700 million at any given time. Included in this was about $13 million in deposits over a three-year period to accounts controlled by the president and his wife—on two occasions, astonishing deposits of $3 million *in cash* were made to the bank, which failed to ask adequate questions about the money, investigators concluded. This was, needless to say, a lot of money for government officials of such a poor country.

A year after the report came out, Riggs would be bought by PNC. The bank that had once been Washington's largest, that had financed the invention of the telegraph and provided gold for the purchase of Alaska, was gone.

The Congressional investigation, using anti–money laundering provisions of the much-maligned Patriot Act signed into law after 9/11, also revealed the complexity of Equatorial Guinea's economic and political web for oil companies, which are often required to enter into production sharing agreements that link them to the governments of the countries in which they operate.

Equatorial Guinea is particularly full of policy land mines for oil companies. Because Obiang and his family dominate sectors from timber to hotels to supermarkets, the Senate subcommittee found that oil companies operating in the country faced particularly fraught concerns around their production-sharing arrangements. In the country, oil companies including Amerada Hess provided a certain percentage of the oil they discovered to Obiang's government and paid Equatorial Guinea taxes on profits earned there.

Records examined by the subcommittee showed that many oil companies' payments went to government oil accounts, including many that went to the nation's oil account at Riggs. However, other accounts also took certain payments, the committee found.

Hess and its predecessor, Triton, made payments to approximately 33 other vendors in Equatorial Guinea between 1997 and 2004, according to documents Amerada Hess provided to the subcommittee. The company emphasized that it had been in the country for only three years by 2004, pulled in by the Triton acquisition.

Of the 28 leases Hess maintained in Malabo, two-thirds were from people connected with Obiang and his government.

"I know you are all in a competitive business and other companies do it," Senator Carl Levin, head of an investigations subcommittee, told representatives of Hess, Exxon, and Marathon at a July 15 hearing.[13] "But I have to tell you, I do not see any fundamental difference between dealing with an Obiang and dealing with a Saddam Hussein. They are both dictators. They are both human rights violators."

Hess told the subcommittee that it planned to cancel all of the leases by April 2004.

Despite these obstacles, in another five years, the country produced 319,100 barrels of oil a day, of which all but 1,000 barrels were exported.

Hess continues to do business in Equatorial Guinea, where the company now produces about 70,000 barrels a day. Hess has now spent over 13 years doing business in a place where 50 percent of the children don't go to school beyond the third grade and 80 percent don't go past the sixth grade.

John Hess is open about the need for charity work to help the company's goals. "One of the things we do to try to help ourselves getting access to energy but also continuing to have a license to operate and having the trust of the government is not just invest to take the oil or the gas out and make money for our shareholders, but just as important as what your economic contribution is, you should have a social contribution," John said in an April 2014 speech in Washington.

The company set up a public-private partnership in 2009 that holds $50 million, of which it paid half, and the government contributed the rest. The partnership has had an effect on 40,000 students, trained 2,000 teachers, and rehabbed 800 schools, focusing on primary education. It's now focused on secondary education and vocational training so that more citizens of Equatorial Guinea are qualified to work for the company.

There has also been some reconsideration of its overseas forays: after years of overseas exploits, the company is now looking to ease back a bit on its foreign jaunts—aiming to get half of its output in the United States and half from overseas (before the company got big into shale, about 25 percent of its production came from the United States).

Chapter 6

Hess in DC

Senator, I'm only here to cooperate with you, I want you to know that. You couldn't get me here with a team of horses.

—Leon Hess, 1990 congressional testimony

L eon Hess was late to the hearing. Fog at the airport delayed his flight to Washington as the November 1, 1990, hearing by the Committee on Governmental Affairs began. It was the last of three hearings on how the Persian Gulf crisis—specifically, Saddam Hussein's invasion of Kuwait—affected oil supplies and prices. The subject of the day was the role of futures markets in oil prices.

A doubling of oil prices had prompted consumer howls and congressional attention, which is always quick to follow. The cost rose from $16.72 a barrel a month before the invasion of Kuwait to $35.23 as coalition soldiers massed on the border before the military response began.

Futures markets, as the name would imply, consist of contracts to buy and sell a commodity at a future date. Most of the traders have no intention of ever actually taking delivery of the oil they are buying or selling. For companies that produce crude, the markets provide a way to hedge against future price fluctuations—if, for example, prices collapse and your supply suddenly has a lower value, you could still make money on oil with a paper bet that they would drop.

As prices spiked, though, lawmakers worried that the markets themselves were somehow broken because they weren't being driven by current supply-demand fundamentals, but rather by future fears. And "speculators" (a designation that encompasses many without necessarily identifying anyone in particular) were benefiting from the price rise. This wouldn't be the first or the last time Congress created a bogeyman it could ceremoniously blame for price spikes, while doing nothing substantive to change the way markets operate.

"I am concerned that the futures market itself has provided too ready a vehicle for sharp price increases that are fueled by rumor, panic, and speculation," Senator Joe Lieberman said at the start of the hearing. "A market that can be so affected by fantasy is, in my opinion, not a rational market."

Leon was also not a fan of the futures market. This was despite the company's more than $200 million profit in the third quarter of that year from futures trading.

In testimony sprinkled with "damns," and abrupt urgings for the senator to give him the next question, Leon told the committee that so-called paper trading was driving worldwide oil prices.

"With the advent of NYMEX oil trading, the law of economics, namely supply and demand, is meaningless," Hess said, referring to the New York Mercantile Exchange.

"We are guilty, we are selling it," he said of oil prices, "but our costs have gone up too." The profit was from hedging against production price swings and refinery costs, not from pure speculation on what market prices would do, he explained.

At one point, he expressed nostalgia for the old days, when producers set oil prices. "If we had left the damn thing alone and we didn't play with WTI [West Texas Intermediate, a U.S. benchmark oil price] and futures market, we would have government sales prices by OPEC of $21 a barrel. That is where they set the official price."

The recent price swings on the market were not driven by a fundamental shift in supply or demand, he said. "It is goddamn speculation."

He suggested the markets should require 100 percent margins, essentially forcing traders to have all the money on hand they would need to settle a contract immediately—something that would have seriously curtailed trading in markets where a little bit of money was often leveraged many times over to make big bets.

Lieberman, a Connecticut Democrat who would eventually be attacked by left-leaning members of his party and lose a primary vote before becoming one of the Senate's few independent lawmakers, agreed with that approach, calling it "some good old-fashioned common sense."

"I hope if a crisis occurs that we find a way to get you right down here quickly," he told Leon.

"I don't think they want me here," Leon responded. "I am a trouble-maker."

■ ■ ■

Leon was no stranger to Washington, so his professed impatience for the place is a little like the longtime incumbent Congressman who declares his intention to change the government.

Leon's eldest daughter, Constance, would describe her father's politics at his funeral like this: "In business, he was a Republican; by marriage, a Democrat; by choice an independent." Leon had married the daughter of a high-powered New Jersey Democrat, former Attorney General David Wilentz. In 1973, he identified himself as a Democrat in an affidavit, by which time he had given substantial funding to support Democratic candidates. (The next generation of Hesses would reflect some of their father's schizophrenic politics: Constance won state office in Pennsylvania as a Democrat after working for a Democratic representative—and an in-law of President Bill Clinton—and ended up running New Jersey Senator Bill Bradley's presidential campaign in her adopted state. Meanwhile, John has become a repeated supporter of Republican candidates. Marlene has followed in her father's footsteps—donating to Democratic and Republican candidates and most recently giving money to Barack Obama's 2008 presidential campaign and then donating to Mitt Romney's bid in the 2012 election cycle.)

Leon threw a substantial amount of money at the 1972 election, pouring more than half a million dollars in total into campaigns on both sides before it was all over. Even with his deep and sometimes contradictory ties to DC, it's still surprising that Leon would become a big contributor to President Richard Nixon's reelection campaign in 1972, a fact that would make him a subject of interest to the Watergate Special Prosecutor.

"I have been an active supporter of various candidates for public office over the years," Leon said in a 1973 affidavit.

"I was a substantial contributor to the 1968 presidential campaign of Senator Hubert Humphrey and have also contributed to the campaigns of candidates for the United States Senate, for the House of Representatives, and for some state and local offices. As in all of my personal, business, charitable, and other activities, I have sought to avoid any publicizing of my contributions. My consistent purpose has been to protect the privacy of my family and to avoid communications from cranks, and other invasions of privacy, which inevitably accompany the publicizing of substantial gifts," he said. "Accordingly, it has been my consistent practice to make contributions as anonymously as possible, both as to the amount of my contributions and as to my personal identification with them. Usually my contributions have been made through bank checks, through business associates, and through my former accountant. Occasionally, I will make small contributions in my own name where the amount is not likely to attract attention, but this is the exception rather than the rule. This approach applied fully to my campaign contributions during the 1972 presidential campaign."

Before getting embroiled in the Watergate affair, Leon had been a major supporter of Humphrey, a Minnesota Democrat who ran unsuccessfully against John F. Kennedy for the 1960 nomination before being tapped as Lyndon Johnson's running mate for 1964. In 1968, he was battling Robert F. Kennedy for the nomination when that opponent was assassinated. Humphrey finally ended up winning the Democratic nomination but, facing another man who'd lost to JFK, he was beaten in the general election by Nixon. It was a campaign that relied heavily on a few people for funding: "[F]ewer than 30 individuals will have provided between one-third and one-half [of] the $10 million to $12 million being spent on the Humphrey campaign," Walter Pincus wrote in the *Washington Post* in 1968. Leon later said he'd agreed to forgive $123,500 of a $250,000 loan to various Humphrey committees from the 1968 bid.

The bouncing back and forth between the political parties would continue up until the end of his life—Leon's name would pop up on a list of people Al Gore called from the White House between November 1995 and May 1996 seeking donations to the Democratic National Committee (the vice president asked for $100,000). That was a few years after he was listed among people who had given more than $100,000 to the GOP.[1]

The 1972 presidential campaign was one that Leon bet particularly heavy on—and he bet on both sides. Before supporting Nixon, Leon pumped $225,000 into Senator Henry "Scoop" Jackson's failed 1972 presidential campaign. Jackson, a Washington Democrat, was head of the committee that oversaw the Interior Department, which at that time (before the creation of the Energy Department in 1977) was a crucial agency for U.S. energy producers like Hess who relied on it for drilling permissions, among other things. Jackson was known as a hawkish Democrat and a strong supporter of Israel. Leon said that he called Jackson in the summer of 1971 and asked what his campaign would cost. He agreed to simply foot the bill for 10 percent of it and told investigators he didn't ask for favors in return. His donations were disguised as coming from others—checks from Leon would be passed through other individuals' accounts, a practice that wasn't yet illegal.

The named parties included Leon's personal accountant, Irving Warshauer, his wife, and other friends or relatives as well as some senior executives at Amerada Hess. "I believe Hess completely when he states that's personal money," Stanley Golub, treasurer for Jackson, told the *Washington Star-News*.[2] "Of course, that's a hell of a lot of personal money, but he is a wealthy man."

Leon would use the same method, including some of the same names, to give $300,000 to President Nixon for the 1972 campaign (Figure 6.1). It was a simple pass-through—the Watergate file for Amerada Hess shows check after check written from his account with the First National State Bank of New Jersey to various individuals, including executives J. D. (Jerry) Callender, Philip Kramer, and H. W. McCollum, for $2,000, $3,000, or even $10,000. The money would flow to Nixon's campaign through checks from the individuals with the same date on them to political committees (organizations with now-ironic names like "United Friends of Government Reform").

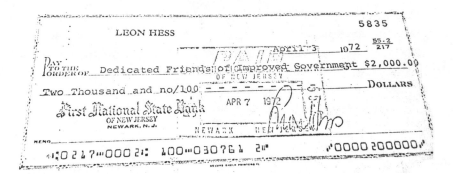

Figure 6.1 A check from Leon Hess to Dedicated Friends of Improved Government, a political organization that supported Richard Nixon's presidential campaign.
SOURCE: National Archives and Records Administration, Watergate Special Prosecution Force, Campaign Contributions Numerical File, Box 132.

Leon's pivot to Nixon came after Jackson faltered in the primary. "When, very early in the primary campaign, I came to the conclusion that Senator Jackson could not win the Democratic Party's nomination for president, I decided to support the reelection of Richard M. Nixon. I made total contributions in the amount of $300,000 to the reelection campaign for President Nixon," Leon said.[3]

Hess was brought into the fold as a Nixon contributor by Bernard "Bunny" Lasker, who until May 1971 was chairman of the New York Stock Exchange. Lasker "volunteered to solicit Leon Hess" at a February 1972 meeting of fundraisers at the Metropolitan Club in New York, he told an investigator from the Watergate Special Prosecution Force in 1974. Hess had contributed to a September 1971 "Salute to the President" dinner that Lasker had organized.

That was the same month that Nixon was recorded in the Oval Office asking Chief of Staff Bob Haldeman for "the names of the Jews. You know, the big Jewish contributors to the Democrats. Could you please investigate some of the cocksuckers?"[4] It was nine months before the Watergate burglary.

"At that time, Hess said that he liked the work the President was doing," Lasker recalled of the September 1971 dinner for Nixon that Leon attended, according to the investigator's notes.[5] Hess handed over checks and about

$3,500 in cash. The treasurer of the dinner committee asked Lasker to return the cash. Subsequently, in March 1972, Lasker went to Hess's office and asked for a donation. "Hess said that he would like to discuss the amount of the contribution with 'someone higher up in the Administration.'"

In response, Lasker set up a meeting with Maurice Stans, a former commerce secretary for Nixon and the finance chairman for the infamous Committee to Re-Elect the President (CREEP). Once again, the meeting was in Hess's office.

"Hess mentioned the fact that he was a Democrat but that he thought the President was doing a great job. Hess then asked, 'What is considered being in the big league as far as a contributor is concerned?'" according to the notes. He was told $200,000, and Stans mentioned that if he gave before April 7 he wouldn't be required to disclose it under the existing law. Lasker recalled there was no discussion of anything Hess wanted in return for his donation.

More than a year later, Hess contacted Lasker, and told him that part of the money he gave to Nixon took the form of funds he had given others to give to the various committees that were supporting the campaign. "Hess said that he had heard from reporters that they were asking about the money and that they were asking whether he had been to the 'Oil Bureau' to ask for anything," Lasker told the investigator. During the call he emphasized the money was his, not from the company, and it was after tax (so as not to violate gift tax laws).

"Hess mentioned that he had the Senate Watergate questionnaire in front of him and he asked Lasker if Lasker knew the names of the nominees [the people through which the Hess funds had passed]. Lasker said that he did not." Two months later, Lasker and Stans had a phone call in which they discussed the Hess contribution and neither of them recalled Hess saying at the time of the donation that any part of his contribution would come through other people.

In the aftermath of the revelations about the Watergate break-in and before the pass-through was publicly acknowledged, reporters were querying the Leon-backed contributions, asking how people who made little money were capable of sending huge sums to the Nixon campaign. Some individuals involved in the pass-through seemed to be unaware of the practice. "I never gave away any money to anybody for President,"

Leigh Tuvin, widow of a Warshauer client who was living on a fixed in-come in Florida at the time, told the *Washington Post*. "I don't have that kind of money to give away."[6]

Hess's name doesn't appear on the list of the New York Commit-tee to Re-Elect the President Inc. (notable names that were on the list included Senator Jacob Javits and Mrs. Henri Bendel).

Leon's reason for concern was obvious: On September 5, 1973, FBI special agents entered Amerada's offices at 51 West 51st Street in Man-hattan and asked to speak with Leon, Callender (an executive vice presi-dent), Kramer (president), and McCollum (chairman of the executive committee). The agents planned to talk to all of the executives at once, to prevent them from coordinating their stories. After a receptionist stalled the agents, Averill Williams, the company's general counsel, met with them and said the men wouldn't be interviewed without their attorneys present. The agents headed to the nearby office of Roger Oresman on the eighth floor of 50 Rockefeller Plaza. He told them he needed time to talk to his clients and would submit affidavits.

In less than a week, the Senate Select Committee investigating Watergate had sent questionnaires to the company asking for details about the campaign contributions. Instead of getting all the executives talking simultaneously, as planned, what the government got was sworn affidavits responding to the Senate's questions.

While Leon was pouring money into the 1972 campaign, Amerada's refinery in the Virgin Islands was under investigation by the Interior Department, a probe that ended less than two months after the Nixon donation. The refinery faced the loss of its special oil import quota be-cause of alleged failures to meet investment and hiring requirements.

The company was fighting a preliminary finding by the head of the department's Oil Import Administration that it hadn't spent enough or hired enough legal residents of the Virgin Islands.

"In August of 1971, [Acting OIA Administrator Ralph] Snyder sent a letter to Hess suggesting that Hess was not in compliance and suggest-ing that Hess re-negotiate its allocation/contract," which allowed it to send 15,000 barrels a day of output from the Virgin Islands refinery to the U.S. East Coast.[7]

"Snyder said that Hess, unlike the other people who had received an allocation, never seemed to want to come in to re-negotiate their contract, or to discuss problems. Snyder attributed Hess's unwillingness to the fact that Hess was a somewhat independent character," according to notes from an investigator's interview.

The company fought the allegations and eventually Snyder decided not to revoke the allocation Hess had to import gasoline and other refined products. The governor of the Virgin Islands opposed any revocation.

"There was no political interference of any kind" in the Interior Department's decision not to revoke the import allowance for finished petroleum products, Leon said.[8]

One tipster to the Special Prosecutor's Office alleged that the OIA maneuver was an attempt to bring Hess into line supporting the Republican administration, but there's little evidence in the file for that conspiracy. Snyder said his probe was meant to ensure that companies were meeting their requirements, and Hess had satisfied him that they were, in most technical respects, so he used his discretion to not strip them of their import allocation.

Newspapers also noted that the donations came before the White House, on January 8, 1973, relaxed import quotas to allow more oil to enter the United States from the Virgin Islands—where there was only one refinery, and it was owned by Hess.

Leon said his main issue with the Interior Department was a delay in getting promised refunds on tariffs. About 6 percent of the cost of crude oil at the refinery in the Virgin Islands was subject to a U.S. customs duty. For a period of 16 years, under a government agreement, that duty was refunded to the company by the Virgin Islands. But Leon said the refund was more like 90 percent. "In addition, the refunds of 90 percent were not being made regularly during 1969 and 1970 and were running approximately 180 days late," he said in 1973. "The corporation was not able to get any satisfactory explanation of this situation from the Virgin Islands Government."

In 1971, Leon met with Interior Secretary Rogers C. B. Morton to discuss the problem. Morton in turn arranged a meeting with Assistant Secretary of the Treasury Eugene Rossides, which was attended by the governor of the Virgin Islands, the Islands' attorney general, and other Interior and Treasury staff. That prompted some action, but not complete resolution of the problem. By September 1973, 6 percent of the duties were being withheld and refunds were about 45 days late, Leon said.

On December 6, 1973, Hess's attorney Robert Morvillo returned a call from investigator John Koeltl. In the course of that conversation, Morvillo (who was at the start of what would be a remarkable career in white-collar criminal law and would later defend Martha Stewart in her insider trading case) said that Hess would testify that he had made one contribution after April 7 of between $15,000 and $20,000 and made another $5,000 donation in another person's name, in violation of the new law. "Morvillo realized that this was a violation of 2 USC Section 440 and asked me what my reaction to such a violation was. . . . He asked if we had prosecuted such violations before and I told him we had not because we had not found any."[9]

Others were not so lucky, Phillips Petroleum CEO William Keeler, caught in the Watergate net, pleaded guilty to making an illegal corporate donation.

Deputy Special Prosecutor Henry S. Ruth Jr. sent a letter dated November 12, 1973, to the head of the Internal Revenue Service asking him to investigate Hess's payments. There's no evidence of any charges being brought, if an investigation was launched. Two weeks before, the FBI was told by the special prosecutor that it didn't need to investigate the Hess contributions any further.

On October 1, 1975, Tom McBride, who investigated campaign contributions for the special prosecutor's office, sent a letter requesting that the file on Amerada Hess be closed. "In spite of extensive investigation there was no evidence of any federal violation. The 'nominee' contributions were pre-April 7, 1972 and thus not violations of 2 USC 440. Nor did the inquiry substantiate any quid pro quo allegations."

The Hess interest in politics continues with John. A registered Republican, John used his connections to raise $285,000 for John McCain's presidential campaign in 2008.[10]

■ ■ ■

"A lot of politics was involved in what has been done for Hess," Senator Russell Long said.[11] Long, a Louisiana Democrat, was talking about the company's refinery in the Virgin Islands and the arrangements that gave it unique advantages over competitors on the mainland. A few years after Nixon resigned, Congress was taking a harder look at the special benefits Hess had won for the facility.

Senator Bennett Johnston was seeking to end a more than 40-year-old exemption that allowed the facility to use tankers that didn't fly a U.S. flag for shipments. Normally goods that are shipped from one U.S. port to another have to travel on a ship with a U.S. flag, a designation that means the ship is owned by a U.S. entity, has U.S. workers, and was built in the United States.[12] Not being subject to the U.S.-flag rule meant the company could save 25 to 65 cents a barrel on shipment costs—costs its refinery competitors, especially in Long and Johnston's home state of Louisiana, were finding hard to swallow in 1976 as the Hess facility expanded to become the biggest refiner in the region.

The Interior Department, which had in 1967 granted Hess the right to build a refinery in the U.S. Virgin Islands to spur economic development of the area, opposed removing the exemption. "It would raise petroleum costs to American consumers and would injure the economic health and development of the Virgin Islands," Assistant Secretary of the Interior John Kyl, a former Iowa Representative (and father of future Arizona Senator Jon Kyl), wrote to the subcommittee considering the legislation.[13] He pointed out that the refinery was competing with Caribbean facilities owned by Exxon, Texaco, and others.

The Jones Act, as it is known, has long been a bugaboo for the refining industry, which depends on tankers to move its product around the world. In a daring game of chicken, refiners in the past few years have actually said they would be willing to risk higher oil prices (in the form of easing U.S. export restrictions), if the government were to remove the Act's onerous requirements that eat into their profit. Of course, that statement is made knowing that shipbuilding and merchant industry supporting members of Congress would never remove the protectionist measure without a vicious fight.

Amerada owned 46 ships at the time, five of them registered in the United States. According to the head of the AFL-CIO's maritime trades department, the company was paying less than the $30,000 going salary for a licensed seafarer on the non-U.S. ships.

At the end of 1975, despite being less than a decade old, the refinery was shipping 300,000 barrels of residual fuel (which weren't subject to import limits) to the United States—the company accounted for more than a quarter of that imported fuel oil. Hess had managed to double its share of the market in two years, Johnston said at the hearing.

Johnston said the exemption was a subsidy for the Hess refinery. "I hope they make a good profit, and I hope they do very well, but not at the expense of our people in the United States who need jobs as seamen and as shipbuilders."[14]

The legislation was in part a response to an article in the *Washington Post*[15] that detailed the company's $400 million "windfall" in 16 months from an entitlements program President Gerald Ford had put in place in late 1975 to help smaller refiners compete with larger oil companies. At the time, Hess was the fourteenth-largest U.S. oil company.

The entitlements were meant as a way to keep independent oil companies operating after OPEC price increases sent the costs of refining crude soaring. It was a heavy thumb on the scales as the government tried to intervene in markets. Since the major integrated oil companies (think Exxon) were able to supply their own production at cheaper rates, the Federal Energy Administration "ordered integrated oil producers with large supplies of domestic oil to share the costs of production incurred by their domestic competitors who lacked access to cheaper domestic oil."[16] That was done by keeping controls on the price of "old oil," which was categorized as domestic wells based on their output from 1972, and letting "new oil" (including imports) fluctuate with the market.

The program was one of many ways the newspaper said the refinery had a leg up on its competitors. Between those entitlements, the ship exemption, the tariff refund provision, a tax agreement with the island government, and its ability to directly import products others had to send through third parties, the growing refinery had "a tremendous per-barrel advantage" courtesy of the U.S. government, Johnston said. The head of the National Marine Engineers Beneficial Association estimated the benefits amounted to 7 or 8 cents per gallon of gasoline.

"For purposes of qualifying for crude oil entitlements, Hess is treated as a domestic refiner. But for purposes of the Jones Act, its refinery is treated as if it were on foreign soil. Hess gets the best of both worlds, and it has used that advantage to selectively undersell its competition," Jesse Calhoon, president of the association, said at a March 1976 hearing.

Calhoon rejected Leon's statement that the company passed the benefits on to its customers, saying Hess's fuel oil sold for 1.9 cents less than competitors and the lighter oils are more expensive.

Long said that of the two island refineries that won development agreements with the U.S. government under an economic development plan from the Johnson administration, Hess had gotten the better deal in the Virgin Islands compared with Phillips's refinery in Puerto Rico.

"[O]f all the islands that the United States owns or operates or has as territories, this is the only one that has this special break where they don't have to employ American seamen and they don't have to use American bottoms [ships]," Johnston said.[17] The former governor of the Virgin Islands, who'd negotiated the deal with Hess, said the territory needed the special exemption from the Jones Act, in a statement that repeatedly referred to the senator as "Johnson" instead of Johnston.

Leon could see the political pressure mounting. Within the year, the Federal Energy Administration rolled back crude prices and the entitlements for imports of foreign residual fuel into East Coast markets. In a bid to silence the critics, Amerada would seek its own legislation: "Your Corporation has requested that Congress enact legislation making our U.S. Virgin Islands refinery a domestic refinery in all respects," the company said in its 1976 annual report. It proposed getting rid of the paradox that had helped it be so profitable: "Presently, that refinery is neither a foreign nor a domestic refinery."

While regulated by the FEA and required to send all of its product to the United States, Hovic was treated as a foreign refinery when it came to license fees and customs duties (duties that were being refunded, however slowly). Amerada requested a Customs Oil Zone be created so it no longer suffered from "discrimination."

Amerada would join with Koch Industries, which also had significant refining interests, to put an ad in the *Wall Street Journal* in September 1975 asking Congress to sustain President Ford's veto of price regulation extensions. In a complaint about gasoline price controls that still lingered in 1976, the company made a statement that seems odd for an entity that was being attacked for its skill at exploiting government programs: "The petroleum industry must be returned to the free market system."[18]

■ ■ ■

Being a major oil company has, since the time of Rockefeller, often meant being a target of public loathing and a political piñata when prices rise. By January 1974, seven of the world's fifteen largest multinational companies sold petroleum. They were Exxon, Gulf, Texaco, Mobil, Standard Oil of California, Royal Dutch Shell, and BP. (Interestingly, on the U.S. side, five of the companies would merge in different deals over the course of time to become just two—ExxonMobil and Chevron.) The seven majors were responsible for 39 percent of U.S. production and 77 percent of OPEC's output.[19]

Thirty years after World War II ended, documents were being declassified that showed the extent of U.S. government involvement in the rush for Arabian petroleum resources during and after the conflict (what Senator Frank Church would call the "mad scramble" for Middle East oil in a series of 1974 hearings trying to figure out whom to blame for the 1970s energy crisis). Two U.S. companies used the lend-lease program (famous for helping the British before Roosevelt had enough public support to enter the war) to get access to Saudi oil as they battled with their British allies for resources.

"Thus was woven the basic pattern which has since that time formed the basis of government-industry relations—the government to provide the diplomatic and financial support for the industry's operations abroad, but denuded of any institutional capability to formulate a policy of its own or to oversee the operations of the petroleum industry abroad," Church said.[20]

Church was looking at ways in which companies influenced the U.S. government's foreign policy over the years, the region that Howard Page had flagged as a major supplier was now essentially controlling oil prices. OPEC successfully shifted control from the "Seven Sisters"—the remnants of Rockefeller's Standard Oil—as U.S. output waned and demand for motor fuels grew by leaps and bounds.

The former Goliaths in the industry were also being challenged by independents, including Hess, Continental, Marathon, and Occidental, which were granted drilling rights in Libya and began to explore in areas beyond their traditional backyard. By 1969, when Libya's king was overthrown, the industry was no longer speaking with one voice about where prices should be, and it was vulnerable to new demands from the colonels now in charge of Libya—and what they wanted was a bigger cut of the oil profits. Those calls would be echoed by the Persian Gulf nations as the balance of power shifted from companies to the nation-states.

"[W]e will not be negotiating on price anymore," George Piercy, senior vice president at Exxon, said at a 1974 Senate hearing. "[W]e do not have the present market forces anymore to bring supply and demand into balance."

In January 1971, the Justice Department allowed the oil companies to avoid antitrust restrictions as they tried to band together to negotiate with OPEC. On Valentine's Day that year, the companies agreed to pay higher payments to producer nations in what was called the Tehran agreement.

"In 1971, OPEC suddenly di overed that W tern companies and governments were unwilling or u ble to organ resistance to illogical and unreasonable demands. This started a mc entum of price demands that ha lerated at a fantastic pace to a l el that endangers the economy an ial framewor of the entire ld," George Schuler, a Bunker Hu Co. executive, said in a 197 s statement.

But wra l strong-armed negotiating nd by 1972, cut Libya and t, coupled with from the Uni caused p e. Posted prices, the agreed-upon levels u ation, no longer to 30 percent above market price. nations, hich through newly enlarged stakes in companies w ee the price climb, came back again looking for higher rate after war broke out between Israel and Arab st in the price, doubling the current level. The two weeks to consider the proposal, but within ee days th told their answer no longer mattered—Gulf ries decided t ere unilaterally increasing posted prices by $2 a bar .

These payments would not be considered royalty payments, however. Under a National Security Council ruling from the 1950s, the government agreed to consider them as taxes, allowing the companies to offset the income taxes paid to the U.S. government by the higher payments to foreign entities. The State Department argued at the time that paying the Middle East governments more would ensure pro-U.S. leadership.

What this resulted in was a drastic drop in U.S. tax receipts from the oil companies. "[T]he largest five oil companies paid an effective rate of tax ranging from 2.9 percent to 5.8 percent," Senator Charles

Vanik wrote in 1974. And at a time when prices had doubled in a year, lawmakers were eager to find a way to punish oil companies that were reporting big profits.

By 1973, the United States had removed all controls over crude oil imports, as declining domestic output was forcing refiners to look farther afield for supplies. The crisis naturally resulted in a slew of congressional inquiries, and legislation was introduced to tax windfall profits that came from the surge in prices. Lawmakers also proposed measures that would break up the integrated oil companies, forcing them to focus on only exploration and production, or only refining and marketing (a breakup that would be much more successful 40 years later when Wall Street investors made a similar argument for a single-minded approach to the business).

■ ■ ■

By the end of the 1970s, inflation was raging at double digits and President Jimmy Carter was trying new methods to control costs. The Council on Wage and Price Stability found in 1979 that a rise in prices between January and April was going mainly into profits for refiners and marketers. The White House specifically named Amerada Hess as violating voluntary price guidelines.[21] The company, for its part, was unapologetic— "We regret that the price guidelines as established by the council do not allow Amerada Hess to comp'   company senior vice president R. K. Stafford wrote in a letter.

Simply put, the company sa   had suffered severely because of price controls earlier in the dec   nd it was now receiving what it termed "a reasonable return" on its investments. Furthermore, a few days after it was publicly named, Hess w a multimillion-dollar contract to supply fuel to the Defense Department, showing that the government's promise to block violators from contracts was basically toothless (according to one news report of the time, the Hess bid would save the Pentagon $49 million). It was a nice way to leverage pressure on the government that was seeking to punish a company for profiteering.

Eventually Vice President Walter Mondale would call Leon, urging that the company comply with the price guidelines, a request that Leon granted. It must've been easy to accede to the government's demands— Hess would report its earnings had tripled in 1979, the biggest gain for any major oil company in the United States as refining margins widened.

A few years later, as the Carter administration wound to a close, Hess would agree to pay $32 million to publicly owned utilities and state and local governments that bought its fuel oil, plus another $3 million to a defense fuel supply center, to settle charges that it overcharged for petroleum products between 1973 and 1980.[22]

Chapter 7

Hess, Refined

The advantage given to Hess by these regulations is so great that there is a good chance that all independent fuel oil marketers will be forced to reduce or terminate altogether.[1]
—Leonard P. Steuart, Competitor

These days, when Hess wants to impress Wall Street equities analysts, who forecast the company's earnings and inform investors' perceptions, it brings them to North Dakota's sprawling Bakken shale formation to see the rigs clacking away, extracting American oil that has altered the global economy and rewritten the company's story.

But five decades ago, the company's pièce de résistance was a beachhead in the Virgin Islands, where it built the largest refinery in the Western Hemisphere. When it started up new equipment in 1969 after rapid-fire construction beset by a few legal and processing difficulties,[2] the company chartered a Boeing 707 to fly the Wall Street crowd down to check it out. The refinery's sprawling tank farm was freshly painted for the event, governed by the same fastidious attention to detail seen everywhere at the company, from its white gas station curbs to its New York office, where employees all wore dark suits under a strict dress code that was kept in place long after neighboring businesses embraced casual Fridays. Protected by a complex set of laws and special tax provisions negotiated by Leon, the plant set Hess apart from its peers, many of whom had less advantageous Caribbean assets.

"The refinery had the imprint of Hess on it, but also of island culture," recalled a former process engineer at the plant, known when it first opened as Hovic. From its start, the refinery was an amalgam of the two coming together—blending attention to detail and desire for precision with the laid-back culture of its home. Sometimes the two worked harmoniously; sometimes they clashed.

Leon's enthusiasm for refining stood out in the oil industry, where the processing of sludgy crude is considered by some to be the redheaded stepchild of energy, looked down upon by the "upstream" sector where the focus is on finding and tapping high-performance reserves, with immediate, clear rewards. The benefits from refining can be harder to realize and are less reliable over the long term.

Refineries take the crude oil that has already been extracted from the ground and process it under extreme pressure and temperatures of about 1,000 degrees Fahrenheit (535 degrees Celsius). Crude is diverted through a maze-like series of units, passing through one to the next, with a little bit siphoned off at each phase to make different products like gasoline, diesel, jet fuel, and naphtha, a petrochemical that's in everything from asphalt to cigarette lighters. The exact configuration of units in any given plant can determine how much of each product the plant manufactures. Refineries can range in size from small plants near a crude oil production field that process limited batches of oil to behemoths, able to make enough gasoline to fill the gas tanks of 271,000 cars in a single day. Refining infrastructure shot up around the first crude oil production fields in Pennsylvania and Texas, and some plants evolved with increasingly complex units, creating night-time skylines dotted with safety lights. While most oil fortunes are usually associated in the popular imagination with gushing wells, there's plenty of money to be made by those who help move the oil from the well, store it, process it, and sell all the various products. Leon cut his teeth on residual oil from refiners and built his business in the logistics around transporting oil to refineries as efficiently as possible and distributing the freshly produced fuel effectively. He came into the industry incrementally—starting with the sale of the end product before working his way backward into fuel storage terminals, refineries, and oil wells. Owning assets along each stage of the process can protect a company from wild swings in prices or supplies. Refiners need to buy the crude they process and then sell the gasoline, diesel, and other fuels. Depending upon the difference in those prices, refiners can get squeezed, seeing razor-thin profit margins that can cause the industry to contract.

For Leon, expanding his refining network was a transitional ticket from running a few storage terminals and trucks to deliver fuel and ultimately a step toward becoming a global player. Buying the huge amounts of oil he needed to feed his refineries put him in the room with some of the most powerful men in the world. To make his mark, though, he needed the right plant: a facility that could take all kinds of Middle Eastern oil and deliver it to his increasingly car-bound customers on the East Coast.

So, after Leon built his first refinery in New Jersey in 1957, he began to scout for additional outposts. In 1963, he bought a Corpus Christi, Texas, refinery, close to oilfields. But he still needed a large, world-class refinery that could deliver highly demanded heating oil to the East Coast. This thick, sludgy fuel was similar to the residual fuel he had first delivered in his oil truck, and was a market he knew deeply and well.

To identify a good place to build a plant, he needed a location with a steady supply of crude and convenient links to gasoline stations where he could distribute the fuel. A great tax package wouldn't hurt, either. He seized upon the Caribbean, which promised a location that would be able to process Middle Eastern crude cheaply and have a straight shot for delivering the products—heating oil, diesel, and gasoline—to the U.S. East Coast. He wasn't the first to look at the Caribbean: Shell founded a refinery in Curaçao in 1918, Standard Oil had built a refinery in Aruba in 1929, and a series of tiny refineries meant to process local oil in Trinidad had resulted in Texaco expanding a plant there in 1956. The Bahamas was home to a refinery as well: just as in the Virgin Islands, the government wanted to industrialize, and had designated a free-trade zone in the Freeport area to attract manufacturers. For Leon and his peers, the Caribbean's proximity to the U.S. East Coast meant a quick way to ship the fuel oil that was needed for manufacturing businesses and to feed power plants. While most U.S. onshore refineries had high volumes of gasoline output, the Caribbean refineries were geared toward fuel oil.

After initially considering a spot in the Bahamas, Leon was urged by New Jersey Governor Harold Hughes[3] to turn his attention to the U.S. Virgin Islands. Unlike the Bahamas, those islands held a key advantage; they were American enough to qualify for tax breaks but not so American that the company would be governed by requirements for U.S.-flagged tankers (the group of islands had been purchased from Denmark in 1917 and the flag exemption was meant to encourage economic activity).

After introductory calls from Hughes and David Rockefeller, who was then the president of Chase Manhattan Bank, Leon arrived in the office of the islands' governor, Ralph Paiewonsky, in 1965. He was determined to do a deal.

"From the day Leon Hess entered my office, he did not leave the Virgin Islands until the deal was consummated," Paiewonsky recalled in his memoirs. Paiewonsky, like Leon, was the son of Jewish Lithuanian immigrants. Raised in the Virgin Islands, Paiewonsky had studied at New York University and had run his family's business, a rum distillery, before being appointed governor by John F. Kennedy. Paiewonsky saw it as his mission to improve life for the residents—an effort he pursued so single-mindedly it made him unpopular in certain quarters. As governor he was eager to bring businesses to the islands—agriculture in the sugar fields was declining as an economic driver with competition rising from other areas, so he was searching for other sources of jobs. Farmland in the largest island, St. Croix, had declined by nearly 40 percent since 1930, and the decrease in the smaller islands of St. John and St. Thomas was even more precipitous. With a population of about 30,000 people, and rapidly growing in the mid-1960s, he was looking for new sources of employment.

Tourism was just beginning to take off in the islands after revolution in Cuba stripped Americans of one major Caribbean destination. But in an era before cheap airfares drew mega-resorts to the area, Paiewonsky looked to industry to provide long-lasting jobs for island residents. The first big industry was aluminum, with a smelter that drew substantial criticism from environmentalists and business leaders alike. The chamber of commerce worried about competition for local labor, and the environmentalists argued that Krause Lagoon, the proposed location for the plant, was environmentally sensitive. Despite a series of court challenges, the smelter was ultimately built. But the governor had learned his lesson. A refinery, he hoped, would turn out differently with a better tax arrangement and preapproval from the legislature. With support from the lawmakers, Paiewonsky was willing to make a lot of concessions to bring business to the islands. The U.S. Interior Department was also eager to spur economic development in the islands and it eventually made a remarkable deal upon the governor's request: only one company would be able to build a refinery in the Virgin Islands. And that company was Hess.

The corporation also received a series of benefits for locating in the area: 16 years tax-free in St. Croix, partial government reimbursement for dredging a channel, and free use of that channel for 16 years. Some of the land for the refinery was under water, so it required a special lease from the U.S. Interior Department. Other parcels were privately held.

To get access to the private land, Leon had to talk to Miss Annie. In 1965, Leon found himself far from the boardrooms of New York, negotiating one of the most important deals of his career in the kitchen of Ansetta de Chabert, who owned some of the land he wished to use for the refinery. A Virgin Islands diplomat, Louis Shulterbrandt, went with Hess to help smooth relations with the landowner, known popularly as Miss Annie. The woman, who was in her mid-50s, had grown up as the daughter of a local merchant, and with her husband, a local government leader, had amassed large estates, converting them to dairy farms. She and her husband were a formidable team, and she also became politically active, taking on the role of treasurer in the island's Democratic party. After her husband's death in 1955, Annie continued to acquire land as she worked to fund her children's education.

As a result of her substantial holdings, Miss Annie was in a position to be a fierce negotiator, and she drove a hard bargain: most of her children opposed her selling the acreage, and she had a competing offer from Globe Oil Company, which was also seeking to establish a facility in St. Croix—besides Leon, others had seen how potentially lucrative the island could be.

"Mr. Hess, you don't have to buy the land. If you can't pay me my price, you don't have to buy it," she told him, while stirring a pot and ironing her grandchildren's diapers. "The land will remain there. Land don't rot."

The negotiations went south. Leon sat on the kitchen stoop waiting for a resolution. Shulterbrandt, who was also an assistant to Paiewonsky, persuaded Miss Annie to call the governor. Fearing the deal would collapse, the governor got on the phone and persuaded Miss Annie to sell four hundred acres in Estates Blessing and Hope, properties she had acquired with her husband, to Leon at his price. The governor told her she would have more leverage for a higher price if Leon later wanted to expand the refinery. After some hesitation, she agreed. (This was one of the governor's promises that did hold up: Within a few short years, Hess was, indeed, looking to expand.)

The deal was done, and building began shortly after. In fewer than 11 months, under the watchful eye of Leon's man on the ground, Robert "Hank" Wright, vice president of Hess and general manager of the refinery, the plant was built. Leon would fly in on a near-weekly basis, and was called the "chief engineer" by some.[4] Wright, a native Texan, quickly developed a reputation as someone who could get things done. He would grill employees who didn't have the right answers and was feared, particularly by junior employees. Some saw him as a sort of junior Leon, the deputy on the ground who carried out Hess's exacting attention to detail.

"It was just an amazing puzzle, watching all these things come together," said John West, an early employee at the plant. "With Hank Wright running this thing, you just had to have someone who was precisely competent and capable."

Hank's main job was to manage the many subcontractors and thousands of workers who constructed the plant on marshy beachfront property on the island. Chicago Bridge & Iron (CB&I), a company that began its life building bridges and water storage tanks before expanding into the oil industry, built the tanks that held crude and fuel. With so many workers swarming around the facility, Leon endeavored to know each employee by name, and expected the same from Hank. By most accounts, Hank succeeded, knowing the workers and even the names of their wives and children. It was the type of family-owned business touch that Leon favored, even as he extended his empire into one of its most complex and risky undertakings. Leon once went through the refinery under construction and handed a worker a $50 bill, telling him he appreciated the work he was doing and wondered if he couldn't do it better.

Hank also had to contend with cultural skirmishes, as workers came from other islands like Puerto Rico and St. Lucia. The workers, known as off-islanders or down-islanders, caused additional tensions from locals who thought those jobs should be theirs. The racial strife generally stayed below the surface, but boiled over in the 1980s, as hourly workers went on strike, leaving managers to work 12-hour shifts. The dispute centered on whether jobs in the plant could be subcontracted to workers who were part-time. While the refinery continued to run during the strike, non-unionized employees from other locations were brought in to help. But the union fought back, distributing pamphlets at a Jets football game, as the employees tried to go beyond the confines of the island to get Hess's attention.

Beyond that, Hank faced harsh demands from headquarters in Woodbridge that clashed with the relaxed island culture. While Hess's structure in New Jersey was described by some former employees as being almost paramilitary, work on the island was less predictable and less easily controlled.

"Leon liked things painted, and in St. Croix, that was a challenge," recalled a Houston consultant, who served as a process engineer at the plant. As a result, along the road in St. Croix that ran to the docks, a maintenance person had to routinely keep the tanks bright white— no small feat, as a large storage tank can be as wide as a football field. Managers would ensure the portion of the tank that faced the road was painted first if Leon was coming. There would be an army of broom pushers out there ahead of his frequent visits.

During construction, one tank, which held jet fuel, blew up as CB&I was welding. One worker remembers standing in an office facing the tank and being knocked across the room. "When those things happened, Mr. Hess and Hank made sure the damage was cleaned up and gone so quickly it would make your head spin," said John West, who worked at the plant for five years before being transferred to the Woodbridge headquarters.

The expansion the governor had anticipated came within only three years. By 1968, phase two of the refinery expansion was being wrapped up and phase three was launching. The plant soon sprawled across 1,500 acres—about the size of Gibraltar. It towered over the palm trees and peaceful ocean views on the south side of the island.

"Until we commenced operations in the Virgin Islands, there was literally no substantial industry in the Virgin Islands and its economy was based primarily on federally subsidized sugar growing and general tourism," Leon said in an August 27, 1972, letter. "Prior to completing our refinery, we at our own cost constructed and staffed the Hess Vocational School. Unfortunately, for the first two years of our Virgin Islands operation, this vocational school was taken over by the Virgin Islands Government as a grade school. Not having the use of this school facility lost for us valuable time and training of Virgin Islanders. Since it has been returned to us, our vocational school has been in full operation and its enrollment limited to legal residents of the Virgin Islands to whom we pay $2.00 an hour while they attend school."

Leon said the facility accounted for about 10 percent of the island's operating budget, directly and indirectly.

As in indication of how important he was to the island, even the queen of England had to share billing with him. After Queen Elizabeth II and Leon both attended the dedication of a school on October 26, 1985, a 50-cent postage stamp was issued in St. Lucia. On the left, it carries a photograph of Queen Elizabeth, and on the right, the Queen and Leon are seen together in front of a plaque recognizing his contribution in the wake of Hurricane Allen. Above the photo, the stamp has text, recognizing the Queen's fiftieth birthday. Leon was nearly royalty for the Virgin Islands.

Hess's refining presence was expanding elsewhere, too, as it purchased a plant in Purvis, Mississippi, in 1973. Hess was becoming a household name because of its U.S. gas stations, and in oil circles, its refineries were also becoming well known, with Leon's reputation as a detail-oriented, demanding boss spreading from Mississippi to St. Croix alongside his thirst for oil (something that would eventually encourage the company to buy Amerada to feed its production needs).

While the network of gas stations spread the Hess name among consumers, it was the refineries that allowed Leon to buy oil from leaders in other countries, and raised his profile and wealth. While all of Amerada Hess's refineries were subject to market fluctuations, nowhere was Leon more successful in using his savvy of negotiating state programs to ride out the downturns than in St. Croix. The mammoth plant was big from the get-go, but at its largest, it grew to process 700,000 barrels of crude a day, making it the largest single plant in the Western Hemisphere at the time.

"I was driving over a hill, [and] all of [a] sudden, a huge refinery appears, and it just scared the daylights out of me," employee John West recalled of his first visit. The job seeker was deterred, and turned around. But in need of money to support his wife, who was expecting their first child, West returned the next day. He was hired for a small job as a concrete expediter, and worked in the trailers around the plant.

Hank Wright decided he liked West and helped him move up the ladder, promoting him first to purchasing, and then making him responsible for setting up a new building at the plant.

That was when West first met Leon. West was bandaged, having accidentally stabbed himself with a screwdriver while assembling some furniture for a new building at the plant. Mr. Hess walked up to him and asked about the injury. After saying that he had stabbed himself, Leon tartly responded, "Well, now, that wasn't real smart."

It was a minor injury among the many things that can go wrong in a facility as large and complex and prone to holding flammable fuels. Refinery accidents can be deadly: units work under high pressure and extreme heat, so if a critical valve fails, major explosions can happen.

Leon had to cope with many small-scale mishaps at the plant. At one point, an attempt to unload a vessel from a transportation barge to land failed, and it rolled off into the sea. Because it was filled with nitrogen for shipment, it floated, but it had to be flushed out, four former workers said. Refinery processing units, which can now fetch up to $1 billion, were not easy to come by, and could be particularly difficult to obtain and maintain on the island. Still, in 1991, the plant managed to install one of the largest fluid catalytic cracking units in the world, used to extract maximum light products, like gasoline, from crude oil, which it could then ship to the United States.

Just as the plant carried physical risk, it also carried financial risk: profits from refineries can fluctuate, and success or failure is determined on how reliably refiners can keep their units running, how cheaply they can buy oil, and the premium they can extract for their fuels. Leon figured out ways to make laws work to his advantage. In one instance, he found that oil would not be considered an import or taxed as one if he brought it from St. Lucia to St. Croix by barge. So he took large ships, had the engine propulsion cut in two and bulkheads welded on each side, and then pinned them back together. The pins were huge, so technically the drive portion could be disconnected from the cargo portion. While it might not appear so the untrained eye, legally, these boats qualified as "barges," so the massive quantities of oil they carried were exempted from the taxes that would otherwise be levied.

One competitor told how Leon showed them how to do more with less, running a facility with 400 people where other companies would have used twice as many workers.

Leon had other ingredients in his success in maintaining refining profits, too—a combination of luck and canny navigation of Washington policies. When he was building his refinery, he applied for a license to import gasoline and heating oil from his refinery, and asked the Department of the Interior to exempt him from the quota on foreign oil imports.[5] One of those who testified on Leon's behalf was Governor Paiewonsky. Allegations of bribes surfaced, with some suggesting that Paiewonsky had taken rides to Washington on Hess's private plane. Paiewonsky dismissed the accusations and said that he had never been on the plane. Hess's request was granted in 1967, in exchange for additional expansion of the plant, and a 50-cent-a-barrel royalty paid to the Virgin Islands Conservation Fund. Others—including legendary Texas oilman Oscar Wyatt—were turned down for the same license, to avoid polluting the Virgin Islands.

Leon may have initially wanted to put the refinery in the Bahamas, but having it in the U.S. territory of the Virgin Islands ended up being a major boon for the plant. An entitlements program put into place by the Ford administration in November 1974 provided a windfall for Amerada Hess, giving the company $13 million in its first month and ultimately adding up to $400 million to the company's balance sheet. The entitlements program aimed to provide a level playing field for oil refiners who owned their own oilfields, and those who didn't, by having oil companies pay into a fund offering a subsidy to refiners who used foreign oil rather than regulated domestic fuel. For all Caribbean refiners, this could have been a boon, but only Amerada Hess had a plant located in a U.S. territory, making it eligible for the payments. Leon said at the time that he got no benefit personally from the subsidies, passing the savings on to his customers. The result was low-cost products for customers, Leon argued. With this advantage, Leon's Amerada Hess beat out competing fuel suppliers, in some cases getting contracts that had been in competitors' hands for decades. "The advantage given to Hess by these regulations is so great that there is a good chance that all independent fuel oil marketers will be forced to reduce or terminate altogether," one competitor complained. The controversy over Amerada Hess's entitlements made headlines, but Leon managed to stay above the fray, avoiding reporters and photographers.

West remembers Leon as a down-to-earth, plainspoken person who didn't talk down to employees—even the lowest ones on the totem pole.

But while Leon was free with handshakes and kind words, he also was known throughout the plant as cutting an imposing figure during his visits, dressing in expensive clothes and having exacting expectations of his workers. Some employees found solace in the fact that Leon had never gone to college—if he could succeed in a cutthroat and highly technical business, despite lacking a diploma, so could they.

In addition to analysts and employees, Hess courted high-ranking oil emissaries at the plant. Because the plant ran Maracaibo crude from Venezuela and Iranian crude bought through arrangements with the Shah, Leon often had visitors from South America or Iran.

On one visit, the Shah's brother, his niece, and another Iranian dignitary visited the plant. As part of the tour, they were also escorted around Puerto Rico, St. Thomas, and St. Croix by Hess employees in a Volkswagen. After dinner one evening, Leon was visibly irritated: the men were obviously visiting for tourism, while he wanted to get them to talk business. Hess also was annoyed by the Shah's niece, who ignored his instructions to meet at 9 A.M. at the Buccaneer Hotel, where the guests were being put up. Leon, his wife, Norma, and the Iranian dignitaries were left, sometimes for as long as an hour, waiting for her.

Her behavior stood as a sharp contrast to the way the employees remember Leon, who they say respected them despite the socioeconomic
gulf between them.

One summer, Leon sent his son, John, to the refinery to learn the
business. He was brought to different departments, including the terminals where oil came in, as well as the purchasing, accounting, and other
departments, rotating through to learn how the plant ran. Unlike his
father, John was introverted and didn't say much, remembers West, who
was charged with taking him to different departments.

Leon, on the other hand, was seen on the ground at Hovensa often, even as he aged, coming around with a large dose of oversight and
handshakes. So he was quick to respond in the summer of 1980, when a
hurricane developed near Cape Verde, gaining lots of power as it crossed
the Atlantic. The storm, called Hurricane Allen, swept through St. Lucia,
destroying the buildings that Hess used as a fuel terminal supporting
the nearby St. Croix refinery. While the refinery was built to withstand
storms and handle any oil spills that resulted from damage to storage
tanks, the island as a whole did not fare well.

Leon established a hurricane fund. While the exact amount in the
fund isn't known, it was used to build 12 new schools on the island on land
the government supplied. Hess also helped to rebuild damaged schools
on the island. On St. Lucia, one of the schools was named after him by
John Compton, the premier of the island, though those around him said
the CEO wasn't looking for recognition for his donation. The school has
continued to operate, and had 700 students by its twenty-fifth anniversary.
They still wear the white and green uniforms that match the Hess corporate colors.

St. Croix also faced major storms: "In September, the twin storms
'David' and 'Frederic' extensively affected the production capacity of
the refinery," refinery manager R. L. Sagebien, who held a long tenure
after Wright had moved on to Woodbridge, wrote in a 1979 newsletter to employees. "But as is often the case, adversity brings out the best
in people, and our employees once again demonstrated their ability to
perform their jobs under most difficult conditions."[6]

Hurricane Hugo, though, is remembered for its strength, and the
damage it did to the plant, as well as for Hess's response. In October
1989, Hugo swept through St. Croix as a Category 4 hurricane before

bashing into the coast near Charleston, South Carolina, where it left nearly 100,000 people without homes.

On St. Croix, over 100 people weathered the gale-force winds of 140 miles an hour at the plant, sleeping in the firehouse or the warehouse. The group took meals in the refinery, eating in the relative safety of the warehouse after the storm whipped through. Just two days after the storm passed, Hess had arrived by jet, walking through each control room. Though he was 75 at the time, "If one person said 'we don't have hot food,' the next day there was hot food in every control room," remembered Joe Esposito, a refinery employee who was responsible for repairing workers' homes adjacent to the plant.

As the damage was repaired slowly, and an oil spill that had resulted from storm damage was cleaned up, Leon would join the thousand-plus workers who gathered in the warehouse to take their meals.

"Mr. Hess was a man of action and could do anything he wanted to at the refinery," Esposito said. His career with Hess had started at the St. Lucia terminal, but he said Leon remembered him even after he took a new job at the St. Croix plant. "One of the things that astounded me was how he could have so many employees and remember me, a guy who was digging ditches for him."

Esposito remembers that people slept up to 10 in a house in a section of land called Figtree, which had sustained less damage, as they waited for the repairs to be done.

"Every night, he'd make a point of sitting down and eating dinner with the guys," said Bill Tabbert, who worked at the plant. Leon would walk around the room, and shake people's hands, saying, "Son, it's miserable, but I can't tell you how much I appreciate your helping me restore my refinery," Tabbert remembered. Others recall a similar attitude.

That kind of recognition brought loyalty from many employees, many of whom describe themselves as being very devoted to him. Tabbert said he liked Leon right off the bat. "He understood that a good handshake made a lot of difference with people." The recovery from storms and mishaps at the plant was made easier by the great esteem so many employees had for Leon.

The refinery stood as Leon's proudest achievement in business,[7] not only because of its grand scale, but also because of the sheer number of people it had trained and provided jobs for, with 2,000 or more people working at the plant at the time of his death. "He believed fervently that something inherently good was achieved by investing in industry to create long-term jobs to the mutual benefit of both business and labor," John Hess recalled.

The refinery was incredibly important to Leon, so when it was most critical, he would fly in every Friday to inspect his refinery, to review its operations, finances, and crude slate. Of course, it helped that he had a vacation home nearby in the Bahamas. Seymour Miller, who worked closely with Hess over a four-decade career with the company, recalls the visits, working to make sure that everything was on track.

Across the refining industry, stories of Leon's persistence at the plant became legend. Bill Klesse, who took the helm at competing refiner Valero after Leon had died, remembers hearing stories about Hess checking units at 2 A.M. to make sure they were running properly.

"I don't know if those were true or false, but that was their pride and joy. They were a refining, heating oil, [and] marketing operation at the time," Klesse said.

Running a plant that size took a great deal of eye for detail, and the facility struggled to find an adequately attentive manager after Wright was promoted and brought back to Woodbridge. It took Leon several tries before he found Rene Sagebien, a manager who was up to his standards, and lasted in the role.

As the reins of the plant shifted from Leon to John, the Hesses became less of a presence at the refinery. "John didn't show up as much as his father had—I only met John Hess a couple of times," said Esposito, who remained at the plant for five years after Leon's death. "A lot of his father was in him. He wasn't aloof, but he was a businessman, too."

After 30 years of operating the refinery, the economics behind the plant were starting to shift. Rising crude prices made it less profitable than it had been in its heyday, and the company's growth engine was increasingly its global drilling profile, as John Hess began eyeing opportunities in Asia and Africa.

The plant's monumental girth and tax-advantaged status protected it as environmental regulations and weak profits forced refineries across the United States to consolidate or close in the 1980s. The market's power over refineries was clear as crude prices rose and demand fell, closing plants from California to the East Coast. While Hovic shut certain units in the 1980s, other Caribbean plants halted operations entirely. In the

Bahamas, a refinery was converted to a tank farm just storing crude and fuel. Hovic had clear advantages, and by 1994, Amerada Hess shut a small refinery it owned in Purvis, Mississippi, choosing instead to invest in Hovic, where it had a geographic advantage and economies of scale.

Hovic was also protected by a shift toward producing more gasoline, and less of the heavy fuel oil that Leon had once used to first make his mark. Utilities no longer wanted the residual fuel oil for power, as they switched to other fuels like natural gas. Hovic's ability to shift strategy and focus on gasoline to serve Hess's East Coast terminals and gas stations was unique among the Caribbean plants, and it was one of the few to survive.

By the late 1990s, profits for U.S. refineries were relatively weak again, though, and larger competitors were beginning to swallow up larger ones in a merger boom that saw conglomerates like ExxonMobil and ConocoPhillips form. To make the expansion and operation of the refinery more affordable in this environment, John Hess brought on a partner: Venezuela's state oil company, Petroleos de Venezuela, known as PdVSA (Ped-a-vesa).

Hess needed a new cheap crude source to refine at the plant so that it could continue to operate profitably. Venezuela wanted a reliable customer for its crude. The deal with the Venezuelans gave the facility access to a steady stream of crude at favorable terms. And the crude was heavy, like the stuff the plant had been using from the Middle East, so no changes were needed to process it.

On October 30, 1998, more than three decades after Leon first secured the land and built the plant, the Hovic refinery became shared property, with the Venezuelans owning a 50 percent stake. For a relatively low price, the country's oil company had found a place to refine its difficult-to-process crude, and Hess had secured a cheap oil source. PdVSA paid just $62.5 million in cash, and a $562.5 million, 10-year note, with a $125 million, 10-year contingent note.

Hess recorded a loss of $106 million from the transaction. The company also reported a write-down of $44 million, saying that the value on paper of its related refining and marketing assets had declined. The deal saved the refinery—at least for a time. After other island refineries had been forced to close, to continue to operate Hovensa (as the refinery would henceforth be known) needed insulation from market fluctuations, and Venezuela provided the plant with a steady stream of crude.

The refinery would now be operated by the parties together. It would also eventually bring the company into partnership with Hugo Chavez, the Venezuelan president who delighted in hurling epithets at America's political leaders even as his oil company refined fuel hand-in-hand with an unabashed capitalist and sold the United States gasoline through Citgo.

The transaction with PdVSA came with a long-term supply contract, entitling the refinery to 155,000 barrels a day of Venezuelan Mesa crude oil. Amerada Hess also agreed to build a delayed coking unit, meant for extracting gasoline and other light products from the heaviest parts of a barrel of fuel oil. After the construction of that coking unit, Hovensa agreed to purchase 115,000 additional barrels of Venezuela's heavy Merey crude oil.

As sport utility vehicles began to dominate American roads early in the 2000s, Hovensa was able to make inexpensive fuel, and ship it off to a coast with a rising appetite for fuel. Refiners became earnings power-houses; Morgan Stanley analyst Doug Terreson dubbed 2005 to 2007 the "Golden Age" of refining. Onshore in the United States, independent oil refiners like Tesoro Corp. and Valero Energy Corp. came into their own, reinventing beleaguered oil drillers into producers and sellers of refined products, as Hess had been at first.

It was a time of strong demand and relatively affordable crude oil, a heady mixture for refiners. Plants ran at full capacity, and things looked relatively healthy for Hess's partnership with PdVSA.

But in refining, things can change on a dime. While the deal may have been intended to keep the plant operating indefinitely, it merely staved off the closure. Demand began to fall off as hybrid cars emerged and a recession rocked the United States, causing economists to rethink demand forecasts as America's thirst for fuel was slaked with less oil than it had consumed in the past. To make matters worse, large-scale Gulf Coast refineries were being upgraded to process the sludgy grades of crude oil that plants like Hovensa had previously been able to get at a discount because of minimal competition.

Some plants became marginal, and independent refiners, who didn't have their own oil production facilities, were hard hit. While some on the Gulf Coast had large-scale plants that they were able to upgrade to take the cheapest grades of crude oil, most East Coast plants lacked that

infrastructure. East Coast refineries particularly struggled to find alternatives to their diet of crudes from the Middle East and Africa, which were
trading at a premium to Latin American crudes.

Beyond finding good crude, running an island refinery brought on
technological complications that refineries on the mainland were spared.

Island refineries, like Hovensa, a Valero plant in Aruba, and PdVSA's
plant in Curaçao, were saddled with a uniquely disadvantaged cost structure that got way out of line as crude prices rose and natural gas prices
fell for onshore refiners. In a commodity business with thin margins,
where pennies matter, these plants were being edged out by Gulf Coast
refineries with growing capacity and more efficient cost structures.

The selling began. Valero first tried to unload its Aruba plant in 2008,
attempting to strike a deal with PetroChina, hoping that for the foreign
buyer the chance to have a refinery close to Venezuelan production and
U.S. markets would be a boon. That deal went south, though—foiled
by politics and the refinery's losing margins. Like Hovensa, it had run
cheap, hard-to-place crude. As the market for so-called heavy oil became
more competitive, the plants were forced to draw on a variety of crude
sources, which were becoming increasingly expensive.

Island refineries faced a huge disadvantage when it came to getting
fuel to power their processing units. They either must make hydrogen
from butane or import butane to make hydrogen. While shale gas in the
United States was a boon to energy companies producing gas and oil
onshore and made it cheaper for U.S. refiners to operate their equipment, it served as just one more blow to Hovensa's ability to compete.
Every dollar per million cubic feet of gas translates to about 25 cents a
barrel cash of a refiner's operating expense, so as U.S. refiners saw shale
gas production boom and natural gas prices tank, their margins were
boosted.

Hovensa was in the same boat as Aruba, buying crude oil, processing
it, loading everything up, and sending it out. While the Hovensa refinery
had a desirable fluid catalytic cracking unit that could produce large volumes of gasoline, which the Aruba plant lacked, it still had to contend with
rising costs. Also, while Hess could capture some vapor like butane and
hydrogen from that unit, it still had to purchase supplies from off the island.

In 2009, the funeral bells for East Coast refining began to ring loudly
as plants that had operated for decades called it quits. Sunoco Inc. CEO

Lynn Elsenhans became the first to announce a planned plant closure, with the intended shutdown of a Pennsylvania refinery. Valero's Bill Klesse followed her, announcing plans to close the company's Paulsboro, New Jersey, plant. Some shut permanently, some reverted to storage terminals, while others were reopened by opportunistic buyers who swept in at the last possible second, seeing a chance to get U.S. refineries on the cheap.

The plants were too far from newly emerging shale oil production in the middle of the continent. Confronted by losses and a bleak outlook, John Hess allegedly quietly circulated word that Hovensa was on the block. While potential bidders looked at Hovensa, his father's era of refining had ended and it just wasn't possible to make the economics work. All of them walked away without buying.

To cut costs, John slashed the refinery's throughput, scaling back to just a few units. But as Gulf Coast plants grew, following renewed crude output in Texas and elsewhere, expansions like Motiva Enterprises LLC's Port Arthur refinery offset the capacity once provided by St. Croix.

With shale oil production rising, the outlook became even grimmer: U.S. crude began to trade at a discount to international benchmark Brent, so as Gulf Coast refiners accessed Canadian or domestic oil that was priced off of the U.S. benchmark, they extracted savings that those like Hovensa, who refined imported crude, couldn't. Refiners that had to pay for the more expensive crude, freight for importing it, and a few extra dollars on natural gas, faced a bleak margin picture.

Continuing to provide jobs at the refinery while also remaining a profitable business became impossible. Hovensa went from providing more than 2,000 jobs to fewer than 600 as the benefits of being just off U.S. shores faded.

With weak U.S. demand, refiners looked to export to Brazil, Mexico, and West Africa, markets that the Gulf Coast had a cost advantage in serving.

John shuttered the company's Port Reading, New Jersey, refinery, which consisted primarily of a fluid catalytic cracker. The unit was processing mostly Algerian condensate, a super-light form of oil that trades at a premium price. Without robust demand, Hess struggled to make a profit from the plant. While a handful of refineries on the East Coast were revived from zombie status by entrepreneurial CEOs who had private equity backing and wanted to run shale oil at the plants, Port Reading became a casualty of shrinking gasoline demand,

and a company that was increasingly focused on oil exploration and production. PBF Energy Inc., one of the companies that was resuscitating East Coast plants, looked at the Hovensa refinery, but despite their ability to find economically workable models for doomed plants, they were unable to come up with a plan that made it economical to operate again.

So, 46 years after it began producing fuels, eventually swelling to become a huge source of fuels for the East Coast and the world, Hovensa shut its doors, its closure a symbol of the end of Leon's era.

A group of investors from the Virgin Islands and New York tried to purchase the refinery in 2014, but their efforts fell flat, stymied by the Virgin Islands legislature, which only wanted to permit Hess to sell to a venture that could afford the environmental cleanup, should the refinery be permanently closed.

■ ■ ■

While the East Coast came to grips with job losses as refineries closed, in the Virgin Islands, Hovensa's closure was a sharp sting. Governor John de Jong said, "Even after the terrible economic realities of these past several years, it is hard to imagine any single piece of economic news worse for this territory than that delivered by Mr. Hess."

The good economic news that his predecessor, Mr. Paiewonsky, and Leon had brought to the island was eventually dashed. Hess's idea was to make it a terminal, and it has continued to run as one, but the territory wants the refinery and the full slate of jobs it brought.

The 90 days after the plant's closure was announced were the worst that retiree Bill Tabbert remembered. "Here's the killer. They said 'Fellows, you're not going to have a job, but you have to hang out here for these 90 days,'" he recalled. "It was awful."

Now, Tabbert can see the old Hovensa stacks from his yard. "It's terrible, having so many years in a place to watch it rot away. It makes me sick."

Chapter 8

When You're a Jet

On a cold December day in New Jersey's Meadowlands, a few stray wisps of snow swirl around the small groups gathered in parking lots surrounding MetLife Stadium. For the most part, they are huddled over fires—either from barbecue smokers, mini grills, or blazes in cauldrons brought solely to warm them.

The Jets are now 3–11 for the 2014–2015 season. For this, the last home game of the year under Coach Rex Ryan, they are playing the 11–3 New England Patriots, led by the league's most glamorous quarterback, Tom Brady (the 2015 Super Bowl winner is the husband of supermodel Gisele Bündchen and devastatingly pretty in his own right). In the cold, after a season of frustration, on the last weekend before Christmas, against a team both more glamorous and more successful than the home squad— these are not fair-weather fans. These people are compelled to be here.

"I've come to the last home game every year since 1972," says Rick Haupt, sitting at a table with friends enjoying what appears to be nice medium-rare steak from the grill at his back. His friend Ron Malcolm leans over and confides that, while the Jets stink, "even a bad dog needs a good hand to feed it."

For the pleasure of sitting in the cold and watching what will probably be a losing endeavor to cap off a season of disappointments, season
ticketholders have to pay thousands of dollars for a "seat license" that
gives them the right to buy game tickets that cost north of $100 each.

Rooting for the Jets can feel like a masochistic exercise. Unlike the
Giants, who share the stadium and won the championship in 2011, the
Jets seem to be in a perpetual state of rebuilding. Every future season is
full of possibility. And yet, like *The Odyssey*'s Penelope unwinding her
tapestry every night after her suitors go to sleep, the Jets don't seem to
advance from prior seasons.

Like the Mets baseball team they used to share a stadium with, the Jets
are the more working-class team for New York fans. In some families, the division is simple—Mets/Jets and Yankees/Giants. It can make the summers as
long as the winters for fans of the first group, who unlike the Yankees and Giants don't have a long and august history of winning. But that hardly matters
to those who bothered to drive an hour or more to get to the stadium on a
cold gray day to watch a game they are heavily expected to lose. "Jets fan for
life, union for life," says Jim Martin. His father, Steve Martin ("the original,"
he notes), nods at his side in agreement. Steve's grandson James stays tucked
inside the car for warmth. The retired sheet-metal worker from Long Island
has been going to games since the team played at Shea and is still not happy
about Hess's decision to move the team to New Jersey. The Jets should be in
New York City, where they belong, the grandfather says. If the proposed West
Side stadium had been built in Manhattan (part of the city's plan to lure the
Olympics in 2012), we could be tailgating in the Village, Jim notes.

When the team left Shea, they became the only ones in the league to
play in another squad's stadium. "This is not our stadium," says Malcolm,
pointing to the gleaming structure to his right. Even if Shea was a mess,
blanketed in bird droppings, "it was our pigeon shit."

As with most NFL franchises, love for the team doesn't often extend into the owners' box—a place where fans paying ever-higher ticket
prices usually direct their ire. Woody Johnson, an heir to the Johnson &
Johnson fortune who bought the team in 1999, "will spend the money
but he won't do it wisely," Martin says.

"The Jets are a blue-collar team," Haupt says. Johnson has turned the
franchise into a corporate outfit, jacking up costs so high that average
families can't afford a trip to the stadium to support them.

"Woody Johnson is just here to make money," says Tom Calabrese, a fan since 1985 who was drawn in by the hard-hitting defensive group that was dubbed "the New York Sack Exchange" for their ability to clobber opposing quarterbacks. Leon, meanwhile, is viewed 15 years after his death as a good man who struggled to find the magic winning formula once he took over the team as sole owner. "I like Hess as a man, but I don't think he was a very smart owner as far as football," says Martin.

Joe Ferrara was still a schoolboy when he got the bug. He remembers the call to his house from Hess's secretary. Leon, who did business with Ferrara's father, an executive at Phelps Dodge, was inviting the boy and a group of friends to see a Jets game in celebration of his thirteenth birthday. "He was a gentleman of the old school," Ferrara says. "He was direct and to the point, a man who shook your hand and kept his word."

His friend Alex Rubin has been a fan since he wore his Jets pajamas as a five-year-old child, taking on the same team his father supported. A signed Joe Namath jersey hangs on his office wall. While he remembers games at Shea fondly, he's watched the team with dismay since the era of the Sack Exchange (and even with the brief excitement that surrounded Chad Pennington's time at quarterback). "It takes character to stick with a team," he says.

With another losing season coming to a close, the men and women dressed in winter coats and Santa costumes had to see a close game slip beyond their grasp as the Jets fell to the Patriots 17–16. A few weeks later, Rex Ryan would be gone, rumored to have packed up his office before the word even came that Johnson was seeking new leadership. As usual, Jets fans hoped next season they would find the winning formula.

■ ■ ■

Leon Hess acquired a 20 percent stake in the franchise in 1963 for $250,000. It was an investment in a team that had struggled to find traction, playing in a league that was challenging the incumbent National Football League. Five years later, one of the owners sold his stake for a reported $2 million.[1] In 1970, the team toyed with a buyout offer from a former coach of the New York Giants. A few years after that, the team owners would reject a $19 million bid to purchase the squad.[2] As the years passed, Leon bought out the four others and eventually became sole owner. By the time the team was sold after his death in 1999, it was valued at $635 million, almost as much as Leon's personal stake in Amerada Hess. The franchise is now ranked as the sixth-most valuable among NFL teams, according to *Forbes* magazine, and worth an estimated $1.8 billion, per its 2014 ranking.

Leon bought the team as a sporting venture, joining with some of his partners from the Monmouth Park racetrack in New Jersey.

While he was sole owner, Leon was involved in the most-high-profile controversy in Jets history (even more high profile than Joe Namath's shaggy haircut or Mark Gastineau dating blond bombshell Brigitte Nielsen). The Jets—who according to legend were named after the planes from LaGuardia that regularly flew over their home stadium in Queens—left New York for suburban New Jersey. The departure from Shea Stadium was the biggest sports blow to the city since the Brooklyn Dodgers left in 1957 for a shiny new stadium in Los Angeles. To this day, the nation's largest city has two professional football teams that bear the state's name—and neither of them actually plays in New York. Instead, fans go about 15 miles west to watch live football in former swampland to a massive stadium that holds 82,500 fans.

The decision to move the team generated the most media coverage of Leon's largely reclusive life, dragging him into a war of words with the mayor of New York, prompting two governors to lobby for his attention, and spawning a lawsuit that accused him of conspiring to keep professional football rivals out of New York City. For a businessman who loved to win, the Jets were a pure expression of his competitive nature, even if they didn't always come through with a victory. They also show some of his deal-making skills and his ability to withstand pressure, sometimes with grace, sometimes with outrage.

For a man who once said he "never wanted to run a football team," the Jets were one of his greatest passions. The team became something of a second family for him—they sported the signature kelly green and white colors, a reversal of the green-on-white logo that was instantly recognizable on the Hess gas stations. For a man who didn't have many hobbies, Sunday football was something he could share with his family, instead of being alone on a golf course or a sailboat. He made the team an extension of that family, establishing the tradition of holding big Thanksgiving meals with players, staff, and their families. He extended many personal generosities to players, including taking care of a paralyzed player for years after his injury and making sure team members received the highest-quality care from his own stable of doctors.

But when he died, he made clear he wanted the families to be split.

"We had observed a number of professional sports franchise transactions, families got into disputes based on who was going to run the team," said Steve Gutman, the former president of the Jets. "He very much wanted to insulate his children from that kind of problem." He also "wanted his son to run the oil business and not get distracted."

The price paid to buy the Jets from the Hess estate was well above any estimate Leon had had. "It was a nice surprise for the estate, more than he would have expected," said Gutman.

Leon made no speculation about who would own the Jets after his death, nor did he have a desire to influence the process in any way. The only thing that he required was that no member of the Hess family would be part of the purchasing syndicate in any way. In fact, there was a very clear penalty if any family member did try to own a part of the team after his death—they would lose a third of their inheritance.

"It was very clear in his will, and not only that, John was very clear in his knowledge and understanding of what his father wanted. There was never even a blink of an eye or a 'what if?'" said Gutman. "He knew that his father wanted the team sold."

Among the suitors for the team were Cablevision Chairman Charles Dolan and owners of the New Jersey Devils hockey team, the Mets, and an Internet investment group that sought to raise fan money to buy the team. John would ultimately recommend the team accept the highest offer, which came from Woody Johnson. Leon was the only Hess family member the Jets would ever have.

■ ■ ■

When Leon took a stake in the football team, "I was one of five partners. The name of the team was the New York Titans," he would testify years later.[3] "They were in bankruptcy and we changed the name to the New York Jets." The Titans before the purchase were "the worst-managed, most-unprofessional professional team of the modern era," one former player, Alex Kroll, wrote in *Sports Illustrated* in 1969.[4] There were bounced checks, player strikes, coach shuffling, questionable player choices. It was hardly a sure investment.

The other owners were Sonny Werblin, Townsend Martin, Donald Lillis, and Philip Iselin. Sonny, the impresario who controlled the team for the group, had initially proposed buying out the other partners, but they ended up buying his stake instead.[5]

"One of our partners sold out and two of our partners died," Leon said in 1986. "I bought their interest and there was a young lady that owned the remaining interest [Lillis's daughter] and she found it necessary to sell out about two years ago."

Leon's progress from one of several owners to eventual sole controller of the squad was a "natural evolution" for the businessman, according to Gutman. "I don't think he really would be comfortable being a significant investor in anything that he didn't have control over or ownership of at some point," he said.

But that comfort took a while to come.

"I didn't have much to do with the Jets or anything to do until my late partner, Phil Iselin, passed away," Leon said. Iselin, who earned his fortune as a dressmaker, served as president of the team after Werblin, who died after suffering a heart attack at the Jets office.

At the time, Leon asked Oakland Raiders owner Al Davis to move to New York and run the Jets. "I offered him a piece of the team for free and to come into New York and run the Jets, and he declined. I did not want to be responsible for running a football team."

Despite his initial ambivalence, the team would take an important role in his life. At a 1990 Senate hearing on oil prices, he would tell the lawmakers: "Let's hope the Jets win on Sunday. That's more important than this testimony. I hate to lose."

■ ■ ■

One of the men who fed Leon's desire to win was the quarterback who put the team, and with it the struggling American Football League, on the map. In the annals of Jets history, there is one name that can still bring a wistful smile to a fan's face—Joe Namath.

The young quarterback, just out of college in Alabama, would sign the most expensive contract in the history of professional football when he was drafted in 1965. Namath realized his bargaining position very early—he was first in talks with the St. Louis Cardinals, asking for $200,000 and a new car, a Lincoln Continental convertible.[6] When they produced paperwork "30 or 40 seconds later" and asked for his signature, he stalled, realizing he could probably get more. Plus, he still had to play in the Orange Bowl for the Crimson Tide.

Werblin was then running the Jets. The talent agent, whose clients included Elizabeth Taylor and Frank Sinatra, figured that football was one part sports and three parts entertainment. And Joe Namath was entertaining, from his dazzling blue eyes to his cleft chin.

Namath was not going to play in St. Louis. The day after the Orange Bowl, he signed with the Jets. "And we were very happy to do it," Werblin said. Namath's convertible was kelly green. His brothers had jobs as scouts for the Jets. His three-year, $427,000 contract was believed to be the largest for any professional sport at the time. The signing was unique in that he used a lawyer to bargain instead of meekly accepting the draft offer (Dick Butkus, another Hall of Famer who was drafted in 1965, said the Chicago Bears contract he signed was half of what he was initially offered). The dealmaking savvy Namath showed with the Jets presaged the larger role of agents in football.

Within four years, Namath delivered on his promise. After joking with reporters that he "guaranteed" a Super Bowl win, the Jets beat Baltimore and won in 1969. It was the third championship game played between the National Football League and the American Football League, and the first win for the younger AFL, which had announced plans to merge with its rival just a few years earlier.

(The year 1969 was full of success for Leon, between the Super Bowl win and the takeover of Amerada.)

Namath not only had talent, he had a charisma that surpassed the game. His autobiography, written at the ripe age of 26, was titled *I Can't Wait Until Tomorrow . . . 'Cause I Get Better-Looking Every Day*. He was a man-about-town in New York, he was "Broadway" Joe—with his shaggy 1960s haircut, he could get away with wearing sheepskin knee-length coats on the sidelines (and would sport a rather infamous fur jacket to help with the coin toss at Super Bowl XLVIII in 2014, showing that his sartorial splendor didn't diminish with age). Men wanted to be him, and women wanted to be with him. Sonny Werblin may have needed a quarterback, but he also needed a star. Namath's appeal would help drive local fans to see the still-young squad, instead of their better-known NFL counterpart, the New York Giants. A year after Namath was signed, the AFL and NFL announced plans to merge, as the latter league saw the television audiences flocking to its rival's games. And in New York, those crowds could be traced to the Namath glamour.

Until the 1980s, when the team had the defensive group known as the New York Sack Exchange, which included Mark Gastineau, Namath was the last time the Jets had anything like that kind of star power. "[H]e's well paid and he's worth it to us and the rest of the league," said Iselin, who handled the last negotiations over Namath's salary.[7]

Joe would say years later how Leon encouraged him to settle down and have a family. "Joe Namath occupied a unique position in Leon's heart," said Gutman. Joe still speaks fondly of Leon and Norma, calling them "very special people."

■ ■ ■

Of course, as with all professional sports teams, the Jets also made some colossal errors. Perhaps the most glaring was picking an unknown Division 2 quarterback from the University of California at Davis, in the first round of the draft when they could've gotten Dan Marino, a future Hall of Famer. As an owner, Leon suffered a lot of disappointments alongside Jets fans.

(The team also got involved in some ill-advised marketing ventures, including the Jets' Christmas album, although in fairness, they weren't the only team to do this in 1969. What fan household doesn't need a recording of NFL players singing "All I Want for Christmas Is My Two Front Teeth" on an album that has cover art featuring a shoulder-pad-wearing Santa gouging out the eyes of an opponent on the field?)

Among other decisions that can only be seen as puzzling in hindsight, Leon would fire Coach Pete Carroll after one losing season (his first as a head coach), perplexing most observers by putting in charge a man who had himself been terminated by the Philadelphia Eagles. Carroll would go on to coach the Seattle Seahawks to several Super Bowl appearances, including his first championship win on the Jets' home field in New Jersey.

Leon hired Rich Kotite to replace Carroll because "I'm 80 years old," he said at a rare press conference appearance for the team. "I want results now." The news came on the heels of a defeat in which it appeared as if players had given up on a game. Leon couldn't abide the quitting mentality. The press reported that Leon liked Kotite's regular-guy approach—he was a "dese" and "dose" New Yorker who lived on Staten Island and, like Leon, had working-class roots. But the result Kotite was supposed to bring, another championship for the team, would elude the owner (when Kotite left after two years of losing, a fan held up a sign calling it "The End of an Error").[8] Leon would die without seeing the Jets win the whole thing again, and it was one of his biggest disappointments. The year he passed away, the team came within one game of the Super Bowl, falling short in the final 30 minutes of the playoffs. As of 2015, they have yet to appear in a second Super Bowl.

To be sure, even if it didn't have them for long, the organization did recruit some of the best coaches, including Bill Parcells, who took the team to the division championship. Leon fought hard for Parcells, who had just been to the Super Bowl with the New England Patriots—even proposing an arrangement that would have his assistant, Bill Belichick, run the team for a year with Parcells as a "consultant" in an attempt to avoid contract issues. Eventually, Leon entered one-on-one discussions with Patriots owner Robert Kraft, who wasn't willing to surrender his coach without recompense (although he was already eyeing former Jets coach Pete Carroll). Leon refused to break for lunch as the talks dragged on for five hours. When the two owners reached an impasse, NFL Commissioner Paul Tagliabue made the final decision.

"I've learned over the years, in negotiations, don't break," he told the New York Times in a rare interview two years before his death.[9] "If there's air conditioning on, shut it off. If there's heat on, shut it off. That's the way I've always been. Stay there until you get it done."

Parcells had complained that the Patriots expected him to cook without letting him shop for the groceries. Leon made clear at a press conference introducing the new coach that he wasn't that kind of owner. "I just want to be the little boy that goes along with him and pushes the cart in the supermarket and lets him fill it up," Leon said. He would be brought to tears by an ovation as the team ended its first season under Parcells at 8–4, the first winning season in four years.[10]

Parcells would later say he wanted a Super Bowl for Leon more than for any other owner he worked for. He was the last coach Leon would ever hire for the team and he would come closer than anyone else. Parcells, a notoriously tough character, admits to crying when he learned of Leon's death.

"All he really wanted to do was win. And as long as we didn't violate the U.S. Constitution, he really didn't care how we did it," Mike Tannenbaum, the head of player negotiations for the team under Parcells, said about Leon in Parcells's quasi-autobiography. Tannenbaum would have more than $100,000 worth of school loans taken care of by Leon, after Parcells rejected the owner's initial desire to double Tannenbaum's salary after the division championship win.

But it seems like most of the Jets coaches did their best work elsewhere—after Leon's death, Parcells's deputy, Bill Belichick, would announce his resignation at a press conference meant to introduce him as the new head coach, in part because he was worried about the ownership change that was in store for the team. Belichick would go on to win several Super Bowls with the New England Patriots.

As an owner, Leon had rare moments of obvious meddling as occurred with the Kotite hiring. He was not an owner in the George Steinbrenner mold—several coaches said he kept in touch but rarely did more than ask how things were going and offer his help. For such a detail-oriented man, he would surrender most of the day-to-day decision making to the coaches and executives he hired to run the team.

"He was the consummate CEO who was not an operating officer. He spit out his goals and his ambitions" and expected you to make them happen, said Gutman. "Leon knew that he was in the oil business and he wasn't in the football business," and he "respected others to do what needed to be done to make it a successful organization."

Parcells tells a story of calling Leon to inform him of yet another expensive player contract. "I don't give a shit," Leon told him. "If you run out of money, come over here to the oil company and we'll get some more for you this afternoon."

Leon was always consulted on two major decisions for the team—the hiring of coaches and trading of the number one draft choice. He sat in on draft discussion meetings, as the team figured out which players it would claim for the coming season. He wasn't prone to emotional outbursts on the field and he didn't ever try to call plays, as some owners have done. Members of the team remember his courtly manners, shaking hands with players and spending time in the locker room after games chatting with the men. Or, in his last years having been declared too ill to fly to an away game, meeting the chartered team plane as it arrived at LaGuardia airport at 2 A.M. and shaking everyone's hands in bone-chilling sleet. Or joining his voice to the players in singing the new "team song" in the locker room after a game.[11] He went to all the home games and most of the away games.

"He was very comfortable with the players and they were with him," said Gutman. Leon would give a speech to the team at the Thanksgiving Day practice each year, gathering the hulking bodies around him to listen to his deep voice. The speeches were usually short and meant to inspire: in 1995, with a 2–9 record, he simply told the men: "Let's go out with dignity and show 'em we're not horses' asses." (They went on to win the next game.)[12]

"There was no mistaking the fact that he was a unique man. He was vastly respected by everyone," said Gutman. "He just had that—I don't want to use the word 'charisma' because it was different than that—he had a magical ability to make himself part of a human's life, part of their ability to help them express themselves, encourage them."

Leon had one box at the stadium for himself and people who understood football. Next door was Norma's box, which was more kid- and family-friendly. In Leon's box, you were quiet and you watched the game, recalls one attendee. You could always tell how well the team was doing by how much Leon had chewed on his (unlit) cigar. If it was chewed right down, things weren't going well.

■ ■ ■

At the time Leon and his partners took over, the Titans played at the Polo Grounds, a complex that was adjacent to the northeast corner of Central Park in Upper Manhattan. The grounds were used for polo in the 1800s but were converted to handle baseball and eventually football. The New York Giants played at the field, as did the Metropolitans (the "Mets").

When Shea Stadium was built in 1964, the New York Jets moved, signing a lease with the city that ran out at the end of the football season in 1983.

After the Dodgers left Brooklyn, teams began leveraging the threat of departure to get better stadium facilities from their host cities. The

Jets threatened to leave Shea in 1977, seeking to end their lease. That prompted the city to go to court, where a judge issued a restraining order to stop the Jets from playing anywhere other than Shea.[13] "Every business that leaves the City; every major corporate home office that departs for the suburbs; every drop in the number of people employed reported by the Bureau of Labor Statistics; every downward thrust in the City's credit standing; each team that leaves for a greener (larger) stadium is another drop of the City's life blood," Judge Harold Baer wrote in 1977. The team was eventually persuaded to stay with the promise of more home games at the baseball stadium (they had been forced to play a long stretch at the start of the season as away games, since the Mets' season took precedence).

By the time the end of the lease rolled around in 1983, Leon was eager to leave the confines of Shea.

"The sanitary facilities were horrible," he said (in contrast, clean restrooms were a hallmark of the Hess gas stations under Leon). "The place leaked. The field was horrible and the security left so much to be desired. . . ." For a man who paid such great attention to detail, operations at Shea must've given him hives.

Iselin publicly complained a decade before that the stadium was too small for the team, pointing to the fact that cities including Kansas City and Buffalo had bigger stadium seating capacity for football.

The Giants eventually moved into a new stadium designed for football games a few miles away in New Jersey. After playing alongside the Jets at the Polo Grounds, the Giants had gone to Yankee Stadium before moving to the Yale Bowl in New Haven and then spending a year at Shea. By 1976, they had their own stadium.

Former New York Governor Hugh Carey said they initially had trouble getting Leon to return calls about renewing the 1983 Shea lease. Realizing they would have to smarten the place up, the city was offering $43 million worth of renovations at the baseball stadium. Nelson Doubleday, owner of the Mets, wanted to keep the Jets in his stadium. The city, he told Howard Cosell in a May 1983 interview, was willing to spend millions to put in luxury boxes and more seats and a give bigger chunk of concession-stand sales.

The city and Leon negotiated for six months off and on about a new lease at Shea. The Jets paid $500,000 a year at that time to the city to use

Shea. Losing the team would cost the city about $33.3 million a year, according to city Comptroller Harrison Goldin.[14]

As talks dragged on, and with the lease expiration looming, city officials took the negotiations public in a pressuring tactic that would blow up in their faces.

On September 28, 1983, New York City Mayor Ed Koch held a press conference in which he brandished a letter to Leon expressing "great shock" that he was not going to let the Jets play at Shea Stadium after the current season. This was the first time any official had publicly said the Jets were leaving Shea.

". . . [Y]ou said that absolutely nothing we can do with respect to Shea Stadium would satisfy you. I fear this attitude is more emotional than substantive," Koch chided in the letter. In fact, Leon told officials that he not only was unsatisfied with playing at Shea, he wanted a whole new stadium built for the team. "For the Jets to leave when they are on the verge of new glory and after we have agreed to address your past problems and to enhance the Stadium enormously is unfair to the fans and to the City," Koch wrote.

The city was offering to add more than 11,000 new seats to Shea, bringing its capacity to 71,530, build new private luxury suites, and double the parking capacity.

Mayor Koch said he thought Leon was moving the team "because of an 'emotional matter' between Mr. Hess and M. Donald Grant, the former chairman of the board of the Mets," the New York Times wrote in its description of the "unusual" press conference the mayor held after talks with Leon broke down.[15]

According to the mayor, Hess complained about Grant and dirty bathrooms and told Koch that there was nothing he could do to make the team stay at Shea. Leon had apparently clashed with Grant, who left the Mets in November 1978, about provisions that prevented the team from starting football games at Shea until the baseball season was over, a prohibition that meant the team had to play its first four games on the road.

Asked whether he found Leon's behavior strange, Koch gave a typical politician's non-denial—"He's not at all odd. He's a billionaire."

Leon, who had donated at least $10,000 to Koch's 1981 reelection campaign, was furious that the mayor had gone public. He responded angrily a week later, saying that Koch had jumped the gun with his press conference. Before the letter, Leon met with a group that included Koch, former New York Governor Carey, and Frederick A. O. Schwarz Jr. (another city official and great-grandson of the toy store owner) in his office. All of the men asked him not to take the team out of the city, but he was not mollified.

"The mayor left our office on a Monday afternoon and said he would come back on Friday with a football stadium program . . . ," Leon testified three years later. "The next thing I received is this letter dated September the twenty-eighth. . . . Instead of coming back on Friday, he came in with this letter and went public by saying that we had moved."

Leon said that he'd long asked the city for a football-specific stadium "back to Mayor Beame's day" in the 1970s. "This was not new."

"The mayor had a fixation that you had to stay at Shea Stadium, and it made no difference how bad the facilities were, and he tried to force us into a new lease at Shea Stadium," Leon recalled.

Gutman remembers a lesson in detail that Leon gave him during the negotiations with the city over the move. "We were receiving the bids for the stadiums from New Jersey and New York, the deadline day, 11 o'clock in the morning," he recalled in an interview. "Leon and his attorney and I were assembled in his office" when a messenger arrived about 10 minutes before the deadline with the city's offer. Leon asked Gutman to get the document time-stamped by his secretary, so Steve went outside and got Leon's secretary, Delores Finley, to time-stamp the front of the document and then went back into the room.

"He looked up at me and said, 'What are you doing here? I asked you to have it time-stamped, every page.'" So Gutman went back outside and made sure each page was time-stamped. By then, it was 20 after 11.

"After he's done, the messenger returns with a new page from the city's offer that changed the share of a percentage of revenue from gross to net—a material change in terms.

"Leon looked to me. He just turned the cigar in his mouth; it wasn't even a lit cigar; and he turned to me and said, 'You'll never forget to time-stamp a document again.'"

Even if Koch had jumped the gun by telling reporters that the Jets were leaving and urging fans to make their displeasure with the idea known, the team was, in fact, on its way out of New York.

"Leon, I ask you, don't leave us," William Shea, namesake of the stadium, said over the public address system at a September 1983 Mets game.[16] But the plea would fall on deaf ears. The Jets would move to Giants Stadium in New Jersey's Meadowlands, a new facility built specifically for football. The move meant the New York Jets would play in a different state and in a place named for a different team. Leon had arranged a deal in which the team would play in the Meadowlands for at least five years, leaving the door open for a return to New York City if an appropriate stadium became available for them. That stadium would not be Shea, he made clear.

Leon sent a letter to Koch the night after meeting with New Jersey officials for lunch to discuss terms of moving the team and talking by phone to that state's governor. Sometime between 4 P.M. and 6 P.M., Leon sat in his office and drafted his response to Koch, including sections in all capitals and underlined portions to convey his anger.

"I don't write many letters for the New York Jets, but that's one I wrote," he said.

In all caps at the start of the letter responding to the mayor, Leon wrote that the Jets would return only if a new stadium was built. He also put into capital letters the list of things he wanted to return: a new stadium, with permits and approvals and financing in hand by February 1, 1986, and guaranteed occupancy by the 1989 season.

"I purposely blocked it up that way so there wouldn't be any chance of a misunderstanding," he said. "Short and brief, which is my style."

"We have been and are still playing our home games in a run-down neglected stadium, which is well known to be the NFL's poorest facility for athletes and spectators alike," Leon wrote to the mayor. "You, Mayor Koch, said that 'Shea Stadium is not suitable for football.'"

He added: "YOU CANNOT FOOL THE PUBLIC, MR. MAYOR. JETS FANS WANT A CLEAN, EFFICIENT, WELL-RUN STADIUM, BUILT FOR FOOTBALL, NOT THE 'UNSUITABLE' SHEA."

When the Jets signed the lease agreement with the New Jersey Sports & Exposition Authority, the arrangement included a $10 million letter of credit and interest payments on the $10 million (which amounted to $1.69 million) to give the team a two-week window in five years to exit the 25-year lease.

When New Jersey offered a 25-year lease at the Meadowlands, "I told them that I would not accept the 25-year lease as they proposed unless the Jets would have the option to return to New York at the end of a [sic] years if a football stadium was built by the City of New York," Leon said, according to a courtroom transcript. "And I also told them that I was willing and I offered voluntarily to give them $5 million that they could hold, invest, they would keep the interest, in order that the Jets at the end of two years could exercise the option to come back to New York."

Leon spoke to New Jersey Governor Thomas Kean, who would later become a Hess Corp. board member, "for three quarters of an hour" about the proposal to move to the state. "I stressed with the governor that I am a citizen, or I was, and I am a citizen of New York City, a vote other [sic] in New York City, a taxpayer in New York City and New York State. I didn't want to come to New Jersey if there was a possible chance that the city would build a football stadium and not have us play at the baseball stadium. I pleaded with the governor that he had to give me an option, and I ended up committing to pay $10 million to have the right at end of two years to exercise that option and come back to New York."

"Ten million got his attention," Leon told the court. "Five million did not."

Kean told him that if he decided to leave the Meadowlands, he could not count on coming back, the NFL's lawyer said, closing off any backup plan if New York didn't have the proposed stadium in place.

"I was told that should we exercise the option and come back to New York, the governor did not want to be used, and at the end of five years, the Jets better have a place to play other than the Meadowlands, that he would go along for [a] $10 million penalty, [and] he would take the abuse for leaving us there for five years, and didn't want us there longer."

While the Jets were a "New York team" with a Manhattan office and training facilities at Hofstra University on Long Island, Leon said the front-office staff had received thousands of calls regarding the move, with only a few fans voicing opposition to the Meadowlands. And it was true; the Long Island fans who had made the short trip to Queens were willing to extend their drive another 30 minutes to an hour to travel across the city to get to the New Jersey facility.

Leon said that about 95 percent of the 55,000 season ticket holders from Shea signed up for season tickets at the Meadowlands (which then had capacity for as many as 76,000 fans).

Hess had promised that the Jets would return if there were plans and permits in place for a stadium and adequate financing by February 1986. The clock was now ticking.

■ ■ ■

Two-and-a-half years after getting Leon's list of requirements, the governor of New York and the mayor, joined by real estate developer Donald Trump, sent him a letter inviting the team to consider returning to the city. They offered to build a new stadium in Flushing Meadows, Queens. The Trump Organization would develop the 82,000-seat project. Trump won the right to build the $286 million domed stadium in Queens if he could attract an NFL team to play there.

This was yet another attempt to put public pressure on Leon. And it backfired again. Discussions on the new stadium had actually begun the year before. In May 1985, Leon met alone with Vincent Tese, head of the Urban Development Corp., the New York state agency responsible for major building projects. The meeting lasted "probably an hour and a half, two hours," Leon said, with an hour spent getting acquainted and discussing Tese's experiences as a gold trader. Leon would call him "a very interesting young man."

Leon said, "I told him in my opinion a domed stadium was too expensive; that all we needed was a plain old open-air football stadium. I told him that the governor had seen Buffalo's stadium, which was built about eight years ago and cost approximately $20 million, and for 10 football games a year I couldn't see any sense in having a domed stadium that had to be air conditioned and heated, air conditioned in the summer and heated in the winter, just to be used 10 days of the year. He said maybe the [Trump-owned] Generals would use for it for 10 days of the year. And I said, 'That makes 20 days a year.' And he said, 'We will use it for other purposes.'"

It is, after all, hard to think that an 82,000-seat stadium in Queens wouldn't attract the largest entertainment acts, who were otherwise limited to using Madison Square Garden, the biggest venue in the city.

The city would put up $120 million in bonds to fund stadium construction, Tese told Leon. He also told Leon that others had tried this but he was going to get it done. "I told him his time was running out," Leon testified. The Urban Development Corp. was already two years behind and $70 million over budget on the Jacob Javits Convention Center, which didn't bode well for its ability to get big developments done on a tight schedule. Leon declined to meet with developers who were bidding to build the new stadium, saying he didn't want to be seen as favoring any of them.

In early December 1985, Leon learned that the city had selected a developer for the stadium. At that time, he was no longer meeting with city or state officials. "I told him [Tese] I didn't want to meet," Leon said. Instead, "I wanted a written proposal from either the city or the state on how they were going to build this, when it was going to be ready, and so forth."

The city said they couldn't get all the permits and the financing until a tenant was in place. Hess refused to meet with Tese until there was a proposal in writing. "Conversation evaporates. You put things in writing."

Tese's recollection of his last meeting with Hess was of the owner's intransigence. "It became quite apparent to us that there wasn't a deal contemplated here, and that we were wasting our time."

Senator Alfonse D'Amato, who was also pushing for the Jets to return, said he thought Leon was giving excuses for not returning to New York City. "He had made a determination that he wasn't coming back, and the story about the environmental impact statements and the permits was at variance with what I knew to be the case," D'Amato testified.

"That is Senator D'Amato's opinion," Leon replied when asked about the comment.

When the proposal came, it was too late and not enough, Leon said. "I received a written proposal in January signed by the governor and by the mayor with less than 30 days to go" before the Jets' option to exit the Meadowlands contract expired.

No permits were in hand by February 1986. "Mr. Tese said they had a way of getting permits in a hurry when they needed them," Leon said. "Tese told me that some of the land was bought and they—the state agency had a special team for condemnation and would get quick results. Which didn't make me very proud."

A group of tenants in the area of the proposed stadium were starting to protest the possible demolition (ironically, most of them would ultimately be put out of business 30 years later as part of development surrounding Citi Field, the replacement for Shea).

The team would be "gypsies" if the new stadium wasn't ready for 1989, "and there was no way I was going to return to Shea Stadium," Leon said.

Plus, instead of government bonds, the new stadium would be built using seat licenses that would cost Jets fans in addition to buying their tickets. Financing for the stadium was unusual—fans would pay $12,000 for certain seats and $2,400 to lease seats on an annual basis, with suite holders paying $90,000. The city and state would invest nothing in the stadium, although they would've paid $75 million to upgrade infrastructure around the site.

"I could not be a party of a husband and wife with two sons having to pay $48,000 for four seats to have the right to buy a ticket to go to each game," Leon said. He asked Tese why they weren't doing the government bonds and Tese told him they didn't want to build the stadium on the backs of the homeless.

Leon replied a week later by laying out the same requirements he made as the team exited New York—he wanted a "first-class" stadium with the Jets as its prime tenant; the stadium had to be built in time for the 1989 season; and the permits, plans, approvals, and financing needed to be in place by February 1 (about two weeks from the date of the letter). It was an impossible task for the city. In all caps and underlined type, the letter expresses Leon's annoyance with the offer, which was made with little time for him to consider it before he entered a two-week window that allowed for him to cancel his agreement to play in New Jersey. "YOUR RESPONSE, WHICH HAS TAKEN 27 MONTHS AND ARRIVED WITHIN 24 DAYS OF THE DEADLINE, DOES NOT SERVE THE INTERESTS OF THE JETS' FANS OR THE PUBLIC INTEREST. . . ."

To Leon, the team was being offered the kind of facility that it felt it already had at Giants Stadium. And he didn't think the city could actually get the stadium built on time. Terminating the contract in the Meadowlands would cost more than $10 million and "would leave our team and its fans in a completely unprotected and risky position; we may not have a football stadium for the 1989 season or thereafter, and we would have no guarantee of an equivalent football stadium in New York," Leon wrote.

The proposal was unfair to the fans, who would have to pay for rights to buy seats. "THE RESULTS: A DOMED STADIUM BUILT ON THE BACKS OF OUR FANS AND OPERATED WITH OUR FANS' MONEY," Leon wrote.

A response from the city did little to calm Leon. On January 23, 1986, Leon sent a letter to Governor Mario Cuomo and Mayor Koch. The team's option to terminate its current lease expired on February 15 and Leon wasn't happy with the alternatives New York was offering to bring the Jets back. "Your January twenty-second letter provides as a fallback (in the event your proposed domed stadium is not ready for the 1989 season), a renovated Shea Stadium which is likewise 'scheduled for completion by 1989.' This is not an acceptable proposal since it would require the Jets to shut out 20,000 of its enthusiastic fans who are now enjoying attendance at our home games," he wrote.

"He was agonizing over the fact that the team would be leaving New York and that New York would be losing its second and final football franchise," Gutman recalled years later of those negotiations. It wasn't something Leon did from a pure profit motive.

"I wanted to come back to New York and I still want to come back to New York," Leon testified. But the team never would. After Leon's death, the Jets would toy with the idea of returning to the city with a proposed stadium on the West Side. But when that plan died with the failed Olympic bid, the team instead would sign on for the new stadium in the Meadow-lands, built to replace Giants Stadium. At least they would no longer have to play in another team's home—the new facility sold naming rights and was now officially known as MetLife Stadium. And fans had to buy seat licenses.

■ ■ ■

While the move to New Jersey was a blow to New York fans, especially all the Queens and Long Island residents who'd been able to see the team in an easy commute from home, there were others who viewed the decision as a conspiracy. In 1984, a group called the U.S. Football League filed suit against the National Football League, accusing the more well-established defendant of creating a monopoly and using its might to prevent the upstart rival from surviving.

The USFL had been attempting to challenge the NFL, making a splash by getting big-name players, like star running back Herschel Walker, and trying to expand to cities that the NFL had been ignoring. (Walker left the University of Georgia early to join the league—something that would've been impossible under NFL rules. He would play three seasons for the USFL before moving to the NFL's Dallas Cowboys.)

The NFL, for its part, was a prime target for fear and loathing. At that time, any rivals who challenged it had either been destroyed or consumed in a merger. Among the supporters of the suit was then-Representative John McCain, who (while running for his Senate seat in Arizona) filed an affidavit telling the court that it should fix the "artificial scarcity" the NFL was creating and allow competition (Phoenix had tried unsuccessfully up to that point to lure football teams from Baltimore, St. Louis, and Philadelphia and had a USFL team that was struggling).

Al Gore, then a Tennessee senator, also weighed in, saying that Memphis needed a team. "The NFL sees no reason to expand," he wrote. "It pools its network TV contracts, with each team receiving an equal portion of an approximately 455-million-dollar pie in 1986. Any new team would reduce the artificially high value of existing franchises." The league had only added two teams (Tampa Bay and Seattle) in more than 10 years, Gore said in his affidavit.

The USFL began playing in March 1983 with 12 teams and TV contracts with ABC and ESPN (a network founded with Getty Oil money). Two years later, it would collapse after suffering losses of about $200 million and losing its legal fight with the NFL. Before it died, the league filed suit in October 1984 seeking $1.701 billion in damages. The lawsuit filed against the NFL, its commission, and 27 of its clubs alleged violations of the Sherman Antitrust Act. The defendants "sought to perpetuate the monopoly position of the NFL member clubs by precluding successful entry by a competing professional football league."

Several leagues had challenged the NFL since it was organized in 1920. The only one that held up for any length of time was the American Football League, which merged with the NFL before the 1970 season. The AFL was formed by a group led by Dallas oil man Lamar Hunt after the NFL rejected efforts to expand the league to new cities. Oil wealth and football had long been on friendly terms.

The lawsuit resulted in 48 days of trial and approximately 7,100 pages of transcripts, plus thousands of pages of additional exhibits (the case now takes up 17 boxes at the National Archives).

The jury deliberated for five days and found that the NFL's unlawful monopolization of professional football had harmed the USFL. The award, however, was just $1 (because of the antitrust nature, the award was trebled to $3 and eventually reached $3.76 including interest, an amount that was paid by the NFL in 1990—plus hundreds of thousands of dollars in legal fees). The bulk of the charges leveled against the NFL were rejected by the jury. "The NFL offered much evidence of self-destructive USFL decisions, and the jury's nominal award suggests that it credited this proof," an appeals court found in 1988.

Leon, who would testify at the trial, had done everything he could to prevent any other teams from playing after he moved the Jets to the Meadowlands in New Jersey, the plaintiffs said. The suit alleged that this son of New Jersey, who was then a proud resident of New York, had moved the team for his own benefit (in part to unload a money-losing racetrack) and then misled city officials into thinking the Jets would return to prevent any other rivals from getting a foothold.

"The purpose of this conspiracy was to block the USFL's New Jersey team [owned by Donald Trump] from moving to a new domed stadium. Proof of this conspiracy consisted of testimony by Senator Alphonse D'Amato and Vincent Tese, chairman and chief executive officer of the New York State Urban Development Corporation, that Leon Hess, owner of the Jets, had promised to return his team to New York," according to the appeals court ruling.

(Ironically, Trump's New Jersey Generals were playing at Giants Stadium at the time. Leon testified that he was a season ticketholder for the team.)

Al Davis, the owner of the Raiders, testified that the NFL had an understanding that it wouldn't allow any other football teams to move to New York City after the Jets and Giants moved to the Meadowlands in New Jersey. Davis had been irked by Hess, who'd opposed his effort to move the Raiders from Oakland to Los Angeles. Davis testified that Hess told NFL owners at a 1983 meeting that he didn't want another football team in the city.

"The conspiracy worked. The New York officials believed the Jets would return; no other NFL team appeared; the Jets reneged; and the USFL was left in the lurch," according to a USFL court filing.

Moving the Jets and Giants to New Jersey raised the real possibility of a competitor in New York, something the other NFL owners agreed wouldn't happen, the USFL alleged. To block another team from coming, the suit charged that the Jets made the city think it would return, when it had no plans to do so, just to prevent officials from finding another team. "It was Hess and Rozelle that fooled New York City—the rest of the NFL aided and abetted."

According to the USFL, NFL Commissioner Pete Rozelle had said he would work to bring the Jets back to the city, but when Trump was selected as developer of the new stadium, he reneged on that commitment.

Donald Trump testified that he was offered an NFL franchise by Commissioner Rozelle if he would block the USFL from moving its season from spring to fall, in direct competition with the NFL (Rozelle denied he made the offer).

In a January 17, 1984, memo to the USFL owners urging them to switch the season from spring to fall quickly to challenge the NFL more directly or force a merger with the other league, Trump said (in typical Trump fashion): "I did not come into this league to be second rate. We are sitting on something much bigger and better than most people realize. We had better get smart and take advantage of it."

Another owner would gripe that "Donald wants to move the League into the fall so that a merger with the NFL could be forced—he told me that in so many words on two occasions and I believe that his comments at the League meeting included that statement as well," Myles Tanenbaum, managing general partner of the USFL's Philadelphia Stars, said in a January 1984 memo.". . . Donald has thought the scenario through to the point where the partner ownership group within our League will have its restructuring in a fashion which gets Donald into the NFL and the rest of us taken care of in some fashion."

Other people involved in the lawsuit were Howard Cosell and Paul Tagliabue, then the outside counsel for the league before he took over as its head.

Hess was served a subpoena to testify in the case at 9:15 A.M. on March 17, 1986. The subpoena describes Leon as about 5'10" and 170 pounds, still lean at the age of 72. It was delivered to him at his apartment on Park Avenue. Robert Fiske, the NFL's lawyer, tried to get the subpoena quashed, saying he wasn't a party to the case and wasn't deposed during discovery and the complaint filed lists no allegations against him.

The lawyers also fought a request for documents, including those related to Monmouth Park Racetrack and any other entity in which Hess had ownership or a substantial stake. His testimony was delayed, and the plaintiffs' attorneys criticized Leon's "sudden" elective surgery, which required hospitalization.

On July 9, he took the stand.

Explaining the reasons for the move, Leon once again complained about Shea (and its bathrooms, in particular): "conditions at Shea Stadium were horrible, our lease was with the City of New York, the city had delegated all the responsibility for operating the stadium to the Mets; the sanitary facilities were horrible, the grounds were maintained in a very bad way. I had advised the City of New York of this many, many times in writing."

Critics of the move alleged that the switch to New Jersey was tied to the sale of Monmouth Park to the New Jersey Sports Authority. In other words, Hess would bring the Jets to New Jersey if the state would take the money-losing racetrack off his hands. Hess denied these accusations.

"I was a member of the board [for Monmouth Racetrack] but there was nothing in the world that would force me to sell my stock," Hess stated. He held a 30 percent stake in the facility, he said. He sold it in September 1985, about two years after he moved the Jets to New Jersey. The New Jersey Sports Authority bought the track, the same people who had negotiated the Jets' move.

Despite being a man who was once described as having no hobbies,[17] Leon viewed the football team and the racetrack as his escape from work. "I had dreams of retiring and running the Monmouth Park Racetrack and running the New York Jets," Leon told the court. "I was going to get out of business."

Under cross-examination, Hess was asked whether he was looking to sell the track after a competing facility was built in the Meadowlands that was paying a lower state tax rate.

"There was absolutely no direct or indirect relationship between the sale of Monmouth Park and our going to the Meadowlands. And I don't care what you say, there wasn't any relationship."

The plaintiffs alleged that Hess was lying; they had a witness—Anne Gibbons—who was on the board of the racetrack and would testify that Hess owned more than 30 percent and that he had browbeaten the board into selling to the state sports authority despite a higher offer from another bidder, and that he hadn't resigned from the board before the vote to sell but merely abstained from it.

On the day she was supposed to appear in court, the lawyers said that despite an "all-night vigil," she was now unwilling to testify. She never spoke about the matter under oath. The idea that Hess had gone to the Meadowlands in part on the promise that New Jersey would buy his faltering racetrack was never supported in court.

Leon testified that he didn't object during that NFL owners' meeting to a third football team playing in New York. He also said there was no agreement among the NFL owners that another team wouldn't be put in the city.

Under NFL terms, teams could move within 75 miles without requiring approval from the league (the Meadowlands was about 15 miles away from Shea). A few years before, Al Davis had ruffled feathers by trying to move his team from Oakland to Los Angeles. The NFL owners rejected his bid, and he went to court and eventually won the right to bring the team to a better stadium. (The league was found guilty of violating antitrust laws in preventing Davis from moving his Raiders to Los Angeles, forking over millions in fines.)

Davis testified in court that he was furious the NFL was allowing Hess to move the Jets after causing problems with his Raiders' relocation. Davis told the court that Hess had said, "We don't want a third team in New York City."

Hess flatly denied that: "I did not say it and it is not true."

Davis testified that he said at the owners' meeting that New York politicians wanted a team in the city. Leon asked Davis if he wanted to move to New York City, but Davis said he was just annoyed at what appeared to be a double standard.

"There is much in that [Davis] testimony that is not true," Leon said.

■ ■ ■

On December 1, 2014, Leon Hess was inducted into the Ring of Honor for the New York Jets, giving him a placard on the 300-level seats at MetLife Stadium, an honorary green jacket, and the rather unwieldy ring that professional football seems to specialize in dispensing. The Ring of Honor includes the most notable names from Jets history, among them Joe Namath, Mark Gastineau, and Weeb Ewbank, the man who coached the team to its only Super Bowl victory.

At a rainy Monday-night game where entry to the game was going for less than the cost of a movie ticket, John Hess accepted the honor on his father's behalf, heralding "the best fans in football." The team was 2–9 for the season and would go on to lose that night's match against the equally hapless Miami Dolphins. A few weeks earlier, someone had paid for a plane to fly over the Jets' practice ground carrying a banner urging the organization to fire General Manager John Idzik. At the game, fans would be shepherded out for holding up signs calling for Idzik's removal as another losing season wound toward its close. The Jets would lose 16–13, blowing a third-quarter lead to let the visitors score 10 unanswered points in the last part of the game. John addressed his remarks to the half-empty stadium. It was a signature mixture of Jets nostalgia and ineptitude from the team that had meant so much to Leon.

Chapter 9

The Hess Truck's Back

O n a cold Saturday after Thanksgiving, more than 100 people gather in the parking lot outside a sports bar in South Philly, waiting patiently in line for about 30 minutes for the chance to see some toy trucks.

For those willing to shuffle their feet to stay warm while they wait, these aren't just any toy trucks. To millions raised on the East Coast, the Hess holiday toy was as much a part of the holiday season as a Christmas tree and stockings on the fireplace mantel. Those waiting for the chance to view the toys include collectors who want to see the years they're missing. Fathers, sons, and grandsons wait for the chance to climb into a specially designed tour bus that has each toy truck from the past 50 years on custom-designed and lit shelves, displayed like priceless Faberge eggs (Figure 9.1). The tour bus has been christened the Hess Mobile Museum.

Figure 9.1   A few of the trucks on display inside the Hess Mobile Museum.
SOURCE: Photograph by Tina Davis.

A local sports radio station has set up a tent nearby. There are two Philadelphia Eagles cheerleaders getting their pictures taken.

There are wheels to spin for prizes, cheap trinkets mostly. There is a chance to get your picture taken with a "Hess—Happy Holidays" background. There's a "kids' zone" set up with miniature tables and chairs and coloring books. There are tablets where you can order the latest toy online, or play the game the company has created for this year's toy. Parents have their phones out, snapping photos of their children in front of the inflatable Hess helicopter. The guy next to us admits his son is more interested in looking at electronic screens than toys. The toy truck may be an anachronism, but it still has its die-hard supporters in this crowd.

It's cold but no one is complaining. For the fiftieth anniversary of Hess's toy trucks, the company is footing the bill for this roaming celebration of a marketing tool that became a collectors' item, stopping at several cities along the East Coast.

Behind us in the line is a woman for whom the toys are a direct link to her dead father. He used to wake up early on Thanksgiving to go down to the local Hess station and buy three of the toys—one for Sue, one for her brother, and one for himself. He died on Christmas Eve. She keeps the trucks out for a few months along with the rest of her Christmas decorations. It brightens up the place for someone who otherwise, as she puts it, comes downstairs on Christmas morning, confronts her empty house, and just turns on the TV.

■ ■ ■

The toy is such an integral part of the Hess brand, and was so closely associated with Leon, that the company made extraordinary efforts to ensure it would continue coming out even after it no longer owned the gasoline stations that used to sell the toy each year. When Hess announced plans to potentially spin off its stations into a separately traded public entity, the regulatory filing included unique language that specified the trucks would be sold even after the retail business became its own entity. The truck's design would continue to be decided by the CEO's office.

When Marathon Petroleum ended up buying the stations before the spinoff was done, Hess made sure that the public knew the trucks would still be sold. While the Hess name may disappear from the corner gas station, the trucks would still be sold online.

We call it a truck, but it's not really just a truck. The toy has appeared in several iterations since it was introduced in 1964 (Figure 9.2)—including helicopters (Figure 9.3), fire trucks, and ships. No one really asks why an oil company is making a space shuttle–launching toy.

Figure 9.2   The original 1964 Hess truck introduced by Leon Hess.
SOURCE: Photograph by Tina Davis.

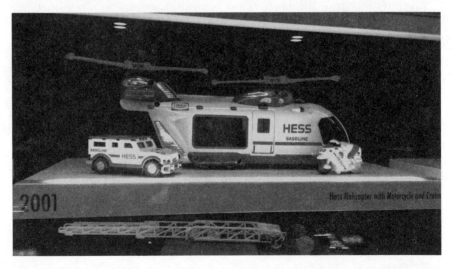

Figure 9.3   The 2001 Hess truck collection, which included a helicopter, motorcycle, and cruiser.
SOURCE: Photograph by Tina Davis.

The toys always had the signature green-and-white Hess logo and for years would make their way onto wish lists courtesy of constant television ads during the holidays. To the tune of "My Boyfriend's Back," viewers would get the earworm of "The Hess truck's back . . ." (somehow turning a 1960s love song into a holiday tune). There followed descriptions of the real working lights and sirens on that year's model. The truck even has pride of place in the company's annual Macy's Thanksgiving Day Parade float (the models used to go on sale on Thanksgiving).

Ray Patterson has been collecting Hess toy trucks since he was a kid. At 58, the retired water treatment worker has turned his love of the toys into a profitable business (so profitable, in fact, that he refuses to have his collection photographed for fear it will encourage burglaries). Even though his two now-grown sons long ago turned to video games and baseball for amusement, Ray is unabashed about his delight in still getting to play with the toys of his youth.

After selling the toys for years on eBay, Ray struck out on his own around the turn of the century, creating a bespoke website devoted to the toys. A business that had consumed time on evenings and weekends became a near full-time calling after his retirement at age 55. The customers vary—"A lot of fathers will call and get the year from when the child was born," he says.

As a marketing tool, Ray thinks it's genius. "Whenever you mention a Hess station, the reaction is not 'Oh, they have cheap gas,' it's 'Those are the guys with the toy trucks,'" he says.

Other companies followed suit in creating branded toys, including Sunoco, BP, and Texaco. "Hess was the first. Hess was the best. Hess was always built the best," according to Patterson. That excludes the "nightmare" boat the company released in 1966, which kids dragged across the floor, resulting in innumerable broken rudders.

But broken toys also mean money for Patterson, who in addition to selling mint pieces in the original box also sells parts to parents who just want to fix an old toy (in case you're wondering, the sideview mirrors are particularly prone to snapping off).

A vintage 1964 truck, which retailed at $1.29, will now cost $1,000 to $2,500, depending on its condition. "The original one, it didn't really do anything except the lights lit up," said Patterson. "It's the smallest of their pieces. It's the only one you can actually fill up with water and drain through the hose."

There are also limited editions that collectors aspire to: in 1969, the company sent out toys to bulk customers as a thank you and in 2006 it gave away trucks to traders on the floor of the New York Stock Exchange when the company representative rang the bell.

And there is the "Red Velvet"—a 1967 edition in which the truck rested atop the eponymous fabric inside the box. Also highly desirable are editions of the 1969 toy, some of which had the old headquarters (Perth Amboy, New Jersey) and some of which feature the company's new home (a few towns away, in Woodbridge).

On release day, Patterson would get up and head to his local Hess station in Oakhurst, New Jersey (the company's first, not far from Leon's hometown of Asbury Park), arriving around 5 A.M. to get his stash of the latest edition.

■ ■ ■

When the company came under attack from Paul Singer's hedge fund, it made clear that even if it had to sell or spin off its gas stations, Hess would continue to make the toy truck. In May 2014, Hess agreed to sell its 1,342 gas stations along the U.S. East Coast to Marathon Petroleum Corp. for $2.6 billion, the largest of the company's multiple asset sales after Elliott Management Corp. launched its attack. In a separate statement the same day, Hess said it would continue to sell the holiday toy trucks at the stations for the 2014 holiday season and after that sell them online.

While an online presence may seem strange for a 50-year-old toy, the company hasn't shied away from its association with Leon's marketing idea, introducing an app for the toy in 2010 and in 2013 linking that app to the physical truck—by honking the truck's horn, players could unlock bonus points in the mobile game, which allowed gamers to move a truck around a course.

Leon was personally involved in designing each toy, according to the company, a tradition that his son has maintained. The concept emerged from a conversation Leon had with a friend who was also a toy manufacturer at a football game in the 1960s. While the idea initially was to create models of working Hess vehicles (one complaint among collectors is that there's never been a tugboat), the toys quickly expanded to include everything from a police car to a space shuttle.

And they drew collectors. One woman in line with her husband at the Mobile Museum confides that they also collect Pez dispensers. Exxon may be five times as large as Hess, but does it incite the kind of nostalgia the trucks do? It's perhaps one of the few positive associations that an oil company has had in the popular imagination.

A few weeks later, over 300 people have gathered at a massive toy expo in Hackensack, New Jersey. Most are there for the toy soldiers and reenactment figures that are the main attraction. At several large tables in the middle of the hall, people are milling about, peeking at a display that has drawn some collectors keen to complete their set.

On plastic shelves and tables, dozens of Hess toy trucks, ranging in condition from used to mint–in–box, line the shelves, all arrayed in chronological order. Prices on the trucks range wildly. A 1974 Hess tanker with a mint-condition caution sticker on it was priced at $475, while mini-vehicles from the past 10 years sold for just $15. Posters nearby with original ads for the oldest trucks disclose their original retail price—from less than $2 for the first trucks going up to $8.99 in 1989 (the 2014 model sold for $29.99).

The displays also include Servco and Wilco trucks, which were made using the Hess molds from the previous year. Hess made a gentleman's agreement so that they could use the molds, if they bought gas exclusively from him, explains a truck reseller, Steve Smiakowski. The bottom and tires still say Amerada Hess.

Other memorabilia crowds the tables, too—Hess lighters, footballs, and drinking glasses. But the trucks are what had drawn a small group of about 10 collectors together, and it is the trucks they are here to talk about.

John Giardina, who goes by Johnny G, has every truck from 1964 to 2014. A dedicated collector, he has them on display in his family room. The interest in the trucks, which are the only thing he collects, started when his son was born in 1972. By the 1980s, he found himself buying four or five of each. His wife, JoAnn, encouraged him to go back and buy the earlier ones. All of his trucks are in mint condition, and to assemble the collection, he's spent up to $2,350, he says.

The family room where the trucks are displayed has a pool table, dart game, and the trucks. JoAnn and Johnny G, who work as perfume distributors, built the custom-lit cases for the trucks together.

"I'm very proud when people come down to the family room," Johnny G says. His wife is proud of the collection, too, but quips that she didn't know how expensive they were when they started collecting them. Johnny G's brother-in-law collected Shell trucks because he worked there. But there was something about the Hess truck—its attention to detail—that attracted Johnny to them.

Ray Doyle, a collector who came from Staten Island for the show in New Jersey, is missing three of the trucks—the 1967, the 1969, and the 1971 "Seasons Greetings" fire truck. They are "toughies" that he hasn't been able to add to his collection, which is understandable since some of them can cost up to $2,500.

Frank Zottola started acquiring the trucks because his grandfather lived near a Hess station, so he would get them as presents—they were the first toy he had that lit up, so in a darkened room it evokes memories for him. While some of the collectors complain that the trucks of recent years look less realistic than the originals, he says he doesn't care as much: to him, their value is still as a toy. Unlike Johnny G and Ray, Frank hasn't collected all of the trucks. "I'm cheaper than those guys," he says, explaining that he doesn't have the earliest trucks.

Like Frank, many collectors say the bond with the toy trucks began in childhood and link them to their fathers, a practice some have tried to continue with their own children. James Galvo's dad started buying him the trucks in the 1970s, as toys, but he now stores them in a room to save as collectors' items. The mementos of his childhood can stay pristine, unopened and untouched.

They are hardly the first or the only toys to be fetishized as collectors' items, but it's hard to think of any toys that were such blatant marketing gimmicks that have grown to be childhood totems. Collectors pore over them and worry about each year—discussion ranges from chrome paint on one truck (starting in 1986, a bad chrome job made the bumpers look gold) to wiring on another.

Mike Roberto, who sends out a monthly newsletter to Hess truck fans on a Facebook fan page (which has more than 2,000 "likes"), says, "Hess trucks are like Pixar movies" because they appeal to both children and adults. He thinks the trucks have created a subconscious affinity for Hess among collectors. As with all fans, he has a few criticisms of the choices over the 50 years. "They really jumped the shark on the space cruiser, but kids love them and they're well made," said Mike.

Since 1964, the company has donated over 750,000 trucks to children's hospitals, and has sent them to the Virgin Islands, Mike says, explaining that the trucks helped him see Hess's philanthropic side.

Steve Smiakowski's affinity for Hess goes beyond the trucks—he holds stock in the company and met Leon twice at shareholders' meetings, believing him to be the "nicest man." In 1973, 1979, and 1981, Steve notes, there were no trucks because of gasoline shortages. Steve believes Leon didn't want parents to have to go buy trucks when there were issues affording gas.

"When they did the fortieth anniversary, there were rumors they would stop. There were rumors again when Leon died," Steve said. But it gave them more exposure than TV commercials or other advertising.

Steve, who worked at Hess for one summer, has always had a fondness for gas station memorabilia. In the mid-1990s, he really got into collecting—so into it, in fact, that the trucks in his basement reside in glass classes within a façade of a Hess gas station.

The company's bid to get the truck into the Toy Hall of Fame at its fiftieth anniversary failed. Instead, the inductees for 2014 included the Rubik's cube and little green army men. Mind you, the blanket and cardboard box have been voted into the Hall of Fame in Rochester, New York. Collectors can view the full array of Hess toys at the company's Woodbridge office, although that building is scheduled to be sold as part of the company's scaling back.

For Ray Patterson, the toys provide a revenue stream and are an indication of the character of the company. People love Hess "because of what Hess does or what Leon has done for their children and themselves. It's a tradition that you want to keep going."

And batteries are included.

Chapter 10

Getting and Spending

You don't name a company after yourself if you are shy. You don't emblazon that name across thousands of gas stations and dozens of enormous storage tanks, not to mention a huge sign at Yankee Stadium and hundreds of thousands of toy trucks being pushed across bedroom floors in homes up and down the U.S. East Coast. The four green block letters HESS on the white background were meant to be bold, recognizable, a symbol of the fastidious man and the company that bore his imprint and followed his lead.

What Leon did with the fortune he raised from those big block letters shows the things he valued most: education, health, faith, culture. But if the large grants reveal the responsibilities a rich man felt to improve the world around him, it's the smaller generosities that give us the measure of who he was as a person. For a man whose fortune was estimated at half a billion dollars by the end of the 1980s (putting him among the top 150 wealthiest Americans),[1] there was awareness that the money had to be used for something beyond the Park Avenue apartment, the Jets football team, and the pony track that he loved. Rising to a tradition that extends from the very early years of the oil barons, Leon Hess put his fortune to use in philanthropic endeavors that expanded the family name beyond just the industry that built him, and he helped to build. The Hess name now appears on schools and medical centers and was even seen at the Bronx Zoo, on the trolleys that ferry visitors around the park (as with so many other things, the trolleys bear the company's name in the same recognizable shade of kelly green that served as Leon's fingerprint).

"Treasure a good name," Leon told his family. He wanted the Hess name to be recognized and respected.

But there's a dissonance between the myriad places his name now appears and his philosophy on giving without recognition during his own lifetime. Some of the most public gifts—a business school, two medical centers, professorships at elite universities—were given by his wife and children after his death, indicative of a man who strove to avoid unwanted attention while he was alive. Leon's reservations contrast with John's tendency to show his devotion through multimillion-dollar gifts honoring his family, and his willingness to be photographed at lavish galas.

Leon's less public philanthropy left its mark on individuals and institutions across the region. John D. Rockefeller was so overwhelmed by his fortune and the attending requests for money that poured in that he often rebuffed efforts to name things after himself. Forty years before his death Leon began the foundation that would ensure his money was being distributed to the often eclectic groups he supported. The foundation was also a way to keep his closest friends and advisers tied to him, with corporate board memberships overlapping with seats on the Hess Foundation in a serpentine way that would raise questions about who was really independent of the Hess family when the company came under attack for its governance. The philosophy of service to the community carried over to the rest of his family—his daughter Marlene was head of corporate giving for JPMorgan, the recently opened Whitney museum in downtown New York features the Susan and John Hess Theater, and Constance Hess Williams has chaired the Philadelphia Museum of Art's board for five years. His grandchildren are often seen at fundraisers for causes that include some of his favorites, like Lincoln Center. But their brand of giving while getting photographed is far more public than Leon's charity. The company that bears his name continues to fund its own charitable projects in areas in which it operates, from New Jersey to Equatorial Guinea.

Beyond the variety of causes that often featured his name, Leon was a man who was quick to perform small favors for friends and employees in need. From helping a colleague who needed medical assistance to funding a whole school, Leon's charitable endeavors were wide ranging, without always being showy. He could slip into the hospital room with a friend and pay for his care, give money from his own accounts to rebuild schools in the Virgin Islands after a hurricane, or just be counted upon to make sure that the poor in Newark had food. Across all of his many philanthropic efforts, the unifying factor was a broad commitment to quality healthcare, education, his faith, and serving those in need in the communities to which he and his business were most attached.

Having grown up in the Depression, Leon understood deeply the feeling of being without, and wanted to use his largesse to benefit others. He was generous with his family and close friends. When he died, his fortune was divided among the foundation, his family, a few close friends and advisers, and his doctors. He didn't sign on to any pact to dedicate the majority of his wealth to charity like some of today's billionaires, including T. Boone Pickens, Harold Hamm, and John Arnold, who have signed off on a Bill Gates–led pledge to donate the majority of their wealth to charity. Upon his death, his children inherited tens of millions of dollars in addition to shares in the company. Still, he knew the importance of giving.

On October 8, 1957, more than a decade before Hess merged with Amerada to establish itself as a leading oil company, Leon created a foundation to support the causes that were most important to him. The contributions to the Hess Foundation grew with his wealth and with the expansion of the company. As the foundation reflected the causes that were most dear to Leon, it also showed the way the company dominated even his charitable activities, with the two entities tied by board members, advisers, and stockholdings.

The gifts from the foundation, initially, were small—many bequests totaling just a few hundred dollars—but their impact stretched across New York from Harlem to Brooklyn, and across New Jersey from

Newark to the Jersey Shore of Leon's youth, and ultimately grew to encompass organizations in other regions that were important to him as his business grew to new areas, like the Virgin Islands.

By 1970, two years after the merger, Leon's foundation held Amerada Hess shares with a market value of nearly $48 million—$299 million in 2015 dollars—and disbursed more than $400,000 (less than 1 percent), which it had earned in interest and dividends on its holdings. Spending just a few hundred dollars on professional fees, Leon and Norma led the foundation with two Hess board members, Harold Gast and H. W. McCollum, and with retired Shell Caribbean Petroleum Corp. president John Walstrom.[2] The company was everything to the foundation, which held few other assets aside from Leon's stock. At that point, the foundation supported primarily educational, cultural, and medical activities, with the largest donations going to the Metropolitan Opera and New York's Mount Sinai Hospital, which each received $50,000. The following year, the foundation shifted its largest contribution to Lenox Hill Hospital, also in New York (and the facility where Leon would eventually die). These two large grants stood out—other recipients continued to get just a few hundred or a few thousand dollars apiece.

Leon joined the Metropolitan Opera Association in 1969, and served as an Advisory Director in 1977. He is credited for contributions to building the Opera House at Lincoln Center and the creation of the Met's first endowment fund. He was often seen at opening night galas, watching from a box he endowed.

In these early years, the recipients included about a half-dozen synagogues, such as the Park Avenue Synagogue that Leon attended, a quiet reflection of his Jewish faith. Smaller grant recipients also included Harvard College and Phillips Academy in Andover, Massachusetts, which John had attended. In the period that ended Nov. 30, 1973, the fund bequeathed $7,500 to Harvard's center for Middle Eastern Studies, an illustration of the family and company's relationship with the oil-producing region. As the foundation reflected the family's values and allegiances, it also illustrated where the company did business, with a growing roster of contributions to Virgin Islands concerns after the Hovensa refinery began operating.

The foundation grew as Hess Corp. grew. When the foundation's coffers reached a fair market value of over $100 million, a manager, Alice

Rocchio, was brought in to handle the family's concerns. Still, Leon remained president of the organization, with Norma as vice president. Rocchio played an administrative role.

By 1997, two years after John was appointed CEO of the company, he had joined the board of the foundation, as had Steve Gutman of the Jets and John Schreyer, Hess's CFO. Among the directors was Squire Bozorth, a lawyer who specialized in estate matters and had cut his teeth representing the Rockefeller Family Offices in the early 1960s, and then advised family members on their estates, including Governor Nelson Rockefeller.[3] Like the Rockefellers, who gave major bequests to both elite institutions and those meant to serve the poorest, the Hess family wanted to give a wide range of grants, and also to fly under the radar with their contributions, so Bozorth was a natural fit for the family's foundation.

While Leon's fortune lagged that of the Rockefellers, you can see in it kernels of the Rockefeller style of philanthropy, which included providing funds for research foundations to carry out good work, particularly in the scientific and medical arenas. John D. Rockefeller, who faced countless requests for cash, opted to divide it primarily between foundations, delegating the giving as he delegated business operations. Leon, too, wanted to avoid being labeled a wealthy patron, saying that it "brings out the cranks." Leon didn't put as much distance between himself and the causes he championed as Rockefeller had—he stayed active on philanthropic boards of the causes he was most passionate about.

The contributions ranged widely, and were sometimes at odds with one another—in 1997, the foundation contributed to both Planned Parenthood of South Eastern Pennsylvania and to the Pro-Life Athletes of Chatham, New Jersey. In the same year, while there were many contributions to Jewish organizations, one of the largest gifts was $350,000 to the archdiocese of Newark, New Jersey. The church of Jesus Christ of Latter-day Saints of Tulsa, Oklahoma, received $1,000, while the Gay Men's Health Crisis received $30,000. As he did with his political donations, Leon's charitable giving sometimes played both sides of the field.

The scale of the foundation was growing. By 1997, it was disbursing over $5.6 million in a single year. The holdings had expanded beyond just shares of Amerada Hess, and as a result, the costs associated with running the foundation were also beginning to ramp up, with $60,000 paid to an investment manager, Darby Emerging Market Fund.

Just as the company began increasing its association with Goldman Sachs in the late 1990s, so too did the foundation, reporting holdings of Goldman Sachs and Templeton funds, alongside its holdings in Darby, by 2000.

After Leon's death in 1999, Norma assumed the role of president of the foundation, with her three children serving as vice presidents, and Burton Lefkowitz joining John Schreyer as a close associate of Leon's from the company, who served at the foundation. Tom Kean, the former New Jersey governor who served on the Hess Corp. board, was also on the roster of foundation directors, illustrating the way the two organizations overlapped. Even after Leon's death, the family chose to surround itself with a small pool of trusted financial advisers at two of the institutions that were most important to him: the company and the foundation.

While the overlaps were initially a source of strength for the family's control over both institutions, it would eventually draw criticism from Elliott Management, as the fund began to agitate for change at Hess. In particular, two long-term board members, Kean and former Treasury Secretary Nicholas Brady, came under fire for their involvement with the Hess charitable trust, which funded the foundation. Kean served as secretary of the charitable trust, while Brady had been involved with investing for the trust.

As John took on additional responsibilities at the company, his role in the foundation expanded, too. He became the executive vice president, while his sisters remained vice presidents. Fueled by contributions of $9 million a year or more from a charitable bequest Leon had made in his will, the fair market value of the foundation's assets rose to $807 million. With the growing asset base, the cost of managing the philanthropy also rose, ballooning from an enterprise spending tens of thousands of dollars to one that doled out nearly a million, paying management fees to accountants, lawyers, an entity called Hess Group, and to Goldman Sachs.

While the commitment to medical, educational, and cultural institutions remained prominent, the size of the grants rose, and Leon's children's preferences began to show through more clearly, with an $8 million donation to the Philadelphia Museum of Art and a $3 million grant to the Philadelphia Orchestra, both organizations near Constance's home in Pennsylvania. Deerfield Academy, which all three of John's sons had attended, received $1.5 million from the foundation in 2012. At Deerfield, the decision to rename the Memorial Building the "Hess Center for the Arts" was a controversial one, as the school had not historically named buildings after donors. After renaming the building, which had been a memorial to alumni who died in World War II, a flagpole and plaque at one of the center's entrances served as a memorial instead.

Contributions to the Park Avenue Synagogue continued, but Mount Sinai and the Metropolitan Opera were no longer the top two recipients, as the broader family's philanthropic priorities became clearer.

"Hess Foundation grant-making can be better understood as John's grants, Marlene's grants, and Connie's grants," according to a 2015 report on the foundation. "Independent and insular, this generation of Hess family members came to their roles in the foundation at the middle stages of their lives and careers, and seem to have left little room to make the foundation any more prominent or strategic."[4]

Upon his mother's death, John became president of the foundation, which held shares valued at more than $555 million in 2012.

Despite its role as a distributor of cash, the foundation has not been free of detractors, in part because of its secrecy compared with other grant makers of similar size. A 2015 study found the foundation lacked transparency and access—it has no website, no paid executive, and "no way for potential nonprofit or foundation partners to reach out to its leadership," according to the National Committee for Responsive Philanthropy. That organization found that, despite efforts to diversify, the Hess Foundation and the Charitable Lead Trust (CLT) that provides income to the foundation are heavily invested in Hess Corp. "The charitable vehicles and associated investments enable the family to retain ownership of Hess stock, free from capital gains or inheritance taxes, until 2035 when one vehicle, the CLT, is scheduled to revert to Hess heirs," the report found. "The lack of asset diversification may benefit the Hess family, but it places the foundation's charitable assets at risk and does not represent best investment practice."

■ ■ ■

While the foundation is Leon's largest charitable legacy, some remember simple gestures of help. His more personal acts of giving, unlike large bequests to the opera or a hospital, reveal his humanity.

More than anything else, Leon's appearance in a hospital room could be a gift, as he offered access to doctors and funding at crucial times.

Into his nineties, Seymour Miller remained a notable opponent in tennis at the club where he plays in Deal, New Jersey. The reason, he said, is simple: Leon Hess. Decades ago, long before he retired from Hess, Sy broke his elbow, and found himself at a small, nondescript hospital in New Jersey. Almost immediately, he said, Leon arrived with an expert physician from New York. The doctor treated Sy, and he was healed. He still attributes the recovery to Leon's involvement. Other Hess employees received similar interventions from Leon, and he was always concerned about the health of those he was close to, Sy recalled. A close adviser, Sy started as an accountant and had worked his way up through the ranks during more than four decades with the company.

Leon's gestures continued and grew, decade after decade. In 1992, two Jets players, Dennis Byrd and Scott Mersereau, collided, leaving Byrd crumpled on the turf, with a broken neck and a prognosis that he would never walk again.[5] Football is a brutal sport and can be an even more brutal business (players sometimes say the NFL stands for "Not For Long") as season- and career-ending injuries have killed the promise of many a recruit who saw a life on the gridiron. As team owner, Leon stepped in, going above and beyond the normal actions that could be expected of someone who had just lost a promising player he'd spent considerable money to acquire.[6] Leon visited Dennis often, and took an active role in supporting the player's wife, Angela, and daughters, paying the final two years of the player's contract—over $1 million—without being required to.[7]

Leon visited Dennis first at Lenox Hill Hospital, where the player spent two weeks, and then at Mount Sinai Hospital where he remained for two months. On the almost nightly visits, they talked about everything from family and Dennis's rehabilitation to their shared love of fishing and passion for hard work. Leon, a slim (5'9"), had a commanding presence that intimidated even a (6'5") defensive tackle. "Mr. Hess would come in, after everyone else was gone" late in the evenings, Byrd recounts in his autobiography. "When I'd gotten hurt Sunday afternoon, Mr. Hess hadn't been far behind the ambulance. He was at the hospital through that evening, making sure I'd have everything I needed. When my parents came on Monday, it was Mr. Hess who flew them up and got them a hotel room nearby. He got Angela a room, too, so she could be right [there] with me for the duration."

Hess told Byrd's agent at the time, "If I had known something like this was ever going to happen, I would never have bought the team."

"[H]e had treated me like one of his own children," Byrd wrote. "I'd come to look up to him much the way I'd look up to a grandfather." Dennis made a recovery that was heralded as miraculous in the medical community, boosted by some of the best doctors in the country and by the devotion of a team owner who didn't discard him when the injury ended his playing.

Dennis tried to thank Leon, saying, "Thank you for what you've done, 'cause you didn't have to do it." Leon's response was: I know I didn't have to do it, but I did it anyway. Byrd's number would be retired; no other Jet could play in a number 90 jersey on the team, out of deference to him.

The fierce devotion he showed to those around him fostered a fierce respect by those who worked for him. "I really wanted to win a Super Bowl for him," said Jets cornerback Ray Mickens. "That's the main thing I wanted to do. I wish I could have done that."

While his will left a large bequest for the foundation, it also offered direct gifts to those who he felt needed them and had been close to him.

It was only natural that Leon, who could strike up a conversation with his taxi driver or a ditch digger at his refinery, would show his gratitude to those who had supported him and helped him most, even if they were connected in a purely professional capacity without being close friends. That meant that his will not only included bequeaths to family members, it released friends, including the Jets' Gutman and Hess general counsel J. Barclay Collins II, from debts.

Leon's brand of philanthropy at times recognized the hard work of employees who were expected to work long hours at the company. While Leon asked for nothing in return for his gifts, the respect his generosity engendered was paid back in loyalty: Sy Miller, who came to the company in 1950, stayed until his retirement four decades later. Dolores Finley, Hess's special assistant, served in the role for three decades. His primary driver, Charles Harris, worked for Hess for nearly 25 years. The tycoon inspired devoted loyalty from those around him and seemed to pay it back in kind. As a result, a sort of brotherhood of Amerada Hess emerged.[8] His secretary and driver were beneficiaries of

Leon's will, which focused on his family, but also included charities, key Hess employees, certain Jets, and doctors who treated Leon. In addition to the doctors who helped him fight the blood disorder that weakened him during the final years of his life, Leon included others, like a pair of ophthalmologists who had treated him. Leon recognized at least four doctors in his will, leaving as much as $1,000,000 to one. One doctor who received $250,000 from Leon said their relationship never went beyond the purely medical—still, he was recognized in Leon's will for that connection during his final years.

His of giving to those about whom he felt protective extended beyond his family members and company to the players of the Jets. In 1965, in the midst of building his oil giant oil refinery in the Virgin Islands, Hess learned that Jets quarterback Joe Namath was having his first knee surgery. Each night after the operation, Hess dropped by to see how Namath was doing.

His tireless dedication to the players spanned decades. When a defensive lineman's wife was injured in a car crash halfway across the country, Hess sent a private jet to return her to New York, where he paid for her to receive some of the best medical care in the world.[9]

■ ■ ■

Leon's largest legacies are medical: the Leon and Norma Hess Center for Science and Medicine at Mount Sinai and the Leon Hess Cancer Center at Monmouth Medical Center. Both centers focus on cancer treatment and research.

The Leon and Norma Hess Center for Science and Medicine at Mount Sinai was announced in 2009 and opened in late 2012, accommodating patients just as Hurricane Sandy struck New York. The half-million-square-foot center in Manhattan was designed to include six floors of laboratories and two of outpatient clinical space, according to plans laid out by the school. The center houses most of Mount Sinai's cancer-related research and clinics, and was a "game changer for the future of health care," not with its spectacular facility, but with its efforts to transform the way doctors collaborate and treat disease, board chairman Peter May said in the opening ceremony for the center, which included a panel of doctors and a handful of community leaders. The Hess family was not on the panel.

The center was conceived in the early 2000s but hit a rut when the organization that was going to be building the residential tower behind the center decided not to go forward with the project because of the recession of 2008, according to Dr. Kenneth Davis, the CEO of Mount Sinai Health System. The medical school decided to continue with the project, and sought philanthropic support from others, including John Hess, who asked that the facility be named after his parents. The school developed a multigenerational relationship with the Hesses, dating back to Leon's service on the board starting in 1966. John now is set to chair the school's research committee, which meets quarterly.

While Mount Sinai did not disclose the size of the grant that funded the facility, it has said that the center has created 650 permanent new employment opportunities with an annual payroll of nearly $40 million. Dr. Davis credited John Hess with an "extraordinary amount of philanthropy" behind the project. Leon and Norma's names stand behind the reception desk at the center's Madison Avenue lobby, and are below those of the Icahn family, the benefactor of the medical school, and next to that of the Tisch family, which has funded the cancer institute.

The Leon Hess Cancer Center at Monmouth Medical Center in New Jersey may have been even closer to home in some ways. The medical center sees itself as part of the Hess "extended family" fabric, with a breast cancer center named after Norma's brother Robert's wife, Jacqueline Wilentz. The Hess Foundation's $3 million gift to Monmouth was made possible by the medical center's former chief of surgery, Dr. Lester Barnett, whom Leon had known in childhood and with whom he kept a lifelong friendship through the Hesses' nearby summer residence.

■ ■ ■

After a 1980 hurricane wiped out 70 schools that served about 30,000 children in St. Lucia, where the company operated a large oil-storage terminal, Leon rebuilt all of the schools. The deed was recognized by the island's governor, who insisted upon naming one of the comprehensive schools after Leon.

Yet, his family said this less flamboyant giving illustrated some of Leon's more understated charitable endeavors. "That characteristic—to find reward in giving, quietly and privately, to others—was one that distinguished my father during his entire life," John Hess remembered.[10]

The gift to St. Lucia was emblematic of the way Leon often wanted to donate: its effects were wide-ranging, but there was not direct, ongoing contact between them and those who benefited from their generosity.

Leaving a postdoctoral position at Colby College, computer scientist Daniel Bilar was thrilled to receive the first Norma Wilentz Hess fellowship at Wellesley College. The two-year position that the Hess family had established provided a reprieve from the rat race of academia that often requires newly minted professors to do multiple fellowships to amass the research they need for at tenure-track job. The grant was meant to foster research by emerging scholars, and offers a generous stipend for travel and research expenses, while only requiring the fellow to teach a single course each semester, allowing them to devote more energy to research.

Bilar used the money to attend a NATO conference in Estonia on cyber security and publish papers that helped establish his reputation as an expert in the field. While others had to struggle to put together grants for each event they wished to attend, Bilar found that the Hess family's generosity had paved the way to a smoother start for his career.

Once his two years at Wellesley as the first Hess fellow were completed, despite a downturn in the economy, he found a position, landing at the University of New Orleans. Because of the research funding Bilar had secured while at Wellesley, hiring him changed the University of New Orleans's status among research institutions with National Security Agency (NSA) backing, increasing the university's eligibility for grants. The result was that the university's students could qualify for four-year full scholarships from the NSA, previously available only to students at two dozen top research schools like the University of Texas and the University of Southern California.

Bilar credited the Hesses' generosity for creating the opportunities he had and the ripple effect for students at the University of New Orleans. He was never actually able to meet Norma Hess, though. (He made a request through Wellesley that he be allowed to shake her hand and say thanks in 2007, while he had the fellowship, but consistent with the Hess family's quiet brand of giving, she didn't want acknowledgment, and she died several years later.)

At the Leon Hess Business School at Monmouth University, founded just a few miles from Leon's birthplace with a gift Norma made in her husband's honor, the interest from the gift has allowed the construction of a trading lab, in which students practice using Bloomberg terminals and other specialty software to gain experience needed to land jobs. The lab, in turn, has attracted professors like John Burke, a hedge fund manager. Still, the name and bequest haven't formed a relationship with the company or with John Hess, who has never given an address at the school.

Giving with no expectation of acknowledgment was one hallmark of Leon's efforts.

Picking up the phone to call Theodore McCarrick, then the archbishop of Newark, was routine for him. Unconstrained by religion, Leon would call the archbishop, without being asked, to offer something to feed the poor, help handle the cost of the Pope's visit to New Jersey, or to buy presents for families who didn't have enough money for Christmas presents. "Leon would almost seem embarrassed as if this was something completely ordinary, something he just had to do," McCarrick recalled at Leon's funeral.[11] For this work, the bishop asked Pope John Paul II to confer the order of Saint Sylvester upon Leon, in recognition of great humanitarian and community services, just two years before his death. The order had previously recognized Oskar Schindler and Bob Hope. In the United Kingdom, recipients have included Muslims and Jews, though it is unusual for Americans to be recognized by the order.

Chapter 11

A New Hess

We are now a bigger fish in a smaller pond.

—John Hess

F rom the age of seven, John Hess was being groomed to take over Hess. When he officially joined the company as a graduate trainee, he came with substantial educational preparation: a graduate of Phillips Andover, Harvard College, and Harvard Business School, and he spoke Farsi as well as Arabic. He was comfortable in a boardroom with bankers, lawyers, and other top executives, having accompanied his peripatetic father on trips to Texas, Peru, and Iran. But he also spent time in the trenches, learning the business by pumping gas at a station in New Jersey, doing accounting for a refinery, taking part in operations in St. Croix and at oilfields in Oklahoma. Trained by his father and his father's top lieutenants, he had learned how to evaluate oil prospects, run a refinery, and operate a trading floor. His rise through the ranks was swift and unsurprising—everyone realized that the young "coordinator of planning and control" who was named to the board at the ripe age of 22 was destined for the CEO's office. John eventually became a senior vice president and worked beside his father until he was named CEO in 1995. When Leon finally surrendered the role of CEO at the age of 81, it was many years after anyone thought he might. The man had once talked of retiring at 65, but then he started counting his birthdays backward. It was a Hess trait to keep a hand in the business, after all; Leon's father stayed with the company until shortly before his death at the age of 94. By 1999, Leon's health was fading and a longstanding illness that required blood transfusions was taking its toll. A broken hip early in the year, from which he never fully recovered, sent him to the hospital.

When Leon died in the spring, John was four years into his tenure as CEO. He would become one of the longest-standing energy CEOs. While he didn't have the challenge of building a new venture from scratch, he had to navigate some of the most complicated and surprising energy markets the world has seen, as a major shift between suppliers and producers once again upended most business plans. With Leon's passing, one thing was clear: with his son steering the ship, the Hesses were in control of Hess and that would continue for a good, long time. Leon even sold the Jets football team to make sure the company was the only major entity that John was responsible for.

John's tenure with the company included new realities of global tensions and domestic growth that were only beginning to be felt in the late 1990s. On this very different landscape, John, who was viewed as more conservative in his business approach than his father, tried to make it the biggest little oil company he could, stretching Hess to become a major integrated energy producer—even though it was less than a tenth the size of Chevron, he wanted to have the same global grasp that his largest rivals held. He aggressively hired top talent from competitors and built up his own reserve of inside advisers, with whom he made major decisions on the company's future. The future, he thought, would require all kinds of energy, so he helped Hess diversify, pushing the company into frontiers like fuel cells, where it hadn't operated before. When the shale revolution took hold in the United States, reshaping the world's energy landscape, John shifted course aggressively, acquiring more oil and gas acreage and jettisoning some of his other non-oil ventures, as investors and analysts rewarded companies that were focused on producing ever more quantities of fossil fuel from shale.

Ultimately, he would expand the company into many new areas and regions and be criticized for being too much like his father (holding on to most of the same board members that were there when he first became CEO) and for dallying in businesses his father wouldn't have stomached.

■ ■ ■

Despite the considerable exploration and production exposure gained with the Amerada acquisition in the 1960s, 30 years later, the company was recognized by the public primarily for its East Coast gasoline stations. A year after Leon Hess's death, the company was still domestically focused, with only 13 percent of its oil reserves outside of the United States.

While Amerada Hess had a reputation as a player in certain global petroleum circles—Leon's relationship with the Shah, negotiations with Qaddafi, and rank as a top oil producer in the North Sea had ensured that—there were still petroleum hotspots that remained untouched by Hess. Tempting basins off the coast of Africa and in South America and Asia beckoned, and John was determined to grow the company's presence in those areas.

Armed with all his father had taught him, plus an MBA from Harvard and strong connections in the banking world, John began to shift the company's focus to seeking exploration and production assets outside the United States. The man who symbolically left his father's office untouched after the latter's death was starting to flex his muscles and shift the corporate strategy to the sexier business of exploring and producing oil in far-flung places.

Mergers and acquisitions activity was heating up, reaching a fever pitch in the late 1990s as the petroleum companies known as the Seven Sisters were combining and growing. To keep up, Amerada Hess needed to expand by acquisition, too.

In one of his first major strategic acts as CEO, John set his sights on Lasmo, the United Kingdom's second-largest oil exploration and production company. He would learn a very public lesson about mergers and acquisitions.

Lasmo had been founded in the 1970s as London & Scottish Marine Oil, with a focus on the North Sea. It was a company that grabbed for hot assets, often biting off more than it could chew, and had a tortured history of mergers and acquisitions. It had become an industry soap opera, the actor in a hostile takeover and then the subject of hostile takeover bids. In 1991, it acquired Ultramar, a gasoline marketer, refiner, and retailer, for about $2 billion and then spun off the company's North American refining and marketing operations.

By the late 1990s Lasmo was faltering after a rocky run—rival U.K. producer Enterprise had taken a hostile run at the company in 1994, and it hadn't regained a solid footing. When John first sniffed around it, the company desperately needed to streamline its assets, and limit exposure to Venezuela (never a straightforward place for an oil producer to do business). Lasmo was generating about 8 percent of its sales from Venezuela and 20 percent from Indonesia in 1999. It had bought its Venezuela assets for $453 million in June 1997, shortly before oil prices fell, and analysts wanted the company to cut its exposure to the country. At the time, Lasmo was seen as making the same mistake twice—or even three times—repeating its Ultramar overspending with the acquisition of Monument Oil & Gas and then paying a steep premium for its Venezuelan exposure.

Rising oil prices, coupled with Lasmo's increasing production from Venezuela attracted Amerada Hess. By the summer of 2000, Amerada Hess was rumored to be making a $500 million bid for half of Lasmo's Venezuelan assets. By November, Amerada Hess's appetite was larger: the company decided to bid not just on the Venezuela assets, but on all of Lasmo, offering $3.5 billion in cash and stock.

Lasmo's chairman, Antony Hichens, who had been seeking a buyer, praised the string of mergers in the United States, saying scale was increasingly essential for accessing capital and tackling big projects.[1] In Amerada Hess, Lasmo had a suitor that had the cash to invest in the company's Venezuela fields and in those it had acquired from Monument.

For Amerada Hess, the Lasmo acquisition was a chance to reshape the entire company, making it a global producer, with 41 percent of its oil reserves outside of the United States. It would be the biggest jolt of M&A the company experienced since the Amerada deal. The deal was John's opportunity to compete more evenly with the giant oil companies, known as super-majors, which were getting bigger by the day as Rockefeller's original seven trusts hungrily snapped up competitors. John's move followed a spate of corporate oil marriages. It was announced just a month after Chevron made its intentions known on Texaco, and in the previous year Exxon and Mobil had merged and a BP subsidiary bought ARCO. A year before that, BP and Amoco had joined forces.

John saw the acquisition of Lasmo as a chance to make Amerada Hess a big player in the United States and Venezuela, and an even bigger player in the United Kingdom, where it was already the third-largest oil and gas producer, behind BP Amoco and Shell, with interests in 35 fields.[2]

"We are now a bigger fish in a smaller pond," he said at the time. "Exploration and production is the primary engine of income growth."[3] After the sale, the combined company would be spending less than a quarter of its capital on running gasoline stations, and would be largely devoted to exploration and production.

But even as John planned to buy Lasmo at a 28 percent premium to its price, trouble was brewing as other companies awoke to the opportunities the British producer's assets presented. Amerada Hess had yet to reach an agreement to purchase Lasmo when competing suitors started to signal their interest. Chief among them was Eni, the Italian oil company.

"We have monitored the company very closely in the past," Eni's CEO Vittorio Mincato told *Bloomberg News* just a week after Hess's bid was announced. "We don't know what the development of this operation will be. We are monitoring the situation closely because it interests us, though it's clear that Amerada Hess made the offer and not us."

John was about to learn that dating someone was a lot easier than getting him or her to marry you. Hess was armed with a credit line and commercial paper program, and had obtained a $3 billion Goldman Sachs loan to comply with U.K. rules that prohibited loans with restrictive conditions, known as covenants Hess's previously existing revolving credit line from Chase Manhattan had included these limitations. The Goldman loans, which had terms of five years or less, could be replaced with long-term bonds if needed.[4]

When Hess was only about a month away from buying Lasmo, Eni trumped the American company's offer, announcing a $5.59 billion bid for Lasmo—almost double Amerada Hess's offer. The acquisition was the second in the year for Eni, which had already bought British-Borneo Oil & Gas for $1.2 billion, as part of a plan to increase output by 28 percent by 2003.

Amerada Hess didn't counter, letting Lasmo go to the Italians. John was making clear that even though he wanted to join the ranks of the largest energy companies in the world, he was still going to be a conservative spender, and wouldn't let pride or merger fever push him to overspend.

With its higher offer, Eni secured access to Lasmo's production in the U.K. North Sea, North Africa, Venezuela, Indonesia, and Pakistan, as well as potential projects in Iran and Kuwait. By January 12, Hess had bowed out of the race. Eni successfully acquired the company by the end of that month.

Despite losing that round, Hess remained hot on the trail of acquisitions.

"It's no secret that we are waiting for the right opportunity to come along," spokesman Carl Tursi told *Bloomberg* at the time. Amerada Hess maintained the credit line from Goldman Sachs, converting the loans into a general line of credit, thereby getting a type of financing that Goldman had refused to give to other companies, like Ford Motor Co. and Vodafone Group Plc.[5] The bank was trying to limit its less-profitable businesses, like providing credit to companies, to focus instead on merger advising and underwriting share offerings.

This was Goldman's first major loan to Amerada Hess, and the bank declined to say why it had agreed to the request. Goldman and Hess had an "ongoing" relationship, spokeswoman Kathleen Baum told *Bloomberg* at the time. The relationship was seen beyond corporate banking, as John had hired a pair of Goldman traders to run Hetco, the proprietary trading arm of Hess, and Leon had requested in his will that the bank oversee the sales process for the Jets.

John wouldn't leave the cash lying around unused for long.

Six months later, after getting beaten for Lasmo and armed with its loans from Goldman, Amerada Hess announced that it would try to acquire again. This time it was targeting Triton Energy, with a $2.6 billion cash bid that would increase its production growth. The deal offered basins in Africa, Malaysia, and Indonesia, widening Hess's horizons and tilting its portfolio toward global exploration and production. The Triton purchase was approved, but in the months following it, declines of its value would lead analysts to question whether John had made the right move.

In 2002, the company posted a loss after a $530 million after-tax charge related to the Ceiba field in Equatorial Guinea, which had been acquired from Triton, and a $256 million charge related to Gulf of Mexico assets. The company lists Triton's Ceiba among the disappointments it experienced in 2003, as it needed to be produced "at a lower rate and over a longer period than originally planned."

While Triton gave less lift to Amerada Hess's balance sheet than Lasmo would have, and dealt a blow in the form of Ceiba's underperformance, it was John's first major deal and indicated how he planned to remake the company to look less like his father's gasoline retailer and refiner and more like a miniature version of Shell, Exxon, or BP.

■ ■ ■

As John led the company into new markets, he started to look at a strategy that would take its natural gas service all the way through to customers, as it did with oil. With a stronghold in gas production in the North Sea, Amerada Hess was well positioned to take advantage of the United Kingdom's opening of its domestic market to competition in 1996, and became a rival to British Gas, providing gas to power plants, a stop on the way to Amerada Hess then moving into the electricity distribution business in the United Kingdom.

Under John, Amerada Hess had visions of growing into a full-service energy company, not only taking oil from the wellhead to the refinery to the user at the gasoline pump, but also taking gas from wells to consumption at power plants.

With that diversification, John dabbled in several other business lines, including microgeneration. It was part of an effort to give big power users more control over their electricity (and a direct challenge to incumbent utilities, whose staid regulatory compact meant they were not often at the vanguard of new power supplies). The business aimed to capitalize on an age-old principle in electricity by compensating for power loss that occurs naturally between power plants and end users.

By the time a power plant—even a top-notch plant—takes gas or coal, converts it to power, and distributes it, more than 50 percent of the potential kilowatts of the fuel source have been wasted. With microgeneration, power is produced on-site, aiming to lower a business's carbon footprint and raising the efficiency to up to 95 percent by capturing heat from the process and using it for other purposes, according to a former Hess Microgen executive.

When Thomas Edison first envisioned electric power generation, he predicted it would be produced on location where it needed to be consumed because of energy loss. Innovations and government regulations had led to the centralization of power plants, but by the late 1990s, going back to the original Edison concept, cogeneration was thought to be the next big business. By some accounts, harnessing power that was lost through waste heat by a power generator could provide for a fifth of the United States's total energy consumption.[6]

Amerada Hess's microgeneration division capitalized on that opportunity, selling cogeneration units to hotels, factories, and other power consumers. Like rooftop solar units, the idea behind microgeneration was to create an immediate source of power at the location of the end-user. At the time, the company's disparate activities also included investing in a joint venture that aimed to develop fuel cells for electricity generation.

In a small arena, Hess Microgen quickly rose to be a top-tier performer, described as the "world's leading provider of packaged on-site cogeneration systems and services," with more than 100 operating systems, by Illinois-based People's Energy in a press release announcing a plan to provide microgeneration to customers. Power deregulation was spreading from state to state, with officials eager to drive down costs and encourage competition among incumbent utilities to get results like what had occurred from deregulating the telecommucations industry (which resulted in much lower pricing and helped spur innovations like the smartphone you may have in your pocket today). Companies from brick manufacturers to hotels signed on to the Hess service. Hess doesn't break out figures for each of its subsidiaries in its earnings statements, but generally, employees remember that Microgen was initially successful. Still, 100 microsystems pales in comparison to the company's multibillion-dollar offshore oil projects.

"The business was doing quite well," said Rich Sanders, who served as vice president of sales and distribution of Hess Microgen from 2001 to 2005. The business grew each year for its first two years.

Pilot tests of Microgen units emerged, particularly in California, which has long been at the forefront of unusual and sometimes daring energy ideas. Still, by 2003, there was a push to cut costs at the unit, Sanders recalled. Compared with exploration and production, some of the smaller businesses, like Microgen, were seen as less lucrative. John and several other Amerada Hess executives flew to the unit's offices in Kansas to meet with the Hess Microgen group, including Sanders and David Wiltke, the unit's president.

John asked Microgen to cut expenses by 10 percent during the meeting, according to Sanders. While the other Amerada Hess executives agreed with John, Wiltke objected, saying that cutting expenses at a time of growth could be the wrong thing to do and could limit the unit's potential. The discussion moved around the table with each executive giving his own opinion. Sanders remembered being one of the last to speak. He agreed with Wiltke, and recalled saying:

"John, do you want to hear what you said, or do you want the truth? There's a fine line between cutting fat and cutting the company's ability to grow." John opted to trim expenses. Sanders perceived that decision reflected John's valuing his own opinion over that of others, and counted it among the factors leading to the eventual shuttering of the unit. His opinion was echoed by the other corporate executives. Of course, the possibility remains that the venture's performance was below that of other Hess units, making it an attractive place for cost cutting.

As part of the efforts to cut costs, John hired a former GE executive, Ellen Smith, with the intention of implementing the Six Sigma program—a manufacturing program that was developed at Motorola and popularized at GE. The data-driven system trains leaders as "master black-belts" who can help integrate process management responsibilities up the chain and ensure that they're not relegated to floor-level employees. The system gets its name from its guiding tenet that defect limits must be no more than six standard deviations from the mean. Hess had found Smith at a chief executives' dinner: John had asked former GE executive Bob Nardelli, at that point Home Depot's CEO, for advice on whom to hire for implementing Six Sigma. Bob suggested Ellen.

Despite bringing in Smith, the Microgen unit began to spiral—it was mired in a legal battle in California centered on changes to some components of a cogeneration system that had been provided to a client, Xnergy.

As oil prices rose, John's focus began to move back to oil and gas production, as well as refining, and away from some of the smaller businesses that had begun to fill the portfolio, which were divested or shuttered.

Hess still hung on to some presence in the power markets, as the company ramped up its energy marketing business. The marketing business sold power to customers in nearly 20 eastern U.S. states, including to Yankee Stadium. That unit was maintained as part of Hess until 2013, when large-scale divestitures broke out in the wake of activist shareholder complaints. The energy marketing unit was sold to a unit of Centrica, which was led by former Hess executive Sam Laidlaw at the time. By the time of the sale, the unit had sales of more than $6 billion a year.

■ ■ ■

In May 2006, John announced that the company would drop Amerada from its name and once again be known solely as Hess Corp. The Hess brand, he said at the company's annual shareholder meeting, is "readily recognized by our customers and in the communities we operate, and increasingly identified with our global exploration and production activities."

While John tied the move to greater awareness of the Hess brand, it also put the name of his father, whom he revered, and his own last name back at the forefront of the company.

As Hess shifted and grew, John maintained certain vestiges of his father's era: the attention to appearances continued and facial hair was frowned upon at the firm, according to traders who worked there. For those who chose to defy the dictum, careers would be stalled, according to some former employees. While this might have seemed like an odd holdout in the mid-1990s, the company put a high value on appearances. When John, based in New York, visited the Woodbridge, New Jersey, headquarters, for example, a memo would be sent reminding employees to clean up ahead of his visits.

The culture was starkly different from that of the majors he emulated, where beach balls dotted traders' desks and a more relaxed atmosphere was allowed to prevail. Unlike some other companies where traders would bolt after commodities markets closed, Hess traders would make themselves present until the day's end—even paying household bills or doing tasks, just so that they didn't appear to leave early at the company where face time and Leon's values of holidays, evenings, Saturdays and Sundays were still valued.

For those who were willing to comply, the prize was great: lifetime employment. Until 2013, the company had a policy against laying off employees, preferring instead to treat them like family. As a result, even as John put his own stamp on the company, the ranks included many who had worked for Leon as well, serving Hess upon graduation from high school or college, and never leaving.

For younger employees, this could be alienating at times, even though the company had programs for recruiting and retaining top talent. One executive, hired by Leon, used to give speeches to a group of upcoming leaders and would talk about how he had "given his career and life for Mr. Hess." Others who were near retirement would come around the trading floors, just "checking-up" on things. As John worked to remake Amerada Hess in the image of a major oil company, he still had to contend with the trappings of his father's era.

■ ■ ■

Even as John worked to put his stamp on the company, he remained most focused on oil exploration and production and Leon held tightly onto refining and securing an affordable crude supply for his refineries. But the model that had worked when he was first in the business— buying oil on the cheap in the summer and selling it in the winter at the peak of heating demand—was starting to be disrupted by trading on the New York Mercantile Exchange late in his career. But by nature he was a speculator and understood Hess's vulnerability in the markets, as the company had volumes of oil on hand that could be subject to market gyrations.

When Leon Hess was initially buying oil for his refineries, and selling the oil he produced, the process was pretty straightforward: in the United States, major producers like Exxon or Amoco would post a price for a particular grade of oil like West Texas Intermediate or Light Louisiana Sweet, and would periodically raise or lower their postings, setting a fixed point at which domestic crude was bought and sold.[7] The exact amount of oil they could extract and sell was regulated by state agencies, like the Texas Railroad Commission, so prices were controlled.[8]

Domestic crude served as a world benchmark, with foreign oil priced at a discount to the U.S. Gulf Coast price, based upon the rate for transporting it to the coast, rather than a price reflecting the quality of the crude or its proximity to an oil refinery.

But by the 1970s, the ability to produce excess oil was reduced, and with production tightness, price stability declined. With the Arab oil embargo of 1973, the era of stable posted prices was abruptly ended. Prices quadrupled between October 1973 and January 1974. As more crude came online in places like the North Sea, crude was bought and sold on a spot market basis, in response to the forces of supply and demand.

In 1981, when President Ronald Reagan lifted embargo-era price controls in his first executive order, a new era began: the age of the actively traded oil market. In an effort to curb steep oil prices, which had risen to $36 a barrel, Reagan lifted Nixon's price controls to allow the free market to work. Opponents, including Jimmy Carter, disagreed with this tactic, advocating energy rationing instead. Still, Reagan's fiat was enacted, shaping the oil markets irrevocably. Gone were the days of posted prices controlled by a few large players. Banks moved into a position as risk warehouses and oil companies began to hedge their forward production, locking in a price for oil that would be sold at a future date, even if it was still in the ground.

Among the first to make the move was Steve Semlitz, a Goldman Sachs banker in his early 30s. With a single phone call to an incredulous broker, Semlitz set in motion a trade that would change the way Wall Street banks would interact with the oil markets for the next three decades.

Semlitz called Michael Cosgrove, a broker at GFI, in June 1985. Semlitz asked for the price of Brent crude in August and September. Cosgrove told him that August would sell at $28 a barrel. September was still locked in the ground beneath the North Sea, and wasn't on anyone's radar yet Cosgrove told *Energy Risk Magazine*.

Semlitz held fast that he was still interested in September Brent. He wanted to buy barrels of crude for August delivery, sell the contract for September delivery, and pay a quarter for the difference, Cosgrove recalled. This was a first: a banker who was willing to be both a crude buyer and a seller, a complex and forward-looking scheme.

Cosgrove was skeptical of the deal, and was even less certain because he had never heard of J. Aron, the subsidiary of Goldman Sachs that Semlitz worked for. The Cornell MBA laid out the firm's pedigree: it was a limited partnership, nearly a hundred years old, and had Goldman Sachs as its general partner. Semlitz faxed the certificate of limited partnership to Cosgrove, who asked his contacts and verified J. Aron's legitimacy as a trading partner.

Cosgrove brokered the deal, buying a cargo of Brent crude for August delivery from Shell International Trading Company, and selling September oil to Occidental at 25 cents in favor of the August oil price. Bets like this one work because one side is forecasting that the price of oil will rise, while the other, Occidental in this case, expects it to go down. Companies can use these deals to lock in what they think is a good price for the oil they are producing and selling or for oil that they will buy to run their refineries or chemical plants.

After executing the trade, the first such exchange, now known as a cargo spread, Semlitz called Cosgrove and asked to do it again.

Oil companies like Shell were among those to follow suit within the next five years, learning to lock in some of the value of the oil and products they produced in advance of production. Shell, for example, had hedged its jet fuel exposure by locking in contracts tied to futures contracts for gas oil, a type of heavy diesel, as well as jet fuel over-the-counter instruments. These deals allow parties to strike a contract that isn't executed on a regulated exchange like the New York Mercantile Exchange.

Just three years later, in 1988, crude oil began to trade on the International Petroleum Exchange in London. The exchange for Brent crude was one of the final elements needed to create a more transparent buying and selling environment for crude. With the establishment of the Nymex for U.S. crude prices, and the IPE benchmark for Brent, petroleum prices finally moved from a posted system, controlled by a few, to a broader marketplace where financial companies could play where major oil had once ruled.

With oil prices for the major grades—West Texas Intermediate and Dated Brent—(a combination of four North Sea grades)—traded on open exchanges, an increasing number of vehicles for trading emerged. A standard futures contract, like the ones Nymex and IPE offered, gave buyers the right to buy a set amount of oil, generally 1,000 barrels, at a particular date in the future. Over-the-counter swaps allowed buyers to get more creative, structuring more complex deals that worked for their own betting strategy.

While some companies were reluctant to follow Shell into arranging hedging agreements for their production and refined products, the first Gulf War in 1990 triggered price spikes that more than doubled the price of crude to $33 a barrel in just two months, underscoring the value of risk management strategies.

Morgan Stanley, Drexel, Bear Stearns, and others followed Semlitz's J. Aron division into the fray, as Wall Street banks plunged into the oil markets, redefining the way the commodity was traded. As increasingly complex futures, options, swaps, and other contracts emerged, banks developed businesses that ultimately grew to manage billions of barrels of crude.

Goldman had established a futures brokerage in 1978, first paving the way for its entrance to commodities. But the firm's position at the front of Wall Street's move into commodities had been secured by its October 1981 acquisition of J. Aron—with Semlitz among its bounty of nearly 400 new employees. Semlitz was head metals trader at J. Aron, a firm that had a pedigree almost as old and storied as Goldman's own mid-nineteenth-century roots.

Jacob Aron learned about the commodities business from his uncle, who was an agent in meatpacking in Chicago. Alongside his brother-in-law, Aron founded a coffee merchant in New Orleans in 1898.[9] At the time, the city's Magazine Street was dotted with coffee importers, as dozens of companies brought in raw green coffee beans to sell to independent coffee roasters around the country. The importers provided a conduit between small roasters across the United States and foreign coffee growers, where communication was often unreliable. Today, the coffee roasting business is dominated by a few major players including Mars Inc., Starbucks, and Smuckers, diminishing the role of the independent importer. But at the time, bringing in coffee from far-flung locales was a thriving, cutting-edge business.

An unlikely force—the United States' final major yellow fever epidemic—bolstered Aron's success. The 1905 New Orleans outbreak

killed 437 people, and made it difficult for ships to land their commodities in the port city, sending prices for coffee soaring and allowing
the merchant firm to profit as demand continued to grow. Aron then
promoted a friend, William B. Burkenroad, to the partner level and left
him in charge of the New Orleans business, moving his own family and
an office of the business to New York so that he could enter different
commodities markets. In the years that followed, J. Aron became established as a metals brokerage, with Aron's descendants continuing to hold
a stake in the partnership. The firm stopped importing coffee by 1978,
focusing on other goods. It was best known for its metals brokerage that
arranged deals on commodities like gold, and was the only New York–
based trading house with a Telex machine connecting it to London,
where gold was most actively traded, giving it an ability to outsmart
its peers in arbitrage deals.[10] J. Aron operated in the foreign exchange
markets on behalf of banks and other financial institutions, the *New
York Times* explained at the time of its merger with Goldman Sachs. The
acquisition was valued at an estimated $100 million, and privately held
J. Aron's revenues were thought to be about $1 billion.[11] While J. Aron
orchestrated commodities deals, the company itself didn't speculate in
the markets with its own money, insulating itself from price swings and
increasing its appeal to a firm like Goldman.

Goldman was also encouraged by slumping commodities prices,
which had depressed the cost of merchant traders, and by its competitors: it was the fifth major financial institution to merge with a brokerage
with a commodities department within a three-month span. The best-
known of these mergers was the Philipp Brothers' brokerage acquisition
of Salomon Brothers, an investment bank.

Even as it was absorbed into Goldman, J. Aron kept its own name
and identity. A culture clash surfaced at times, with the commodities traders donning red suspenders in their 1983 firm picture to
mock their more serious banking colleagues. Some of the J. Aron
traders were at the start of careers that would bring them to the pin-
nacle of Goldman Sachs's leadership, including future CEO Lloyd
Blankfein and President Gary Cohn. But the first few years after
the merger were fraught. J. Aron's profits waned because of inflation
in the United States, increased competition in arbitrage, and other
market pressures.

Among the traders at J. Aron alongside Blankfein and Semlitz was Stephen Hendel. Like John, Hendel is the grandson of Jewish Eastern European immigrants, and went to a prestigious New England prep school before heading to an Ivy League university. Hilbert Hendel, like Mores Hess, had arrived before the Great Depression, and tried to strike a fortune in sales, starting Hendel Inc.,[12] which grew to include gas stations and furniture stores. Stephen's father, Myron, led the business and became the heating oil distributor to buy fuel from Leon Hess's terminal in Groton, Connecticut. Stephen, who attended Phillips Exeter and Yale, didn't take the most direct route to Wall Street, first getting a law degree at the University of Connecticut and working on corporate matters for a white-shoe law firm. Hendel worked as a lawyer only briefly, before moving to J. Aron to trade metals.

In 1983, the commodities firm instituted mass layoffs, firing 20 percent of J. Aron's headcount as it was integrated with Goldman. The 1983 layoffs were said to follow a study that found that the business could operate with less staffing. The team grew increasingly lean, and by the late 1980s, even as its profits had recovered and surpassed their previous highs, its staff remained small, at just 200, compared with the 400 when it had joined Goldman. Both Semlitz and Hendel weathered the firings. The pair, who would become known as "the Steves," would emerge as the most inventive energy brokers of their time.

In 1985, Semlitz was named co-head of energy trading at Goldman Sachs. Hendel joined him a year later, and the pair would hold the post for the next decade. The Steves both got promoted to partner level at the firm in 1988, joining a group of 132 elite bankers and traders. The promotion came as Goldman was becoming increasingly global, naming its first Japanese citizen as a partner and boosting the presence of its London office on the partnership's rolls.[13] The New York partners included two men who would be among the most important forces in commodity trading in the early 2000s: Blankfein and Gary Gensler, who was later named chairman of the Commodity Futures Trading Commission, where he would be known as one of the "toughest cops policing Wall Street."[14]

By 1989, J. Aron accounted for 3 percent of Goldman's staff, and a whopping 30 percent of its profits. The age of commodities was growing, and there to ride the boom were the two Steves.

Goldman Sachs and Morgan Stanley became known as "Wall Street refiners," banks handling contracts for as much oil as an actual 100,000 barrel-a-day refinery would.

But while Goldman was increasingly focused on trading paper—futures contracts—the Steves saw greater opportunities in the physical market.[15] Men who had traded oil in the form of paper contracts were now going to figure out how to get the oil from point A to point B, and look at the complex logistical issues involving oil, not just the broader geopolitical concepts and production outlook. Under them, J. Aron commissioned a condensate splitter, a piece of equipment that was like a mini-refinery, capable of turning ultra-light oil into substances like naphtha, which could then be sent to a refinery or chemical plant for use in their processes. The unit, which was built in Rotterdam in 1994, provided another means for taking advantage of conditions in the physical market. But the focus on capturing profits from moving and transforming physical barrels of crude oil wasn't in line with the bank's paper trading mission.

In 1997, after a decade leading Goldman's commodities business, the two Steves were tapped for their next challenge. Goldman jettisoned the Rotterdam unit, selling it to Koch Industries just a year later.[16]

■ ■ ■

Leon had grown his business with little help from bankers. He negotiated the biggest merger in his corporation's history, with Amerada, on his own, not relying on the advice of outside bankers who could've taken a hefty fee from such a large deal. When that merger was done, he brought a member of the investment firm Dillon Read & Co. onto his board (Dillon Read had represented Amerada). Hess didn't play much in the debt markets because it didn't acquire many businesses. It was not a juicy target for bankers.

Having done some early borrowing from Chase Manhattan Bank, Hess began to rely more consistently on Goldman as its banker in the late 1990s. The relationship emerged as Goldman assembled major loan packages for Hess, then in the midst of building the huge Hovic refinery in the U.S. Virgin Islands. The bank lined up millions of dollars, including an $8 million offering in 1967, on which Goldman led a syndicate of banks working for Hess.[17] The partnership between the bank and the oil company would be firmed up in the coming decades. Leon knew John Weinberg, who ran Goldman Sachs until 1990, and Goldman banker Robert Higgins oversaw the relationship, managing it even after he retired.

By 1997, John was two years into his time as CEO, but Leon continued to oversee the company's activity in the financial markets, expanding its trading presence even as he remained critical of the unpredictability of commodities markets. Oil markets were growing more complex, and hedging was an increasingly important component of rivals like Koch, a particularly active trader. So Hess turned to the two Steves, the Goldman traders who were looking for an opportunity to go beyond paper trading and make their mark in physical oil.

Goldman's J. Aron division was a natural place to look. The oil company's close ties to Goldman, the growing accomplishments of the Steves, and Leon's encounters with Hendel's father's company made them a clear choice for partners in the fund that Hess would co-own.

So Amerada Hess added a new subsidiary: Hess Energy Trading Company, or Hetco. Tucked away in two 1998 corporate reports was a passing reference to the new venture, which Amerada Hess described as a "trading company" that had been formed as a joint venture with "unrelated parties."[18] Hess held a 50 percent interest in the venture, while Semlitz and Hendel controlled the remaining stake.

It was an odd choice, but it reflected the new power that John was exercising within the company. Seven years before Hetco was founded, Leon testified to a Senate committee that his company was getting out of hedging after wild swings in futures prices in the aftermath of Iraq's invasion of Kuwait.

"When I see a market that can go up $4 or down $4 in one day, that's not my crap game, I am out of it," Leon said at a November 1, 1990, hearing. "I took losses to get out. . . . We have got no damn business speculating."

The start of the futures markets on the Mercantile Exchange (or "Merc") made the law of economics and its supply and demand equations "meaningless," Leon said. "Rumors can drive the prices up five or seven cents a gallon."

He expressed longing for the time when a few players set the prices. "That damn crude shouldn't have been $40," he railed to Senator Joe

Lieberman. Hedging, he said, "at times cushions losses, rarely makes profits."

"I am an old man," he said (this had become a constant refrain at this point in his life), "but I would bet my life that if the Merc was not in operation, there would be ample oil at reasonable prices all over the world without this volatility. I would bet my life on it."

Leon distrusted the markets, but since his refinery consumed vast quantities of oil that was subject to market fluctuations, he wanted the best players at his "craps table."

■ ■ ■

Semlitz became an increasingly active player in oil markets, but even as he helped to build Hetco into a Wall Street heavyweight, his approach to trading and theories behind the deals he executed remained cloaked in secrecy. Semlitz historically hasn't commented for articles on his business, and has only occasionally spoken on panels. When he has spoken, it has been on broad regulatory topics, and not on the specifics of his business. As is common in the Hess mode, Semlitz has entirely shied away from the press.

Hendel is perhaps the better-known Steve, but he, too, has remained tight-lipped about the business, instead rising to fame in New York theater circles for the Tony Award–winning musical *Fela!*, the show he pitched to his theater-producer wife and ultimately saw to fruition. The $11 million production, directed and choreographed by Bill T. Jones, was produced with fellow backers Jay-Z and Will and Jada Pinkett Smith. While the biographic show about the anticapitalist Nigerian singer Fela Kuti, may seem like an odd fit for a businessman from the New York suburbs, Hendel told the *New York Times* that the pairing wasn't as unusual as it might seem. "Over the years, I've learned a great deal about how financial markets can help some economies, but leave others behind," Hendel said at the time of *Fela!*'s production.

At Hetco, the Steves' first hire after founding the firm in 1997 was Guy Merison, who had worked with them at Goldman. Merison, like Semlitz, had come to Goldman after working at a commodities merchant—he had been employed by the sugar firm Czarnikow Schroeder before joining the bank. At the bank, he managed the trading of refined products like gasoline, diesel, jet fuel, and heating oil, as well as grains and commodity derivatives. Merison had left Goldman in 1995 and spent the interim at Odyssey Partners, where he traded commodities, before coming to Hetco as a partner.

Backed by Hess's balance sheet, the three partners created an environment that was similar to the culture they had been steeped in at Goldman: high-pressure, long hours for traders who structured complex deals in energy markets that were rapidly evolving and changing. Unlike the bank, which went public in a 1999 IPO, Hetco remained largely steeped in secrecy. Also unlike the bank, the fund didn't collect fees for managing money for investors.

In the early days, the amount they were trading fluctuated, with about $1 million to $5 million value at risk on a daily basis for Amerada Hess's total trading activities in Hetco's first year. "The value at risk on trading activities, predominantly partnership trading, was $4 million at December 31, 1998 ($2 million at December 31, 1997)," according to the earnings statement for 1998. It is impossible to determine what Hetco's VAR was.

Led by Semlitz, who had strong numbers sense and drove the firm's trading strategy, Hetco earned at least $100 million a year when it started up.[19] While assertions have been made about Hetco's profits, the founders have never verified any of the purported figures. This showed incredible returns, despite its low value at risk. Hendel, the more genial partner, coached traders to stay away from shady deals, while Semlitz, the more numerate, took traders to task when they underperformed.

As profits increased, Hetco expanded the variety of commodities it traded: not only oil, refined products, and gas, but also power contracts as Hess built a wholesale power business. The fund used Hess's balance sheet as a guarantee for counterparties. "The link to Amerada Hess Corporation and the Amerada Hess system provides the group with a presence and understanding of the physical markets, as well as the full credit support of the Fortune 100 company," the fund said in a profile at the end of a presentation.[20]

As the fund grew, one of its early hires was Edward Morse, who joined in 1999. Morse, one of the best-known market analysts of his era, had earned his Ph.D. at Princeton and been Deputy Assistant Secretary of State for International Energy Policy from 1979 to 1981. He would go on to co-found the consulting company PFC Energy and later run Citigroup's commodities research business.

The complexity of the fund's deals grew as it acquired a staff capable of carrying out transactions like weather derivatives: a type of over-the-counter deal that was first executed in the late 1990s. The derivatives allowed companies to protect against the risk of adverse weather conditions that could affect the demand for energy consumption. In 1999, Amerada Hess said the expenses of the partnership were rising, and were reflected in the marketing section of its balance sheet, which reported a loss. By 2000, Hetco entered into the fray of these new weather trades after hiring a small cadre of traders away from Koch. Semlitz said at the time that the company planned to act as a market maker and take proprietary positions in weather markets.[21] The trading company maintained its weather business even as it became increasingly exposed to oil and gas, halting power trading at the end of 2002.[22] At the time, Hetco was said to be exiting because power trading required too large a commitment for them to be a significant player. An Amerada Hess spokesman told *RiskNews* that there were no liquidity concerns driving the exit, and that Hetco's American and European power was profitable.

The exact returns of Hetco are difficult to break out, as they were mixed with Hess's other trading operations on the company's balance sheet. "The Corporation owns an interest in a partnership that trades energy commodities and energy derivatives. The accounts of the partnership are consolidated with those of the Corporation," Hess said in its earliest results that include Hetco. "The Corporation also engages in trading for its own account."[23] Still, after tax, Amerada Hess reported a trading loss of $26 million for the first full year the partnership operated, 1998, followed by gains of $19 million and $22 million in the two years that followed.

Guided by fundamentals analysis from Morse, the fund became a major presence in both the physical and paper markets, particularly on the U.S. East Coast and in Europe, with offices in New York and London. The trading company built itself into one of the largest participants on the New York Mercantile Exchange and the International Petroleum Exchange in London by 2005.

Because a veneer of privacy was critical to conducting their trading operations, as Hetco became an increasingly dominant force in oil, Semlitz, Hendel, and Merison remained largely internal figures: powerful within the organization, but seldom seen from outside. Morse, instead, emerged as an elder statesman of the oil industry, and was an often-heard voice from the silent firm, talking to reporters about the markets and even having opinion pieces on energy policy published in the *New York Times*, tackling issues like oil's 2004 jump to $40 in a joint piece with an adviser to Saudi Arabia,[24] which suggested both the United States and the Saudis had made missteps causing crude to spike.

The fund developed a global presence in the markets, expanding to have offices in seven cities from New York to Singapore, some located within Hess's buildings. While the Amerada Hess company name was often tied to Hetco, Leon and John were rarely mentioned in conjunction with the venture. Leon remained Hetco's champion, and the fund only transitioned to John's handling after his father's death. (Another well-known oil and gas trading company, Phibro, would also be run as a separate fiefdom within a larger entity—Citigroup would own the company until it faced the public embarrassment of owing its head trader more than $100 million in bonus payments after the bank took a government bailout. Phibro would move to Occidental before it was eventually wound down.)

A discussion of the fund, its particular performance, and how it related to Amerada Hess's main mission of exploring for and refining crude and products was largely absent from the company's annual calls and earnings statements. Still, by 2011, Hetco reportedly controlled 30 percent of cargoes of Forties oil—a North Sea grade mixed into Benchmark Brent—and 25 percent of Brent cargoes. At the time, Brent crude's premium to U.S. grades was rising rapidly amid oversupply in the United States.[25]

When Paul Singer's Elliott Management began its campaign to "reassess Hess" in 2013, the question of what Hetco's role at Hess was came front and center. In its evaluation of Hess, Elliott called Hetco a "hedge fund" and labeled it among the assets that were a distraction from the core business. The firm has maintained that it was not a hedge fund, as it did not take in outside investments or use that model.

In its first response to Elliott's attacks, Hess offered a counterproposal, saying it would "transform Hess." After a decade and a half of operating the partnership, Hess announced a plan to sell its stake in Hetco on March 4, 2013, saying it would unlock value as part of a three-phase strategy transforming the company into a pure-play exploration and production company without refining, marketing, or trading. When Elliott and Hess struck their eleventh-hour agreement in May of that year, Hetco was on the list of assets that would be on the auction block.

The liability that the fund created for the company could be seen in a 2014 lawsuit: Hetco and Mercuria Energy Trading, another commodity merchant, were pulled in alongside BP, Royal Dutch Shell, and others, standing accused of conspiring to manipulate Brent crude oil prices. In the case, combining 14 separate lawsuits, the plaintiffs claimed that the companies had conspired to fix the Brent crude market since 2002. Hess had long said market manipulation was not in its interest because the impact on its customer base would be negative. Hetco argued that the case should be dismissed, saying that the data on price movements on the days in question didn't support the claims and that the data was limited. Furthermore, they said the plaintiffs bringing the suit "self-servingly label normal market activity as 'collusive' or as 'aiding' other market participants without reference to a single factual allegation of concerted effort by Hetco."[26] The fund had worked hard to keep compliant, steering away from business in developing countries where compliance can be murky. While the suit was disputed by all of the defendants, it highlighted the risks that big traders face for being considered not just market makers, but alleged price manipulators, given the regular outcry against Wall Street traders that would now emerge every time oil prices rose to politically unpalatable levels.

Jettisoning the unit still faced headwinds: big outfits like Deutsche Bank and Morgan Stanley were looking to shutter or shed their physical commodities businesses, as regulations from the new Dodd-Frank financial reform law put restrictions on banks operating in the commodity space. That cut a significant number of buyers out of the market. Yet, by February 12, 2015, Hess had closed the sale of its stake in Hetco to an affiliate of funds managed by Oaktree Capital Management LP, a hedge fund based in Los Angeles. At the time of the sale, Semlitz said, "Having spent three decades in this space, we see this as the beginning of the next cycle as the fundamentals and participants change." The announced sale marked the end of Hess's role as a key player in the oil markets.

"It is goddamn speculation," Leon said of the futures markets in 1990. The price of oil "will go as high as the people who are speculating and looking for a quick buck want it to go."

■ ■ ■

As Amerada Hess grew and Leon's veteran staff began to retire, the company began recruiting top executives from bigger energy rivals, bringing in tenured leaders with deep experience at the majors. Without his father, John needed to surround himself with new advisers, and he chose those whose backgrounds were at companies that he hoped to model Amerada Hess after. The cast included Bill Drennen, who gave up retirement to join Hess as a senior vice president after decades at Exxon; Lori Ryerkirk, who left Exxon's refining division to run refining and marketing for Hess; Mike Turner from Shell; and John O'Connor, who had a long history with Mobil Oil before moving on to BHP Petroleum and Texaco.

O'Connor joined right after the Triton acquisition, and was schooled in growing an international exploration and production business—he had served as CEO of BHP Petroleum in Melbourne, Australia, and as a worldwide exploration leader of Texaco. O'Connor was brought into Hess's top leadership circle and joined the board.

"He has vast experience in the worldwide exploration and production business and a proven track record of successful leadership and improving financial performance," John said at the time O'Connor was hired. "He will be a valuable member of our senior management team." O'Connor's substantial compensation package, which climbed to over $16 million a year during his time at Hess, was indicative of the lengths the company went to in luring executives from its competitors. Salaries at the company were soaring as the push for top talent continued: John's own compensation rose from about $7 million to nearly $19 million during O'Connor's tenure with the company.

Different things attracted these men and women to the smaller company. Leah Smith, who was hired as director of global new ventures, said she was intrigued by the complexity of Hess, despite its small size. With 30 years of experience in the industry, Smith had had substantial exposure to big corporations, like Exxon, where she had done large exploration projects in the North Sea and in Hungary. She was also no stranger to independents, having spent time at Pogo, where she had been vice president of domestic acquisitions in the United States, helping to build and ultimately sell the company.

Smith thought having a technology group to help in the search for hydrocarbons at a company Hess's size (something that didn't exist under Leon) was an amazing thing, as it was usually a hallmark of mega-corporations. She liked the idea of having in-house resources that a technology group indicated, and was drawn to the company's global reach. "I was very impressed with what I was going into," she said.

Bill Drennen remembered that John wooed him from retirement to join the company. Drennen was taken for dinner in New York and sat through an interview that lasted nearly five hours afterward with John. The pair discussed how to build a balanced portfolio of exploration and production assets that included unconventional resources, like shale and oil sands, as well as conventional oil and gas developments. Drennen immediately thought Hess was a capable leader with an excellent vision of what to do.

"They wanted me to help them to transition from an independent capability skillset to a mini-major, as I would call it," he said. The company had been operating very comfortably as an independent, but Hess saw it needed to up its exploration game if it wanted to compete globally, so that it could use its own resources to grow instead of relying on entering the tricky world of M&A to increase its size. Drennen was no stranger to Hess—while at Exxon, he had partnered with the company for projects in Norway and the Gulf of Mexico. He considered the company a fine independent with an envious history, especially on the downstream and marketing side. While Drennen never met Leon Hess, he became good friends with John, and believed that the company had historically been so focused on the marketing side that Leon could recite the margins of every gasoline station on the East Coast.

"I was very familiar with them, but what I recognized was they were not a technology-focused company, but they were acquisition-focused," he said. While the company had a technology department, it was not growing organically, expanding its discoveries, but instead acquiring rivals. In joining Hess, Drennen said he aimed to increase the company's technical acumen and workflow, and focus on exploration and production. When he arrived in 2007, the company was 85 percent focused on downstream—refining and marketing—and was going through a process to turn the old model on its head. The change was one that managers thought Leon might have been reluctant to make.

Once O'Connor, Drennen, and others joined the fold to reshape Hess's exploration and production portfolio, they were confronted with a difficult landscape of fiefdoms and a constant push to remain ahead of the super-majors with a smaller staff and budget. These hires, who were

generally older than John, had all had storied careers with major exploration and production companies. While they may have lacked some of
John's academic pedigree, they brought a track record of managing the
types of companies that he wanted Hess to become.

One of the first things that Smith and other managers say they
noticed was how siloed the organization was. There were exploration
teams dedicated to different geographies that didn't communicate well
with one another, and dialogue between exploration and development
divisions was absent or antagonistic and lacked collaboration. Despite
how varied the portfolio was, former managers and executives say they
thought there was a lack of an overarching effort to cull through the
assets and make them into a whole that complemented one another.

"Mr. [John] Hess was willing to go for big, high-risk, high-reward
plays," said Smith. But together, those plays accounted for only about
15 percent of the portfolio. Drennen was responsible for reconciling the
disparate elements of the portfolio and trying to make it more cohesive
while trying to keep up with demands to stay ahead of competitors.

On occasion, John would see reports of competitors' discoveries in
trade journals, showing progress in areas where Hess had no portfolio.
He would call his top executives directly, asking why they weren't in a
particular area in their push to be more global.

In 2009, Greg Hill came to Hess after heading Shell's Asia operations, taking the mantle as the president for worldwide exploration and
production. The latest in a series of hires from competitors, Hill pushed
Hess executives to compete with majors, according to Drennen and
other former Hess executives. The corporate culture became intense,
with a driven focus on keeping ahead of much larger competitors, Drennen said. At times, Drennen thought they were forced to make decisions
too quickly, and others agreed that in shale formations, particularly, the
timelines were unrealistic.

Within this competitive corporate structure, it became difficult to
leverage the powerful network of exploration managers that the company
had built up. There was a huge network of up to 15 exploration managers
who were the leaders below the director and vice president level, and three
or four were dedicated to each region—the Gulf of Mexico, Europe and
the Mideast, Southeast Asia, the new ventures team, and the unconventional
team. These managers were responsible for deep technical work around the

world. Still, the group wasn't gathered to discuss wells or technological advances, but rather their dialogue was focused on people and administrative management issues. The result was a lack of communication that might have helped Hess advance its wells, according to former executives.

The culture was also punctuated by competition—as a result, there were slights, either real or imagined, in which certain units were perceived to be slowing down work if they had to do it for particular executives. After leaving, Drennen heard rumors that units that were not his own were instructed, at times, to complete projects more slowly if they were for him, rather than for their own direct managers.

The company was entering new markets at a rapid pace, sometimes doing so with partners but often taking large solo risks on wells in uncharted territory. And while the go-it-alone strategy was risky, some of the partnerships had even poorer results. For example, partnerships like those with small companies like Petroceltic in Kurdistan and ZaZa Energy Corp. in the Eagle Ford Shale and France's Paris Basin, were fraught. The ZaZa partnership ended up costing Hess millions: the partnership started in the lucrative Eagle Ford formation in 2010, and Hess agreed to pay ZaZa to acquire $500 million in acreage, and give the company a working interest in every well it drilled. Three years later, Hess and ZaZa had drilled about 50 wells at about $10 million a well. But with all those wells in the ground, ZaZa took issue with Hess's plan to slow down drilling in the formation and exited the partnership. The company's exit left Hess with just 43,000 acres in the formation, with an output of less than 5,000 barrels a day of crude oil.

For the first time, the company was at the forefront of the most exciting oil plays in the world. Through aggressive hires and increased spending on exploration and production, John had built up a portfolio of some of the best discoveries. Exploration of this nature can be risky, though—companies pour money into projects and may drill a dry hole, without commercially viable oil prospects. As a result, oil companies often "farm in" to others' projects, sharing the risks and partaking in the rewards.

As Hess drilled in Indonesia, the company had lucrative offers to share the risks of exploration, but declined them, and drilled a dry hole. This attitude was attributed by some to Greg Hill, who led the production organization from the front, creating the perception that decisions had to go through him.

"The demands were to explore everywhere globally that the majors work, but stay beneath the radar and a step ahead of them," said Drennen. "And do it with 300 guys instead of 3,000. And on top of all of that there was the new resource focus in the world for the unconventional space."

The demands created conflict between Hill and Drennen, and some former executives say the company faced increasing management concerns as different divisions competed for attention and funding in the race to go global.

Still, the company did make an effort to prioritize its upstream spending. When Larry Ornstein, the senior vice president of downstream, was up for a budget review in about 2010, he was struck by how easy it was for his upstream peers to get funding—landing billions of dollars for projects after 45-minute PowerPoint presentations, while he struggled to get $50 million to invest in refining and marketing efforts.

One of the areas where Hess was increasing spending was in unconventional oil shale production. By the time Smith arrived at Hess, the Eagle Ford Shale in Texas had been identified as a play, and she was responsible for capturing 100,000 acres there and overseeing drilling of the first two exploration wells. The Monterey Shale, with basins running beneath Los Angeles and Bakersfield, California, was also on her radar. It was a totally new play, and Hess acquired another 100,000 acres there and drilled two exploratory wells.

But the silos hurt the exploration and production in the unconventional plays like shale formations: the exploration team and engineers were divided, competitive, and antagonistic. In the Eagle Ford, managers said, exploration led the charge without sufficient engineering. The converse happened in the Utica Shale, where a lot of engineering was done absent the exploration team. "We did not bring all of the things to bear that a lot of companies would," said Drennen. Often, he said, one discipline would lead the way with the other getting involved a little late. Drennen takes responsibility for some of the schisms—in France, for example, he says he should have brought in engineering teams, responsible for designing the best way to drill a well, sooner than he did.

One day, Smith was informed that the Eagle Ford was a new priority, with a partner already chosen. The deal had already been completed, and the company had negotiated its net revenue interest, or NRI, an industry term used to indicate the share of production Hess would receive after all royalty burdens were deducted. Smith was concerned because she felt that the NRI was too low, and she had been instructed to keep the company's price at just $3,000 an acre, while shooting for the most profitable parts of the play.

"I know the deal structure was made way up the line," she said. And getting a deal of $3,000 an acre in Texas was going to be difficult for her and others working down the line—Texas landowners are savvy at negotiating royalty rights, and exploration companies are lucky to get a 75 percent NRI. Overall, in the United States, Hess was looking for closer to 78 percent. In this deal, the partnership structure was complex, and further cut into the earnings. "They gave the partner a 3 percent override," Smith said. "They paid the partner 10 percent in dollars on every acre that they brought to Hess that Hess acquired." The deal created a rough economic landscape for Hess to negotiate in. "We got into the play in early 2010, when the [cost of] acreage was zooming up," Smith said. Hess bought 100,000 acres in a year, drilled two exploration wells, and honed in on one select part of the formation.

For Smith, the Eagle Ford Shale became all-consuming. "I did not look up for 18 months. But that's not the way to do it." At other companies, the pace would have been more measured, bringing all of the resources to bear over with a longer lead time. Ultimately, the exploration project was completed and transitioned into development, but, she said, that wasn't the best approach to the project. Rather, she said, before beginning an exploration program, there should be a handle on what the economics of the formation are, and what the NRI will be.

Hess, it seems, is learning from its mistakes. In late 2013 and early 2014 the company reached out to employees who had been involved in the early days of the Eagle Ford, even those who had left. Hess did a postmortem on the Eagle Ford, conducting audit interviews and looking at how projects of that scope could be better handled going forward.

Some of the difficulties in shale formations reflected John's top-down management style, which were perceived from the smallest ventures, like Microgen, to some of the most critical ones, like oil drilling in North Dakota's Bakken. Decisions in North Dakota were made from the top down rather than starting with a bottom-up engineering assessment of where to focus spending. Following a mandate that came from John and Greg Hill, the company focused intently on the Bakken, giving a mandate to gather as much acreage as possible. The approach had mixed results: the driven focus on this particular play resulted in Hess landing nearly a million acres in the formation. While that included a good bit of the Bakken's lucrative sweet spot, they had additional less-desirable acreage that lowered the average returns. While Hess has been successful in the Bakken, becoming one of the largest operators there, the road to its position wasn't straight. "They kind of took the long way around to get to that point," Smith said, reflecting on the breadth of their acquisitions in the play. In the Marcellus natural gas formation in the eastern United States, Hess ended up with acreage in New York that is inaccessible because of the state's ban on hydraulic fracturing.

By 2012, the company's spending and acreage was split nearly evenly between unconventional wells, like shale, and conventional wells, like its Gulf of Mexico projects. The speed with which Hess had immersed itself in the unconventional space was unlike the pace that longer-term executives with histories in large conventional projects were used to and it caught them by surprise. As companies like Pioneer Natural Resources shed their overseas assets to focus on U.S. unconventional plays, Hess remained divided between dedicating resources, technology, and people to two very different types of exploration and production.

Growing the unconventional shale space was especially difficult overseas—Hess's course took it into China. Despite an opportunity to work with top Chinese producers like Sinopec and Petrochina, there were still obstacles to growth—even the biggest fields had wells that produced only 10 barrels a day, as opposed to the thousands of barrels that could be produced in a large deepwater offshore well in other regions. Margins were slim, executives said. Some of Hess's Chinese production took it far afield, to the western part of China where there was minimal infrastructure for the development. "We just got too expanded, and we couldn't cover the bases for what needed to get done," Drennen said.

As John took the company through its transition from being primarily a downstream refiner and marketer to a more integrated oil production model, there were growing pains, not only around funding, but also around the timelines that oil development projects required. Some big oil production projects may not result in actual crude for ten years, and Hess struggled with that timeline, pushing for a faster turnaround that wasn't always achievable, former executives recounted.

As part of the effort to stake out a new beachhead for exploration, Hess joined forces with PetroCeltic in Kurdistan. In an example of Hess's siloed approach, though, the project was first spearheaded by an engineering team that didn't seek out the full support of the exploration team, which would be seen as collaborative at other companies. By the time exploration came to the table, Hess was already involved with PetroCeltic, but the project had moved quickly, and there were key questions that remained unanswered. Drennen said he wondered about the rocks underlying the formation. He asked the teams what was known about the history and quality of the oil-bearing formation. The teams, he feared, had gotten ahead of themselves, and wouldn't have as many opportunities as they had hoped. Although the exploration team helped figure out where to drill in the formations, ultimately, the first well was noncommercial, filled with gas condensate rather than oil. By 2011, the companies paused this effort in order to return later and reexamine it. These geological problems were separate from further problems in the region, where geopolitical issues were heated: Iraq's government in Baghdad didn't recognize Kurdistan as an autonomous region, with the ability to set its own laws and levy its own oil royalties, causing great difficulty for companies operating there.

While the executives John imported from ExxonMobil, Shell, and BP had experience keeping a steady course as their companies weathered price crashes, dry holes, and other downturns, Hess had to be more careful because of its smaller scale and was more vulnerable to external factors than its larger competitors.

Some of the top names that John brought in to lead exploration and production lasted many years, including Hill, who is still with the company, but many of the senior vice presidents came to Hess after lengthy careers elsewhere, and have since retired. "I think in the end, my sense is Hess did not have that stomach to go about with the big exploration program [and] the big cost that would be associated with it to make that growth engine," Drennen said.

■ ■ ■

Beyond that, Hess was forced to contend with a revolution that no one—including John—saw coming.

Catching everyone from planners in North Dakota to royals in Saudi Arabia off-guard, it has been called the biggest revolution to affect the United States since the Internet.[27] Referring to the ramifications of expanded U.S. oil and natural gas production from shale as a "revolution" may still be understating things.

In 2005, the United States got 4 percent of its gas from shale. Seven years later, that figure was 40 percent. For 2013, 80 percent of the wells drilling in the United States were "fracked"—the process of hydraulically fracturing a well by shooting fluids underground to open fissures in rock and release oil and gas. Shale has long been known as a source of oil. In fact, many companies drilled through it to get to reserves during the twentieth century. What has proven difficult was finding a method of extracting the hydrocarbons from the dense rock formations at an economical price.

"I visited a plant making oil from shale in 1931," Wirt Franklin, the first president of the Independent Petroleum Association of America, told a Senate committee in 1946. "I spent several days there. It was put up to make oil from shale. I witnessed all the operations, but at that time it was costing the man who had invented that process—a man by the name of Harry Brown of Denver—about $3.50 a barrel, and of course he could not operate at that time in competition with well oil," which was priced at about $1.10 a barrel at the time. By the time World War II was over, shale was being produced at about $2.25 a barrel, still almost twice the going rate.[28]

Franklin would testify that one formation in Colorado and Utah could alone hold 80 billion barrels of oil. But it would be decades before companies would successfully tap the source rock.

After years of tinkering, a few U.S. companies found the winning formula for combining water, sand, and chemicals to break apart a layer of dense rock known as shale. With a way to finally get at the fuel, companies engaged in a sort of gold rush in the first decade of the 2000s, amassing millions of acres of leaseholds and starting to pump out oil and natural gas in places where it hadn't been produced in a long time—places where drilling rigs hadn't been seen since the Rockefeller era.

After years of politicians promising to reduce the nation's reliance on foreign oil, the United States is now expected to be energy self-sufficient by 2035, according to BP's annual energy outlook.[29] It has already risen to become the world's largest oil producer, surpassing Russia and Saudi

Arabia, the International Energy Agency has said. The boom fundamentally changed many things. It made North Dakota into a state crowded with "man camps" full of workers flocking to help produce the oil. Overnight, McDonald's restaurant workers in the Williston basin reaped $18 an hour as jobs boomed in the region.

Even the mayor of Houston, no stranger to the energy business, said his son took a year off from college to make $150,000 in the sector—but instead of hanging around home, he headed north to the Bakken formation, which stretches from North Dakota to Montana and Canada's province of Saskatchewan. In North Dakota, oil production surged to more than 12 times its level from a decade before, while OPEC members saw only a 2 percent gain in output in that same period.

A plunge in U.S. oil imports pushed the trade deficit in 2013 to its lowest level in four years. A narrowing of the gap between goods exported and imported is generally good news for a country's currency.

"I think there's a fundamental rebalancing of world trade in oil that's going to continue to unfold," said Daniel Yergin, an energy historian and vice chairman of consultancy IHS Inc. "It's a different world where Nissan is going to produce more cars in Mexico than it does in Japan." Access to cheap gas from shale formations makes North American manufacturing attractive again, and has drawn billions of dollars of investment to the U.S. Gulf Coast.

Fracking has also galvanized the environmental movement in a way it hasn't been in years. With its signature (and startling) footage of a man lighting the water from a faucet on fire, the movie *Gasland* won wide distribution, an Emmy, and was nominated for an Academy Award for best documentary (unlike Al Gore's *An Inconvenient Truth*, it didn't win). The film was attacked by industry backers. Naturally, the creators made a sequel.

The fear of fracking fluids contaminating water supplies led some in Congress to voice support for federal standards on the practice, an idea that the industry has fought, saying state regulations were sufficient. In an effort to allay some fears, the industry has reported some data voluntarily, but in general, the frackers have been unwilling to publicly post all of the secret ingredients for fracking fluids because the mixtures are often proprietary. That has only stoked concerns that water supplies may be harmed by the practice.

Not only are there direct concerns about fracking and its effect on the environment, expanding oil production in Canada and elsewhere in the United States has resulted in a lack of adequate pipeline capacity to move the fuel to storage hubs and refineries. That led to TransCanada Corp.'s proposal to build the $8 billion Keystone XL pipeline, a system that would measure about 2,000 miles and connect oil production in Alberta's oil sands and the Bakken to refineries on the U.S. Gulf Coast. Environmentalists opposed to development of oil (or tar) sands have chained themselves to equipment to stop the pipeline's construction. The Keystone system became a physical manifestation of rising energy output and environmentalists have leapt on it as representing all that's wrong with potential damage from that production.

As with anything else that has stoked strong emotions, the issue drew the attention of members of Congress eager to portray themselves as for or against Keystone. In an elaborate Washington ritual, Republicans forced the Obama administration to make a decision on the project before a proposed reroute through Nebraska had been finalized. The inevitable rejection gave the GOP a chance to bash Democrats as stymieing U.S. energy security and being against jobs that would come from the pipeline's construction. The administration's inability to make a final decision on the project in its revised form has allowed opponents to heat up their rhetoric. In the meantime, Canadian government officials question the sanity of their southern neighbor as the approval process stretches beyond its sixth year. Given that Canada has normally supplied a lot of the United States' oil needs, they can be forgiven for wondering at the outrage Keystone has entailed. While not giving up on the project, Canada has made it clear that its output will go somewhere, and the prospect of sending the oil and natural gas to Asia has been raised more than once, albeit in an always polite Canadian way. As one Canadian newspaper put it about the nation's effort to get the project through the U.S. government, "Sorry, but would you like to buy our oil?"[30]

A lack of pipelines has also resulted in gas being flared from wells in North Dakota, a wasteful process that could be avoided if the infrastructure were in place to economically move that gas to demand centers. In 2014, North Dakota announced new plans to curb flaring, which also releases greenhouse gases.

"Keystone or no Keystone, the United States is going to be a lot more integrated with Canada and possibly Mexico," said Yergin. "The flows in the Western Hemisphere will be north-south and south-north, and the oil that used to come from the Eastern Hemisphere to the Western Hemisphere will just go farther east to south Asia and east Asia."

The surplus of cheap gas has already been a game changer for U.S. companies that have decided to reshore jobs, proposing billions of dollars of chemical plants for the U.S. Gulf Coast. Among the employers flocking to the Gulf Coast, steel-maker Nucor said it wouldn't have built its direct-reduced iron facility in the United States without cheap shale gas.

"Ten years ago, we moved a DRI plant from Louisiana to Trinidad because of high natural gas pricing in the U.S. and our ability to secure a long-term supply of natural gas in Trinidad at a very attractive price," Nucor CEO John Ferriola said in 2014. "Here we are 10 years later and that situation is very different as a result of horizontal drilling and natural gas production in shale areas." The plant—the largest in the world—will be the first one to open in the United States in five years.[31]

Beyond steel and chemical plants, new jobs have emerged in the rail sector, which has boomed as a lack of pipelines forced oil into railcars for transportation from the Bakken and Eagle Ford fields to refineries in New Jersey, Texas, and even California. While some oil has always been transported by rail, the number of cars carrying petroleum products tripled in a decade, with grain purveyors complaining about congestion on the rail lines they had long used to ship harvested food products around the country.

Refining in the United States, in the doldrums since the recession of 2008, was resuscitated by shale as cheap gas made some nearby plants inexpensive to run, and discounted crude gave the operators an advantage in a business that can be cutthroat.

While Hess opted to close its refineries at Port Reading and St. Croix despite the shale advantage, others saw the ability to rail Bakken crude to the East Coast as a savior for a dying industry, rescuing thousands of jobs in Philadelphia and New Jersey as companies like PBF Energy Inc. bought up and reopened shuttered refineries.

Seeing the glut of oil on rail lines, pipelines struggled to keep up, with three new oil pipelines from shale fields in Colorado to the storage hub at Cushing, Oklahoma, introduced in 2014, and reversals of existing lines, like Magellan's Longhorn pipeline in Texas. Once used to carry imported crude from Houston to refineries serving El Paso and Arizona, the line was reversed to bring cargoes of crude from burgeoning fields in the Permian Basin to the coast.

It's also having geopolitical ramifications. "Our ability to put the sanctions on Iran was made partially possible by the fact that the U.S. is putting more oil into the market and therefore we could pull out a billion, a billion and a half [barrels a day] from the market, which is what Iran was contributing. Five years earlier, if you talk to the people in the Bush administration, when they looked at the same set of measures, they couldn't do it because the market was too tight," Admiral Dennis Blair, the former director of National Intelligence, said.[32] Between 2004 and 2014, oil production in Texas surged from 1.1 million barrels a day to 2.8 million barrels, while Iran's production precipitously declined from 4 million barrels to just 2.7 million.

Drilling for oil and gas had become a lot less unpredictable with the advent of shale—in shale, there is pretty much no such thing as a dry hole. The most important thing now is finding the right mix of fracking fluid to extract the fuel. That can be expensive.

Because shale wells tend not to be gushers (in the Bakken, Hess's wells can start producing 500 barrels a day, a rate that will fall to 100 barrels a day), they require more in the way of preinvestment to get a good pad in place from which multiple wells can be drilled. So, as with any technical enterprise, the winners become those who can execute efficiently.

Hess was attacked by Elliott Management for the high costs of its Bakken wells. The company cut its drilling costs from about $13.5 million a well to $7.5 million in two years.

John now says the huge sell-off of assets that included everything from refineries to gasoline stations was necessary to help feed the $2 billion a year the company needed to make the investments in equipment and workers to get shale output flowing.

Between the costs of fracking and the exploration for oil and gas in ever-deeper wells offshore, there is no "middle class" in drilling anymore, according to Troy Eckhard, CEO of Eckhard Global LLC, a Texas-based energy investment company.

Shale "totally changed our strategy," John said in an April 2014 speech.

Without once mentioning the shareholder pressure he was under, John told a group gathered at the Center for Strategic and International Studies in Washington: "In the past, our company was way too dependent on high-impact, high-risk exploration and we were drilling, or participating in drilling, very expensive wells offshore Brazil, offshore Gulf of Mexico, offshore Africa, offshore Indonesia. And some of these wells could cost $200 million and there's not many companies that can afford a dry hole at that rate."

Hess was no stranger to dry holes. In 2009, Hess reported poor results in a well off the coast of Brazil, leading the shares to tumble. Hess shares dropped 19 percent in about a month on the news that there was no commercially recoverable oil in the Guarani well. The Guarani well was in the same formation as Lula, the largest crude discovery in three decades.

"The great thing about shale is, once you find it, it's really low-risk growth," John said. It's not cheap, of course, and if prices were to fall below $70 or $75 a barrel, "you'd start cutting back on your drilling," he said.

His memory is a bit selective on the shale revolution, though. While acknowledging in one breath that the company was "lucky" to get in on the Bakken acreage in 2010 (where it plans to more than double production by 2018, to 150,000 barrels a day from 70,000 in 2014), he also seems to want some credit for having foreseen the coming output boom from fracking.

"About five years ago, we saw that shale was a game changer and if you were going to be a resource growing company in hydrocarbons, in oil and gas, you had to have a seat at the table in terms of shale," John said in 2014. It was a very different John from the man who spoke to the annual CERAweek conference in Houston (a huge industry powwow that draws the CEOs and Saudi leaders) in 2011: "As demand grows in the next decade," a somber John predicted, "we will not have the production capacity we will need to meet demand."

Oil prices at $140 are "not an aberration," he warned the crowd. The price of Brent, an international benchmark, fell below $90 a barrel a year later. While it has occasionally been supported by disruptions in Libya and Iraq, prices have fallen steeply, below $100 a barrel, indicating a new normal that takes shale production into account.

A Saudi decision to try to maintain market share by keeping OPEC's production high in November 2014 sent prices crashing, leading them to fall more than 50 percent in seven months. While some oil wells were plugged and drilling slowed, prices crashed below the $70-a-barrel threshold that John had identified a year earlier, and tested where the pressure point for U.S. drillers really lies. In key basins, like the Bakken, drilling has persisted, with companies, including Hess, calling for new laws that would allow them to export their crude and compete more internationally.

Of course, predicting energy prices has long been a loser's game and you can hardly blame John for missing the coming output boom (even if you question his revised version of history). Some of the leading figures in the industry failed to predict the coming shale boom, including ExxonMobil, which boarded the fracking bandwagon at the height of the market, as added supply spurred a downward spiral of gas prices from $13 to less than $2. Another company that made the wrong bet on gas is private equity firm KKR & Co., which helped lead the biggest-ever leveraged buyout in history with the $43 billion takeover of Texas power company TXU Corp. in 2007. That deal, which saddled the company with debt that came from buying up all its outstanding shares, went south after gas prices fell, which in turn caused power prices in Texas to drop precipitously, leaving TXU's plants in a bad position. Seven years later, parts of the company would enter bankruptcy, drowning in the initial debt that had been exacerbated by falling gas prices.

Hess's prominent place in shale has put John in a position to talk more publicly about public policy than his father did. Agitating for a gasoline tax at a public speech or appearing on television to further his agenda on cutting U.S. oil export restrictions, John, while reserved, has been more vocal in speaking to the public to call for changes, appearing on CNBC, and doing interviews with the *Wall Street Journal* and other major outlets.

■ ■ ■

No matter how much John expanded Hess—stretching it from the Bakken shale to Brazil and Equatorial Guinea—he preserved the ties to

New Jersey and New York that Leon had cultivated. Even as Hess built a 29-story tower in Houston in 2008, the foothold in the country's energy capital was considered a "regional" headquarters, and New York remained the company's major center. Hess was interwoven with the city, from the company's float in the Macy's Thanksgiving Parade to the sign at Yankee Stadium.

But New Jersey residents were still fast to complain about Hess when Hurricane Katrina struck the Gulf Coast in 2005, limiting oil production and reducing the availability of gasoline and diesel, leading to a price spike along the East Coast.

New Jersey's attorney general accused three companies, including Amerada Hess, of violating a law that forbids gas stations from changing their prices more than once a day, as gasoline climbed as much as 40 cents a gallon a day. Amerada Hess settled with the state for just over $372,000, but said at the time that it had been well intentioned, as it had kept prices lower by raising prices slowly.

"What we did is not price gouging," Amerada Hess spokesman Jay Wilson said at the time. "Some of our competitors took their prices up 50, 60 cents per day. I guess they did the right thing. What we did was a technical violation of the statute." The company said in a statement that these "measured" price increases actually had resulted in lower prices than drivers would have paid otherwise. Hess did not agree to any wrongdoing.[33]

Hess had better publicity and public acceptance for its response when Hurricane Sandy hit its core area of New York and New Jersey in the fall of 2012, causing about $32 billion of damage to homes, subway stops, gasoline stations, and power lines.

The company was the first to make a major donation immediately after the storm struck, giving $2.5 million as one of the largest corporate donors to New Jersey's Hurricane Sandy Relief Fund. "John Hess is a New Jerseyan. He is someone who cares about this state," Governor Chris Christie said at the time. Hess gave an additional $550,000 on the storm's anniversary, and John serves as an honorary advisory board member of the relief fund, alongside famous residents of the Garden State like musician Bruce Springsteen, boxer Sugar Ray Leonard, and celebrity doctor Mehmet Oz.[34]

In New York, the corporation responded as well, donating $2.5 million to the Mayor's Fund to Advance New York City. It also made logistical efforts, allowing New York City to use 10 of its locations—two in each borough—for refueling emergency equipment exclusively, as the city set up its largest-ever fuel-sharing program.

As the hurricane struck the city and the Jersey coast, the response went beyond checkbooks, one employee at Hess's Woodbridge, New Jersey, office recalled. He had previously worked together with an official at a local hospital on a project and as the storm struck, the hospital was running out of fuel it needed to run its generator. The hospital official had the employee's cell number, and called him long after Hess's offices had closed ahead of the storm. But the employee, who had worked at Hess for more than a decade, knew that he had the resources to respond, and that he had the leeway to help in New Jersey's time of need. After a few phone calls to coworkers, he was able to line up fuel for the hospital and trucks to deliver it to keep things running. The response to the storm, with employees pitching in to help with response and, later, recovery efforts, was one of Hess's signature moves as a family-style company with deep community ties.

Nearly two weeks after Hurricane Sandy, New York and New Jersey were still crippled without fully functional transportation systems. Gas lines stretched out, reminiscent of the 1970s, as only a quarter of New York City's 800 gas stations were open due largely to the difficulty of getting the fuel to retailers. But Hess had reopened nearly all of its 186 gas stations in the New York City metro area.[35] With generators at many of its stations and access to storage depots around the city and a terminal at its Port Reading, New Jersey, refinery, the company was uniquely positioned to help the hobbled city return to its feet.

Even though Hess has kept its New York headquarters, less than two years after Sandy, its ability to respond to a similar crisis has been curtailed with the sale of its gasoline stations and the divestment of its trading group, at Elliott Management's behest.

When Hess came under fire from Elliott, the hedge fund was quick to criticize some of the company's more idiosyncratic customs. They questioned the tenure of directors, some of whom had deep connections to Leon, and examined the company's approach to exploration and production, both in shale formations and in foreign basins. While the reorganization that has followed has made Hess more palatable to investors, some employees wonder whether the new Hess will have the same level of philanthropy as it did before. Without its network of gas stations, it will be unable to provide fuel during storms like Sandy, and if the culture that John has developed at the company is eroded, some of the Hess legacy of public service may disappear as well, lost in the corporation.

■ ■ ■

John has talked with his subordinates openly about his plans for the company's future, explaining that he expects his son Michael to be his successor as CEO of the company. Like Leon Hess, John has said he doesn't see himself working until age 65, and then suddenly saying, "I'm going to retire." His love of the business compels him to stay working as long as he can. The expectation of continuing to work will also allow his oldest son, Michael, to get more experience in the business. His son's training has already started, and John seems keen to give him the same experiences he received at Leon's side. Like John, Michael attended Harvard College as an undergraduate, but unlike his father, Michael drew attention for his lavish lifestyle.

John has brought Michael on trips to the Middle East for work, introducing him to key players in the business. Attending trips with Drennen and other executives, Michael dealt easily with high-level officials, proving himself primed to eventually take the reins of the company. Interacting with top global oil firms, he is perceived as serious and focused, like Leon and John.

While John's two oldest sons were each seen at Hess, Michael was perceived as the only one with a serious interest in the business. While the rise of activist shareholders threatened Michael Hess's eventual ascendance at the company, former executives and friends say it would be devastating for John if the CEO role were passed to someone who was not a Hess.

Since Elliott became involved with the company, though, John has taken a more measured approach publicly. In a 2014 interview with the *Wall Street Journal*, he was elusive on whether the company's future would lie with his sons. "If their passion happens to take them to Hess, they will have to compete on the same terms as anyone else, because we're a public company."[36]

Chapter 12

Fight for Control

J ohn Hess is only the second CEO to lead Hess Corp. in its 80-year history. The company, which began delivering fuel from a second-hand truck, had blossomed into a $25 billion multinational conglomerate, doing business in more than 20 countries and managing everything from oil wells to a power plant to sales of beef jerky in the local corner gasoline station, all under the distinctive green-and-white Hess logo. And there had always been a Hess in charge of Hess.

In 2013, that model was now being criticized as a "dynasty" that wasn't benefiting the average shareholder, a family business approach that was better suited for a grocery store than a large integrated oil company. Eighteen years after taking over from his father, John Hess's ability to manage the company was being questioned, as was a board that had very close ties to the legacy of Leon Hess. Leon's shadow, even 14 years after his death, continued to loom over the venture he'd built as the son of a butcher in the small seaside town of Asbury Park, New Jersey. It wasn't just his name on the company stationery, it was his buddies still in the boardroom and his oversized ambition evident in an expansive corporate strategy that modeled itself after the world's largest oil companies. Leon's American dream had dominated his company, creating a conglomerate that, according to its critics, was now both too big to focus adequately on all its business units and too small to compete with the "major" oil companies like ExxonMobil Corp.

Hess is considered an anomaly in the energy business, with its headquarters in New York (when most U.S. energy companies are based in Houston) and a long history in the Northeast from its founding. It also had disparate parts that didn't always make sense to investors. Why keep the gas stations, when they generated so little profit? The holiday toy trucks, for example, did that ever make any money? Did it make any sense to do it, except for the fact that it was a program Leon Hess had wanted? And why did Hess include a commodity trading house that had grown into a large player in the shadowy world of energy derivatives?

Holding its annual shareholder meeting in Houston was a tactical decision by Hess. With its gleaming towers in a downtown that often seems empty even during a workday, Houston wouldn't give any home-field advantage to the financial players who were now pounding on the company's doors demanding a new direction. While Houston certainly has its share of bankers and financiers, activist investors like Paul Singer and Carl Icahn tended to stay in their Manhattan skyscrapers, far removed from the self-styled "energy capital of the United States."

Previously, Hess had held the annual shareholders' gathering at its headquarters in midtown Manhattan, near Rockefeller Center. The tower at 1185 Avenue of the Americas, designed by Emery Roth & Sons, is an imposingly bland monument of concrete and glass, akin to other 1960s corporate fortresses in New York the firm created for General Motors and MetLife. Having the meeting in Hess's hometown this year may have seemed risky, just months after Singer's Elliott Management Corp. filled a banquet room at Le Parker Meridien Hotel a few blocks away in New York with rows and rows of analysts and shareholders for what it was calling a Hess "town hall."

At that meeting, Elliott introduced its roster of proposed Hess board members and let the attendees pepper the candidates with questions. The bulk of the discussion was about what would happen to Hess when (not if) the new members joined. The fund had launched its attack on Hess in January, criticizing the company for "17 years of underperformance" (John was starting his eighteenth year as chairman and CEO). "Hess is a public corporation and should not be run as a private company in deference to a family and at the expense of 90 percent of shareholders," Quentin Koffey, portfolio manager for New York–based Elliott, said at the April meeting. The fund was pitting the 90 percent of shareholders against the 10 percent held by John and his family in various trusts.

Elliott was no stranger to controversy and certainly hadn't shied away from a fight before. This was the same organization, after all, that had forced the leader of Argentina out of her own presidential plane.

The $21.6 billion hedge fund was formed in 1977 by Paul Elliott Singer. Singer, born and raised in New Jersey, started his firm after leaving Donaldson Lufkin & Jenrette. The Harvard Law School graduate made his fortune in a maneuver known as convertible arbitrage, betting that an underlying stock would drop in value. He invested in some of the most distressed companies of recent times, including Trans World Airlines, Enron, and WorldCom. His prowess was remarkable— the firm's flagship fund lost money in only two calendar years since 1977 and its investors include large institutions, colleges, and charitable endowments.

Singer was known for making gambles on debt that few other investors would touch. In perhaps his most high-profile effort, Singer was among a group of bondholders that forced Cristina Fernandez de Kirchner, the president of Argentina, to charter an international flight out of fear that her presidential plane, the Tango 01, would be seized when she left her own airspace for overseas trade talks. President Fernandez left her plane at home for a January trade trip to Indonesia, Vietnam, and the United Arab Emirates, calling the Singer group "vulture funds."

Singer and the other bondholders were chasing Argentine assets after the nation defaulted on $95 billion worth of sovereign bonds in 2001. The holdouts were a minority that rejected the nation's offer of 30 cents on the dollar for their investment, filing lawsuits instead, seeking national assets as payment. Ghana detained an Argentine navy ship briefly in response to bondholders' demands for payment.

Singer and John Hess would not speak one-on-one for months as the battle between the two raged through shareholder letters and press releases that accused each other of misleading investors. Despite the increasingly aggressive back-and-forth, the two men shared more similarities. Both were raised Jewish in New Jersey and now mingled in the stratosphere of 1 percenters who were not just rich but rich by New York City standards, where apartments with $100 million price tags no longer make front-page news. They were both prolific fundraisers for John McCain's presidential bid in 2008, bundling more than half a million dollars each for the Republican candidate's campaign.

While both men were press shy, Singer kept a particularly private life on Manhattan's Upper West Side. A supporter of Republican candidates, Singer gained press attention for his public support of gay marriage in New York's state legislature, explaining his take on the issue in a rare interview in which he revealed that he has a gay son. State lawmakers who faced stiff challenges after voting in favor of the controversial proposal got backing from Singer's political action committee.

John Hess and his wife are the parents of three sons and live on Park Avenue, on the tony east side of town. They are more notable figures on the gala circuit, often photographed at society events, including parties for the Whitney Museum, with celebrities like Regis Philbin and John McEnroe. John also attended Harvard (both undergrad and the business school) and was raised in privilege as his father's fortune grew, graduating from the exclusive boarding school Phillips Academy (motto "not for oneself").

Despite their similar backgrounds, the two men communicated their beliefs for much of this battle largely through competing websites— transforminghess.com and reassesshess.com (you may be forgiven for not being able to recognize which belonged to the company and which to the hedge fund). There were also copious press releases stuffed with quotes from analysts and advisory companies that endlessly recycled broad statements of support for either side's case.

The company had been caught off-guard by Elliott's approach. A few months before Singer's approach, Hess had heard from Relational Investors, another activist hedge fund. Over the course of two cordial meetings, they managed to convince the fund's David Batchelder that the changes he saw as necessary were coming, if slowly.

The battle with Singer began late on a Friday. On January 25, 2013, the company got a letter saying Elliott had bought a chunk of its shares and was going to seek seats on the board. Elliott had managed to quickly

and quietly amass a 4 percent stake in the company, making it the second-largest publicly declared shareholder in Hess. There had been no
warning, no outreach. It was a sign, according to one participant, that
things were "about to get nasty." There would be no private meetings
to discuss the way forward for Hess. The company was underperforming
its peers, Elliott said, and it was now going to face a very public confron-
tation with a shareholder that was looking for results immediately.

The company had a weekend to work up its response. On the following Monday, when they were obligated by Securities and Exchange
Commission rules to reveal what they knew about the Elliott stake, they
made their first effort to cut the activist investor off at the knees. Hess
was willing to make changes, but it would end up being not far enough
and not fast enough for Elliott.

Hess announced that morning that it was exiting the refining and
terminal businesses that had formed the foundation stones for it 80 years
earlier. Leon built the company's first oil terminal in Perth Amboy, New
Jersey, not far from his childhood home. His son was now proposing to
dismantle some of the original corporation, years after some of his competitors had pulled out of that messy, unpredictable side of the business.

Several other companies had been closing refineries in the past year,
as the margins for East Coast facilities in particular were suffering because a glut of U.S. oil producers were struggling to deliver to the coasts.
Refinery owners with plants in the middle of North America were
reaping handsome rewards, while Hess, Sunoco Energy Inc., and Valero
Energy announced they would shut unprofitable plants on the coasts
or turn them into storage points. Among the facilities being closed was
the Hovensa project, a joint venture with Hugo Chavez's Petroleos de
Venezuela on the island of St. Croix, in the U.S. Virgin Islands, a venture
Leon Hess had established and made profitable with special exemptions
he'd lobbied for.

Hess's decision to exit refining and sell 19 terminals along the East
Coast was a divergence from its roots, but it wasn't a surprise for those
who followed the business. The next press release was.

Ten minutes after telling the market about its plans to "complete its
transformation" to a company that predominantly focuses on finding
and producing oil and gas, Hess gave a hint about why it was suddenly
eager to cut extra units—the company announced that Elliott had given

notice the prior Friday that it was acquiring more than $800 million of Hess stock and was considering nominating board members.

That news caught Wall Street's attention. Singer was known as a canny investor and what he did mattered. His fund had pushed BMC Software Inc., a maker of cloud computing software, into adding new board members in the previous year, after saying a sale of the company made more sense. That stock had climbed more than 30 percent since Singer's involvement.

After the dual announcements, Hess recorded its biggest increase in 15 months, with shares rising 6.1 percent—almost exceeding in one day the total amount it had gained in the entire preceding year. Investors could smell something coming for the normally sleepy Hess. Would the company be broken into pieces and sold? Was Elliott going to bring in a buyer?

"This is the most undermanaged major oil company in the world," investment talking head Jim Cramer said on CNBC. One day later, Elliott made its intentions clear: Hess needed to stop pretending it was a "major oil company."

The company, which had been trading at about $50 a share, was really worth more than $126 when you looked at the actual assets it held, Elliott argued. By maintaining so many different businesses in so many parts of the world, the company had created an "unfocused" model and obfuscated its true worth for analysts and investors. The problem derived from a "governance failure," the hedge fund said, and Hess needed to shake up its board and its strategy to make itself appealing to shareholders again.

To start, the company needed five new board members with what the fund called "relevant experience." Outside of company executives who served on the board, none of the directors had any oil or gas experience. Plus, many board members had simply been there too long—the average tenure was 13 years, compared with about nine years among 10 "peer" companies that included ExxonMobil and ConocoPhillips.

Corporate board memberships can be chummy arrangements for retired or semi-retired executives who can claim payments in cash or stock for attending a few meetings a year. In Elliott's view, the Hess board represented some of the worst aspects of the corporate boardroom, with several members having personal or financial ties to the Hess family. It had become a "Golden Meal Ticket" for those lucky to get a seat, Elliott said.

That included former New Jersey Governor Tom Kean, who used to attend Jets football games in the owner's box with John's father and was one of several board members who had been executors of Leon's will. Others served on the board of the Hess Foundation, part of Leon's philanthropic efforts, with more than $600 million in assets and donations to Lincoln Center, Harvard University, and other institutions. In total, the Hess family estate had paid $8 million to board members over the years.

Four of the 14 board members had been there since Leon Hess was in charge, 18 years before.

"The confluence of these dynamics call into extreme question the ability of this board to effectively oversee John Hess," Elliott said. John Hess is "focused more on maintaining a family dynasty than instilling accountability and addressing chronic underperformance." Leon's approach to board membership did not include challenging management—in 1986, he would testify that he saw a very limited role for corporate directors: "If you are not going to support management, you have no business being on the board."

Surprisingly, even with all of its calls for changes in corporate governance, the hedge fund stopped short of calling for John to step down as CEO of the company, despite attacking the $195 million in payments he'd received for the preceding five years (putting him among the top 25 of highest-paid CEOs on *Fortune* magazine's list for three of those years). A change in CEO would be up to the board, said John Pike, a portfolio manager for Elliott. What the company needed was a board strong enough to control John and save him from his worst excesses and the devotion to a myriad of business lines that were no longer profitable.

Instead, Elliott proposed five new candidates: Rodney Chase, a former deputy group chief executive for London-based BP; Harvey Golub, former CEO of American Express and chairman of AIG; Karl Kurz, the former chief operating officer of Anadarko Petroleum; David McManus, former executive vice president of Pioneer Natural Resources, and Mark Smith, chief financial officer of Ultra Petroleum.

Once the new members were on board, the company should undertake a full strategic review, including spinning off its Bakken assets.

The company had made a string of bad business decisions in recent years, including entering areas that were later put under drilling moratoria. That included 91,000 acres in a joint venture in the Marcellus Shale—an area that covered parts of Pennsylvania and New York—and a venture in France where drilling had also been banned.

Hess also had failed to give any cash back to shareholders, leaving its dividend unchanged since 2002 and not buying back any stock (a method to increase the value) in more than a decade.

Elliott's stake in Hess was worth more than $1 billion, in what it said was the largest initial equity investment in the fund's 35-year history. The fund had been studying Hess for a year and started quietly buying the shares in the latter part of 2012.

Despite management's statement that Hess had "the portfolio of a major," the company had neither the size nor the balance sheet to compete with Exxon or the other big oil companies whose operations spanned exploration, production, and refining of crude. Hess was losing money by drilling the wrong type of wells in the Bakken shale. It was also taking on too much risk itself instead of farming out some costs and bringing in partners, as many in the industry did for riskier projects. The company repeatedly said it was focusing on a few primary areas, and would then start projects in Kurdistan and other areas that were outside the self-proclaimed regions of focus, according to Elliott. Elliott contended the company had squandered $4 billion in risky (and failed) exploration ventures. It was also spending an average of $3 million more per well in the Bakken than its peers because it had been using drilling techniques better suited for deep-water wells when the hard rocks required more of a manufacturing approach that focused on process and getting the right formula of water to sand to chemicals to free trapped fossil fuels. The company should spin off its Bakken assets, sell its "downstream distractions," including the refineries and gas stations, spin off or sell its pipeline and processing businesses, and streamline its international assets to focus on the best prospects.

In addition to far-flung international operations across five continents, the company had a commodity trading house known as Hetco. It ran a power plant and sold electricity and gas service to 21,000 customers, among them Yankee Stadium. It invested in fuel cell technology, an alternative energy option.

Integration on that level may work at larger companies, which has the cash to sustain itself and can capture more dollars as they trickle from the oil field to the gasoline station. That approach doesn't make sense for a company like Hess, which was one-twenty-third the size of Exxon, Elliott said. Hess behaved liked a major oil company and had the attendant headaches of a major oil company (like Exxon). What it didn't have was the "wherewithal" to compete like a major oil company.

The true value in the company lay in its Bakken holdings, one of the most prolific oil plays in the United States this century, and in what Elliott called the "crown jewel" offshore assets in the Gulf of Mexico, the North Sea, West Africa, and Southeast Asia.

Keeping the Bakken assets mixed in with other struggling businesses was depressing Hess's price, reducing the multiple at which the stock traded compared with the amount of cash it was taking in. Hess traded at three times its cash flow when other companies with big holdings in the Bakken were trading at 8.4 times. The board should split the assets into a separate company and give the shares to its investors in a tax-free spinoff, letting the separate company trade on its own and raise its own operating funds.

Furthermore, the company's "hastily announced" plan to exit refining and sell the terminals business did little to show a "credible commitment" to change.

Indeed, Hess's claims of transformation were perpetual, Elliott said, like a caterpillar that just kept building cocoons without ever blossoming into a butterfly. The hedge fund pulled up 16-year-old analyst quotes, including one from long-defunct Wall Street firm PaineWebber, which said in 1997 that "Hess continues to be the perennial turnaround story."

The need for turnaround at energy companies was becoming a more prevalent theme in late 2012 and early 2013. Hess wasn't the only oil and gas producer to attract unwanted attention as shareholders increasingly challenged corporate leadership on returns that trailed the performance of oil prices.

Elliott's interest in reforming Hess came after a slew of activist shareholder actions that had shaken up the usually staid energy industry. The stock prices of oil and natural gas producers had trailed the price of crude for the preceding five years. The Standard & Poor's energy index dropped 2.1 percent during that period, compared with an 18.4 percent gain in Brent oil prices, an international benchmark. Several U.S.

companies struggled as gas prices collapsed from a supply boom driven by production from shale formations.

All that production was coming from the more widespread use of hydraulic fracturing and, crucially, wells that could now be drilled down thousands of feet and then curved horizontally to get more access to an oil- or gas-rich layer under the earth's surface.

With the boom in production, an industry shakeout was in order. Gas companies saw their stocks crater and began to sell assets and seek joint venture partners to fund drilling and hold on to leases that allowed them access to land. Oil producers were initially buffered from the volatility, although some Canadian companies began to suffer from bottlenecks north of the forty-ninth parallel and pushed for more ways to get their product to market, including liquefying the gas for overseas transport and adding pipelines and railcars.

Refiners were a mixed bag, with some gaining based on where their facilities were and others sinking under an unprofitable need to buy more expensive crude from overseas.

The message to CEOs from large shareholders was clear: simplify. Sell assets you don't need, or spin them off into other companies. Stop trying to be a one-stop shop for energy (unless, that is, you were as big as Exxon). By making a company "pure," the argument was, it would be more attractive to investors of that particular business model—those seeking steady returns could buy into master-limited partnerships for, say, pipelines that gave regular payouts while avoiding federal income taxes. Those seeking riskier high-return investments could try an exploration and production company that was heavily into deep-water production. Those who wanted to invest in the booming shale output could seek out companies specializing in the Bakken or other formations.

Splitting assets would also reduce the drag of funding on more profitable arms of a business, the argument went, cutting off dead weight that had held back a stock's value and possibly increased the cost of doing business. Getting pure meant no longer trying to do multiple things at once. Stick with what you know.

Marathon Oil responded in 2012 by splitting off its refining and marketing assets into Marathon Petroleum—a move it had repeatedly deferred for five years. ConocoPhillips spun its refining business into Phillips 66.

Holders of energy company debt were noticing the pressure by stock investors and driving up the costs of borrowing money amid fears that those targeted would use the cash for dividends and other payouts in lieu of reducing debt.

CVR Energy Inc., owner of refineries and a fertilizer plant, had been among the first targets of shareholders unhappy with returns in the new boom.

Calling them "activists" makes the shareholders sound like grassroots organizers, but as with most things on Wall Street, more often these players were rich people going after other rich people. Billionaire investor Carl Icahn is arguably the highest-profile and most feared of these activists.

Having Icahn buy into your company usually gives a company a quick boost in share price, but directors and management know this hike in their net worth is likely to come with substantial headaches as Icahn proposes changes to the corporate structure.

In the case of CVR, Icahn's stake was announced through a regulatory filing and the company immediately took a defensive position. Shortly after, Icahn made his demands clear: CVR needed to sell assets. The company's refineries, located near the booming oil fields, should be worth substantially more than the company was valued at by the market.

After fighting for a while, Icahn eventually bought the majority of the company's shares and, when no willing buyers showed up for the refineries, spun the assets into a partnership. A short time later, the company declared a $2-per-share dividend, the largest in its history, giving the new owner a hefty payout for his $2 billion investment.

Icahn had several other balls in the air on energy stocks, including putting pressure on drilling rig company Transocean Ltd. to boost its dividend (the Swiss company successfully fought this off in a shareholder vote) and joining with hedge fund Southeastern Asset Management to get management changes at Chesapeake Energy Corp. after CEO Aubrey McClendon was found to have engaged in personal transactions approaching $1 billion with some of the company's lenders, using Chesapeake wells as collateral.

Icahn wasn't the only one. Hedge fund Jana Partners sent shivers through the management of Marathon Petroleum when it acquired its stake. The company, itself, the product of a recent spinoff, shortly afterward announced plans to put some of its pipelines into a separate company. Another hedge fund, Daniel Loeb's Third Point LLC, persuaded Murphy Oil Corp. to sell its gasoline stations in 2012. Loeb's interest in Murphy came just after he pressured Yahoo to fire its CEO after raising questions about the veracity of his resume.

What had been a relatively easy job on the board of a major energy company became significantly more fraught as the normally staid boardrooms were buffeted like never before. Companies beefed up their investor relations departments and made more outreach to shareholders. Several CEOs began a program of "engagement," making sure their biggest investors were happy before the barbarians began to attack the gate. You could no longer rely on the comfortable money to back you when something bad happened. It was time to shake hands and kiss babies and shore up your support.

As the fight with Elliott started to heat up, John worked the phones and flew all over North America to talk to the company's investors. Most CEOs of publicly traded companies will regularly talk to their 20 largest investors. John ended up reaching out to investors who were ranked outside of the top 100 shareholders, meeting folks who held fractional percentages instead of focusing solely on the big boys. The company got the Wachtell Lipton law firm on board early to defend it against what was turning into a proxy fight—a battle for control that would culminate in investors voting at a May 16 meeting to determine who would hold Hess board seats. Wachtell, in turn, suggested MacKenzie Partners to head its investor outreach. MacKenzie knew Elliott's tactics well—the company had worked for it for years before the hedge fund hired rival proxy solicitor Okapi Partners as it was beginning a battle with Compuware. When the hedge fund began to steadily acquire Hess shares, Okapi had a new campaign to manage.

John was being told by some shareholders that the company needed to do away with some "sacred cows"—specifically, its retail business, which included more than 1,000 gasoline stations with the iconic Hess logo. That was not something the company was eager to do, for a mixture of reasons both business and emotional—without a retail branch, the name that had been so proudly displayed by Leon Hess, representing all the accomplishments of an immigrant's son, would largely disappear from public view. The company also couldn't do the sort of things it'd gotten accomplished after Hurricane Sandy, when it ensured that key outlets in New Jersey and elsewhere in the Northeast had fuel.

But the gas stations were a big drain on capital for what was only an incremental source of profit. If you wanted to spend money, some investors told Hess, you should be spending it where you can get the biggest returns—in producing oil and natural gas. Oil prices in 2013 would average over $100 a barrel. As bank robber Willie Sutton would say, that's where the money is.

Although the landscape for investor response is changing, some shareholders in a proxy fight will always vote with management. Others can be pretty reliably expected to support activists seeking to disrupt a company. Certain investors vote depending on the recommendations of outside proxy advisory firms like ISS or Glass-Lewis. Before going into war with a company, an activist has to know who owns the shares, how favorably inclined the investors are to the company, and what relationships exist.

Hess posed certain problems to Elliott as it considered its approach: first of all, it was really big, easily the biggest company Elliott had ever gone after. Second a large chunk of the company, estimated at a little over 10 percent, was controlled by family, and the Hesses were not about to split into factions like the Bancrofts did when Rupert Murdoch came calling to buy the *Wall Street Journal*. Finally, the company had protections in place to make it harder for an outsider to shake up the organization.

Over the course of the months leading up to the big meeting, Elliott's solicitation adviser was getting calls from folks seeking information on how to vote their shares. Some of those calls were coming from Hess employees, calling on Hess phone lines. While Okapi was wary of a trap, in some instances they were disgruntled employees who were sympathetic to Elliott's stand.

There are many ways a company can respond to a proxy fight. For some companies attacked by activist investors seeking changes, there is only one response (according to one veteran): "Fuck 'em and fight 'em."

Other companies will go out of the way to assuage investor concerns, immediately folding to whatever demands are made. Hess's response was somewhere in the middle—they were willing to make changes, both to the board and by way of asset sales that had been pondered, but they would make the changes on their own schedule and they were not looking for a new board to oversee the CEO and chairman. But neither side seemed interested in negotiations as the fight wore on and the company's May shareholder meeting came closer.

While John was making some changes, he didn't want to appear to yield to what his company called Elliott's "bare-knuckled" tactics. A decade earlier, his father had remained calm when members of the Bass family, known for shaking up other businesses, invested in the company. "This has happened before many times and it will probably happen again," Leon said. That approach wouldn't work so well this time.

Three days before the vote, John picked up the phone and called Singer for the first time. According to the *New York Times*, Singer made him wait two hours before returning the phone call. John, whom Elliott had called a "CEO who denies and seemingly misleads," was at last talking directly to his accuser. The investor was stunned by the CEO's tone, according to people told about the call. Singer had prepped for the discussion, going over the fund's position, its bargaining chips, and what it knew about the current vote tally (which was in its favor). John, however, perhaps borrowing a page from his father's playbook, seemed to think he could approach this as one jovial billionaire to another. John had been raised by a CEO who would often stop an executive's breathless phone call with a request to hear about the wife and children before business talk began. For Elliott's team, who were putting in 80-plus-hour weeks on the campaign, the tone wasn't congenial; it was jarring. They felt like John was acting as if the whole thing could be worked out over a few glasses of scotch at the club. The naïveté of the CEO was amazing, Elliott staffers said.

In a brief conversation, Singer told him repeatedly to "talk to Pike," meaning John Pike, the man at Elliott Management who was leading the fight against Hess. Singer wasn't interested in negotiating an investment that was being led by one of his lieutenants. At the time, Singer's fund was almost the same size as Hess's market value, each worth about $20 billion. Singer gave his deputies autonomy to run the campaigns as needed, rarely interfering as Quentin Koffey and Pike led the charge against Hess. Elliott's COO would also chime in for big decisions.

Despite that aborted attempt at negotiation, no one involved believed that John was really the problem (although he would voluntarily give up his role as chairman of the board in a bid to head off accusations that the company wasn't governed independently). John was well liked and his network with the company's investors may not have been rock solid, but it was there. If he wasn't seen by Elliott as being particularly good at making money for Hess shareholders, John was very good at having money—his charitable efforts connected him with some of the wealthiest investors on Wall Street and Elliott knew it would face an uphill battle convincing some of the more staid funds to shake up the company drastically.

One large shareholder, Franklin Templeton, had ties with three existing Hess board members, so they were a likely "no" vote for Elliott's campaign, the hedge fund believed. The chief investment officer of T. Rowe Price, Brian Rogers, wouldn't support the activists because he served on a board with Marty Lipton, whose law firm was representing the company. (In the end, his fund's vote was split, with Rogers voting with management and the rest of the fund managers going with Elliott.) Even in the cutthroat world of high-stakes capitalism, it sometimes still boils down to simply who you know.

John hated the idea of selling off prized assets, saying the company needed a balance of onshore and offshore oil and gas fields. Keeping the international projects in places like Libya and the North Sea would help to fund the drilling into shale fields in North Dakota's Bakken and the Utica formation in Ohio, he argued. He vowed to hold on to the businesses his father had championed, including the gasoline stations. Keeping another unit that sold gas and electricity to retail customers made sense because it was profitable and would eventually pay off more handsomely once the company was producing gas from the Utica shale, a field that covers much of Ohio.

A day after Elliott released its proposal asking shareholders to "Reassess Hess," the CEO had a chance to make his case to analysts on an earnings conference call.

Like most smaller exploration and production companies, Hess was expected to spend more than it took in during 2013. Markets had begun to frown on that approach as domestic oil and gas prices were no longer rewarding that long-term outlook for always-higher commodity gains. Plus, Hess wasn't exactly a pure exploration company, Elliott argued, where that kind of shortfall would be understood, so it was getting punished twice—by investors comfortable with an integrated model company that saw the cash flow and disapproved of it, and by investors seeking production assets who couldn't see the value of the Bakken holdings before they were producing at full capacity.

Hess would see its cash outflow and inflow "balance" in 2014, the CEO said. Until then, it would cut back spending and sell assets while it pursued a more focused exploration program.

The loss of production from the asset sales would be offset by more output from the Bakken as well as the Valhall field off the coast of Norway and a Gulf of Mexico project known as Tubular Bells (not to be confused with the Mike Oldfield instrumental album—the oilfield is one of many projects in the Gulf given whimsical names by their owners, see also: Davy Jones, in reference to the pirate's treasure, and the Laphroaig field, which sadly doesn't consist of deep reserves of scotch, as its name would imply).

Hess had a position in the Bakken since the 1950s, but the acreage wasn't worth much until fracking and horizontal wells made production from the fields prolific. During the last three months of 2012, Hess's output from the field rose 87 percent from the prior fourth quarter and was forecast to double again in the next five years. John called it "arguably one of the best shale oil plays in the world," and he wasn't alone in doing so.

The Bakken is part of a shale revolution that has erased earlier talk that oil production had already peaked in the United States and the nation would in the future always be beholden to other countries (mostly in the Middle East) for its energy supply.

The U.S. Geological Survey declared the Williston Basin, which includes the Bakken and Three Forks areas, as the largest continuous accumulation of oil it has found, with an estimated 7.4 billion barrels of crude under North and South Dakota and Montana. The wealth of resources spurred output from North Dakota to surpass that of OPEC member Ecuador in November 2012. The promise of that production continuing to rise has led to some calls for the United States to end its ban on exporting oil.

The boom led to what some call a "distortion" of U.S. crude prices, as stored oil piled up at a major terminal hub in Cushing, Oklahoma, where costs are set. The Cushing bottleneck caused the price difference between U.S. and international oil to grow as wide as $29.96 a barrel in 2011, a record. It would eventually help cause a cratering in oil prices at the end of 2014, as demand forecasts dropped.

Unlike tricky deep-water wells, so-called unconventional oil, drawn from shale formations, is supposed to be a safer investment for companies. The practice has proven to be controversial, however, as environmentalists question the safety of water resources when oil companies are shooting thousands of gallons of water, sand, and a secret mixture of chemicals underground to break up the rock and get access to the supplies. Fracking has also been linked to earthquakes in Oklahoma, and some communities, including New York State, have halted it while more studies are carried out.

The company had so far squandered its position in the Bakken, Elliott argued. It persisted in drilling dual lateral wells, a technology not suited to the area. Instead of admitting fault, Hess transitioned to a cheaper design for completing wells and blamed the need for "pad drilling," in which companies build structures that house several wellheads close together with equipment for easily moving rigs between wellheads, for its slowing rate of production growth.

The Bakken assets, coupled with holdings in the Eagle Ford of Texas, the Utica holdings in Ohio and Pennsylvania and other assets, could be worth as much as $14 billion on their own (Hess's market value at the time was $22 billion), according to Elliott.

Selling a gas processing plant and rail line in the Bakken would yield as much as $2.5 billion, and divesting downstream "distractions," including the gas stations, terminals, and power plants, would be worth $3 billion.

Hess said its costs in the Bakken were down 36 percent. The company had 550,000 to 600,000 net acres in what it called the "core" of the Bakken. It was the second-largest leaseholder in the formation, after Continental Resources (a company that essentially bet its whole strategy on the area). Hess said selling off the Bakken and other shale assets was a mistake, since they couldn't get access to the credit markets on their own and they would essentially be starved of the funding they needed without being part of a larger integrated company. Elliott was proposing changes that would "effectively dismantle" the company.[1] Hess was making the course corrections it needed to, proposing some new board members and asset sales that would leave it with fields that promised a five-year combined annual growth rate at a healthy 5 to 8 percent. Singer's Elliott was after a short-term gain that would ultimately harm shareholders, the company said.

For the other offshore projects, Hess's investments typified the industry's approach—going deeper and further afield to find the oil and gas that would feed global demand. The Gulf of Mexico project was in deep water and was a complicated and risky endeavor, as BP high-lighted with its Macondo well in 2010, a more than six-mile drilling endeavor that erupted and eventually sent 4.9 million barrels of oil into the Gulf.

The company was also going into areas that hadn't always appealed to the bigger oil producers. Finds off the coast of Ghana were paying off for smaller companies like Tullow Oil and Kosmos Exploration and drawing interest from larger producers.

John acknowledged the company's three-prong strategy had been too focused on what it called "high-impact exploration"—the very big but very risky finds like those in Ghana. The company wasn't too spread out, he said, pointing out that it had actually gotten rid of about a third of its assets. In sum: the strategy to focus and streamline was already under way and working.

"We have no sacred cows in the business or in the boardroom," John told analysts.

The company had just reported fourth-quarter results that were posi-tive after a stinging loss in the previous year. The profit narrowly missed analysts' estimates. The changes Elliott was agitating for were already coming, the company's argument went. It complained the hedge fund had made no attempt to talk to management before launching its attack.

Meanwhile, Hess hunkered down and seemed prepared for a long battle over its course. The company hired reinforcements, bringing in crisis communications specialists Saard Verbinnen & Co. to handle the press and MacKenzie Partners for outreach to investors.

For its part, Elliott had acquired a big-name ally in its fight—Relational Investors, another activist shareholder, said it supported "significant" board changes. The fund, owner of a 2.7 percent stake, called on the company to compromise with Elliott and avoid the shareholder vote.

Relational co-founder Ralph Whitworth was perhaps best known for shaking up the board of Hewlett-Packard, the computer maker that had become a symbol of corporate mismanagement after going through four CEOs in three years. Whitworth was named interim chairman of Hewlett-Packard in April by CEO Meg Whitman, the former eBay head who spent $180 million in a failed 2010 bid to be the governor of California.

No stranger to throwing its shareholder weight around a boardroom, Relational seemed happy to take a backseat in the Hess battle, voicing occasional support for Elliott but otherwise sitting out the day-to-day warfare between the two. Hess should take "some or all" of the Elliott nominees onto its board, Relational said, and avoid a bruising proxy fight in which shareholders would have to vote for either the company's board or the Elliott slate of nominees. Relational proved to be a helpful friend for Elliott almost before the public fight began. Elliott, for its part, wasn't aware of Relational's Hess holding going in (hedge funds can keep their investments secret unless and until they trip certain size triggers). The two firms were sympatico in their approaches, although Relational was much less confrontational. With Elliott leading the charge, Relational could afford to wait while the other fund made a lot of noise, sending the share price up, as Wall Street smelled blood in the water. Eventually, Relational would take the Solomon-like approach of supporting a board that was evenly split, with five Hess nominees and five from Elliott.

Nine weeks after the initial announcement, Hess made its first real concession. The company proposed a slate of six new board members and said it would sell the 1,350 Hess-brand gasoline stations that dotted 16 states and had become famous in the Northeast for the holiday toy trucks sold each year since Leon Hess introduced them in 1964. It would also buy back shares and more than double the dividend payment to shareholders.

The company said this time it will "fully" exit what the industry calls "downstream" businesses—basically anything beyond finding and producing oil or gas. That meant selling its energy trading and sales business and getting rid of some pipeline assets. It also announced it would exit Indonesia and Thailand, where it had drilled offshore wells with partners including Exxon.

The six nominees it wanted to bring to the board didn't include any of Elliott's candidates. They were, however, heavy with oil and gas experience. Under Hess's proposal, the new board would have John Krenicki, the former head of General Electric's energy division; William Schrader, former chief operating officer of TNK-BP Russia, the sometimes tumultuous joint venture of U.K. oil company BP and its Russian partner; Mark Williams, a former Royal Dutch Shell executive;

James Quigley, former CEO of accounting firm Deloitte; Kevin Meyer, former senior vice president of ConocoPhillips; and Frederic Reynolds, former chief financial officer of CBS. Hess said one of its executives had already given up his seat on the board to make way for the group. Five others, including former Senator Sam Nunn, who'd just joined the prior year, would be replaced if shareholders voted in support of the company's plan.

The sale of the gasoline stations, which Hess had said in January it was committed to keeping, seemed to show for the first time the effect Elliott was having, causing the company to second-guess its strategy less than two months after announcing the initial round of asset sales.

John pooh-poohed the notion that the company was moving with haste in response to the attacks.

"This is not a response to an activist," John said in an interview with *Bloomberg News* at the time, not even naming Elliott. Paul Singer's "proposals demonstrate no meaningful operational insight into our business," the CEO told shareholders.

If it had been meant as a response, it wasn't mollifying. Elliott called the action "incomplete" and said the company still "lacks accountability." Relational chimed in that the actions weren't sufficient and a week later Elliott announced its stake in Hess had increased, as it boosted its valuation of the shares to $128 apiece (they were then trading at $71).

Elliott's main stumble during the campaign was including a payment program that was designed to reward its board nominees if the company's performance exceeded an industry average. Uncertain investors viewed the payments, which would come from Elliott even after the board members were in place, warily. Hess called the payments an incentive for the nominees to sell off the assets for their own short-term gain—candidates could've been paid up to $9 million by the hedge fund if certain share-performance measures were hit. The payments included bonuses of $10,000 for each 1 percent that Hess exceeded the average total return of its peers' shares in the first three years the new directors were on the board. The payments were the perfect example of Elliott's motivation "to pursue short-term goals in an industry that requires long-term patience," Hess said. The average oil or gas project takes five to seven years to start producing, the company argued, and destabilizing the board by bringing in "a divisive element" posed a risk to shareholders.

Elliott contended they were a way to ensure the candidates had a stake in the company's success, much as the existing board members had longstanding stock options to make their interests align with other shareholders.

Jana Partners, another activist investor, had used similar payments in its attempt to make changes to the board of Agrium, a Canadian agriculture company. The uproar that ensued cost that company, and Hess used a similar playbook to sow discontent among investors with the practice.

Hess also went on the attack against Elliott's nominees, saying Harvey Golub's 11 months at AIG showed his divisiveness, as the chairman clashed with CEO Robert Benmosche and continued to urge a breakup of the company after its takeover by the U.S. government. The insurance company's revival eventually yielded 305 percent returns, Hess pointed out.

Rodney Chase, the former BP executive, was in charge while the company cut budgets in the run-up to the Texas City refinery explosion and fire, which killed 15 people and led to the company paying about $2 billion to settle claims. Ultra Petroleum's Marshall Smith oversaw the company during a 37 percent decline in its stock price, Hess said.

Elliott at first defended the payments to its candidates, saying Hess was engaged in "scare tactics" and the payments ensured nominees were working for the best interest of the shareholders without requiring them to buy huge quantities of stock. One corporate governance expert called the payout scheme "highly unusual." Elliott eventually bagged the idea, after hearing from enough investors who were expressing concern.

On April 1, Hess announced it had found a buyer for its stake in its Russian company Samara Nafta. A $25 million acquisition in 2005 was now valued at $2.05 billion, an admirable 8,100 percent return by anyone's measurement. Hess touted the sale, its biggest ever, as an example of the new streamlined approach. Elliott took the rare opportunity to decline comment.

Instead, a few days after that, the hedge fund filed its case with shareholders, more than a hundred pages of proxy materials that sought to sway voters to its nominees. "John Hess has never been able to articulate a plausible strategy" for the company, Elliott wrote. The hedge fund was seeking to disentangle the company from the family.

Further letters to shareholders by the company and the hedge fund followed that month. Elliott accused Hess of losing almost $800 million on the Eagle Ford, an oil field in Texas that it says was so prolific that it was hard to lose money in it "even if you try." In particular, the fund attacked a disastrous joint-venture agreement with ZaZa Energy Corp. (whose name in Hebrew "implies movement," according to the developer's website). The movement was not good for Hess.

Under the agreement, Hess paid ZaZa to buy acreage in the Eagle Ford without regard to cost or quality and without having to bear any risk for Hess's losses, Elliott said. When the company realized too late that it had lost out on the most prized portions of the field, it ended the arrangement and paid ZaZa $175 million plus 60,000 acres in the field.

Along with the cost of acquiring and drilling in the area and subtracting cash flows, Elliott calculated that the company had lost $771 million in the region.

Meanwhile, proxy advisory companies, which are supposed to serve as an independent voice on shareholder vote items, were starting to line up against Hess and express support for the Elliott nominees.

"The question is never whether an incumbent board, having presided over a long destruction of value, has suddenly awakened to the need for change; it is whether, when the heightened scrutiny of the proxy contest ends, the same board is likely to remain as reinvigorated as it now professes to be," Institutional Shareholder Services said in a report.

Hess responded by attacking the advisers' reputations, saying Glass Lewis & Co. "has done a disservice to its clients" and that ISS "betrayed its own principles" in choosing the dissident slate.

Elliott said Hess was suffering from a "complete denial of reality and increasingly desperate 'bunker mentality.'"

Less than a week before the May 16 vote, Hess made another move to appease the shareholders, promising to strip John of the chairmanship. Krenicki, who had stepped down as head of General Electric's energy division the previous year, would be the new chairman if he won election to the board as part of Hess's slate of nominees.

Splitting the two roles would ensure proper board oversight. "We understand our shareholders' views, and recognize that our corporate governance structure should have been improved sooner," said John Mullin III, the company's new lead director.

Mullin, now a gentleman farmer in rural Virginia, had gained notoriety as a board member the previous year after he complained in a letter to the *Wall Street Journal* that a last-minute switch of CEOs by Duke Energy Corp. in its acquisition of Progress Energy Inc. was "corporate deceit." The former managing director for investment bank Dillon Read spurred state investigations of the transaction, after which the CEO of Duke eventually agreed to step down in 2013. Mullin was the voice of the outsider on that transaction, bumped off the Progress board as the merger closed, and furious at the course the new board took.

This time he was defending an incumbent board from shareholders who cried foul.

In any event, Elliott said the move to change chairmen wasn't a concession, but a reaction to the company's losing vote count.

As the vote neared, Hess offered another conciliation—it would add two of Elliott's five proposed members if all five of its nominees were approved. The hedge fund called the proposal a "PR stunt" and said Hess should be engaging in "substantive conversation" not just blasting out "desperate press releases."

In a signal of how strong its position was, one day later Elliott proposed a "resolution" to the fight—if Hess would accept all five of its nominees and add all of its own new candidates, Elliott would agree to support the full slate.

■ ■ ■

By the night before the meeting, Hess's advisers had given up. They were in the bar at the Four Seasons Hotel a few blocks from the company's offices in Houston. They were drinking. It was getting late and they knew they didn't have the votes to win a proxy fight in the morning that would give Elliott Management five board members, wresting governance out of the careful family control that had been its hallmark for so long.

Elliott representatives, however, hadn't declared victory just yet. Even if they had the majority they needed to win the proxy battle and get their nominees onto the board, they knew two things: Hess could try to lean on an investor to change a vote and, more important, Hess owned the clock during this voting process.

The company could've spent all day, maybe even multiple days, "counting votes" from the proxy fight. During that time, the company could persuade one of the many money managers who knew Leon or who served on a charitable board with John to switch sides and support management. That would leave Elliott with nothing to show for its $1 billion investment as well as several months of research and millions paid to advisers in the fight.

Even if it won the board battle, Elliott might lose the war for Hess by adding five members who were in a minority on an otherwise hostile board. If both slates of board nominees could be combined in some way, Hess could operate with an infusion of fresh blood and no lingering animosity about the directional changes Elliott was seeking.

BlackRock, a large shareholder in Hess, was pushing for the company to make a deal. Despite the fact that the "stunt" offer prompted the first face-to-face talks with the investor, Elliott thought it wasn't a real settlement bid. Big investors like Vanguard were free to vote with the company's management without compunction if they felt that Hess had made a good-faith effort to settle. Furthermore, another investor, State Street, wasn't yet saying how it would vote and it remained to be seen how many votes it controlled, given the investor had lent out stock for complex financial transactions.

So Elliott reached out: they contacted Hess's general counsel—were the Hess lawyers willing to talk?

With Hess folks in the hotel bar and Elliott representatives taking up two conference rooms in the Four Seasons, talks began in earnest. Singer was in Europe and John was checking in on the talks occasionally by phone. The goal was to get a deal together by 7:30 A.M. Houston time, at the latest, before the next tally of votes was due. No one was going to get any sleep tonight.

At least this all-nighter would be in a nice hotel. Another company under attack from investors, Stillwater Mining, had held a proxy vote meeting in the cafeteria of one of its operating mines to try to keep problematic voters from casting their shares with the enemy. Investors don't have to be physically present for the votes, but holding them in far-flung places can ensure that rabble-rousers don't bother to attend. Some of the players were just happy Hess hadn't moved the meeting to its historic headquarters building in Woodbridge, New Jersey.

From around 10 P.M. until 5:30 A.M., talks at the Four Seasons dragged on, with representatives shuttling between the bar (and later, the hotel lobby) and rooms Elliott had reserved in the hotel. While an agreement on the number of Elliott-backed board nominees that Hess would add to its board came quickly, the company and investor battled over minutiae as the hours ticked down before the shareholder meeting. Around 4 A.M., staff began vacuuming the hotel lobby as the sides continued to argue over which committees the board members would serve on. One attendant went to his room and came back in sweatpants and a hoodie through the overnight hours, but most of the Hess team remained in rumpled suits for the session. With hours to go before the meeting in Houston was due to get started, a deal was reached. Hess would add three of the Elliott nominees (instead of the two they suggested in their "final" offer) and five of its own new candidates to the 14-member board. "I'm glad it's over," John told reporters after the meeting.[2]

Ninety minutes before shareholders were due to assemble at Hess's Houston office, the two sides announced an agreement. Elliott would withdraw its proxy and in return Hess agreed to add three of its five nominees to the board and allow board members to come up for election every year instead of every three years. With the addition of Hess's five proposed candidates, nine of the company's 14 directors were new.

John, as promised, gave up his chairmanship, although Krenicki was not named chairman and former Shell executive Mark Williams took over as head of the board instead.

Months after the fight, John spoke at an energy conference. Singer, he told the crowd, was "happy" with the progress being made at the company. A short while later, he got a call from Singer. "I'm not happy," the investor told him. "I'm not unhappy, but I'm not happy." Elliott had made $700 million on the approximately $1 billion investment in Hess, from the time its investment was announced until the middle of 2014. That return should keep anyone from being unhappy, at least.

The compromise between Elliott and Hess ultimately led to a transformation of the company, away from the gas stations and refineries of Leon's era, toward a new age with a focus on domestic and international exploration and production. The company's shares, which had taken a

beating during 2012, began to rise, first boosted by the announcement
of Elliott's plan to take the stock price from about $60 a share to $129 a
share, and later driven by the company's efforts to shed underperforming
assets from Russia to the East Coast of the United States. The company's
exploration strategy, which once drew criticism for being too far-flung,
has become more focused on opportunities in the Atlantic basin.

While the company did not immediately hit the storied heights
Elliott had forecast, Hess was successful in increasing its value to more
than $100 a share within 18 months of the compromise. Investors appre-
ciated that Hess was becoming easier to value with oil exploration and
production as its clear priority. Still, the company's increased focus on oil
production from shale formations left it vulnerable to stock price fluctuations as oil prices declined in 2014 and in the first half of 2015. Hess
fared better than some producers, due largely to its competitive position
in the Bakken formation of North Dakota and its robust financing. "Our
first, second, and third priority is to keep our financial strength in the
current environment that we think will be with us for some time and
to come out of this environment strong," John Hess told investors at the
end of the second quarter of 2015.

Chapter 13

The Last

What a blessing the oil has been to mankind!
                                    —John D. Rockefeller[1]

"Please don't write this book." John Hess made the plea directly to us, after rebuffing all of our prior offers to participate in this book (and, in fact, hours after he turned quickly on his heel upon being introduced to us). Leon was an intensely private man, John explained, and out of respect for his father, he and his family didn't want this book to be written. The family had circled its wagons, declining all interview requests. And it wasn't only the Hesses—many friends, business associates, and acquaintances who initially appeared eager to talk about Leon would clam up when they heard the family wasn't cooperating.

This wasn't terribly surprising given the reluctance of our subject to talk while he was alive. "I have been brought up all my life to stay out of the limelight and I'm never going to change," Leon told one reporter.[2]

Not having direct access to immediate family is a challenge for any biographer. But it can also be a gift, preventing you from being co-opted by your subject, from being romanced by the views of those who loved him most (in what is already a complicated relationship with a person who inevitably burrows into the deepest parts of your brain). It was a challenge we were willing to take because we think this extraordinary man lived an extraordinary life, and while the signs that bear his name are getting taken down from gasoline stations across more than a dozen states, he should not disappear from public view.

While we were excited by the many interesting facets of his life before getting started on the book, the actual research yielded even more evidence of the way his life and his company exemplified changes in the United States and global energy industry in the twentieth century. We are both the better for having known Leon, even if no one outside of his family members will ever fully know the man who so often shunned the spotlight.

What makes Leon the "last" oil baron?

Don't get us wrong—there will still be oil millionaires and billionaires. The relatively recent expansion of production from so-called tight oil—which includes the oil sands in Canada and formations in hard shale rock—has already produced several new billionaires, including Harold Hamm, whose bet on output from the Bakken Shale in North Dakota helped make put him at number 54 on the *Forbes* magazine list of richest people, with an estimated net worth of $16 billion (of course, that was before the recent drop in oil prices and a divorce that forced him to write a $975 million check to his former wife). Other nations may have the same wealth of resources locked in shale rock, which requires that companies find the right blend of water, sand, and chemicals to free the trapped oil and/or gas through hydraulic fracturing. So yes, there is still wealth to be had from fossil fuels even as the developed nations of the world try to wean themselves from energy sources that produce large amounts of greenhouse gases.

The reason we call Hess the last oil baron is that we believe him to be the last of his kind—the last man who could create a multibillion-dollar, multinational, vertically integrated energy behemoth that could do everything from finding oil in far-flung fields off the coast of Indonesia to selling you a tank of gas and a pack of gum at the local station on the corner.

Beyond just the wealth associated with such an enterprise, we would argue that Leon Hess was a baron in the sense that he was able to create a dynasty with his company. He is the last man who could pass that large of an oil business on to his son, treating a company with thousands of shareholders as if it were the local family-owned corner store. With the possible exception of the media business—Rupert Murdoch being perhaps the most notable example—there are few billionaire businessmen who are able to put their children in charge of a publicly traded venture.

Which is not to say that in the energy industry family-owned or controlled businesses are that unusual. One of the sons of H. L. Hunt continues to run Hunt Oil (in a complicated family history that includes several other children the founder sired in a series of polygamous relationships). The daughter of Charles Schusterman took over his oil and gas company after her father died, as Oklahoma-based Samson Resources quietly became a huge enterprise worth more than $7 billion when private equity firm KKR & Co. bought them in 2011. W. A. "Tex" Moncrief Jr. took over the oil business from W. A. "Monty" Moncrief, a legendary wildcatter. But these are all examples of privately owned family businesses being passed down. In most cases, the family business passes on to the child only when there aren't a slew of shareholders to appease. And there are almost always lawsuits as relatives jostle for their share of the dearly departed paterfamilias's fortune (perhaps one of the most notorious being oilman J. Howard Marshall II and the Supreme Court case over his bequest to wife Anna Nicole Smith).

"Call it a wish to perpetuate a dynasty if you will, but I had always visualized passing what I had built on to my sons," J. Paul Getty wrote in his 1976 autobiography.[3] After having built his father's oil venture into a multinational business, Getty wasn't able to pass the company on to any of his five sons—two of whom predeceased him. The heir to the Murphy Oil Co. founder serves on the board but doesn't have an executive role at that company. While John Hess appears to be grooming his son Michael to take over for him, that will require board approval and may incite activist shareholders.

So the deeding of a company to a child isn't that easy or that usual for a publicly traded energy company, given shareholder pressure to find the best person for the job (and not simply pass it on like a birthright).

It's one thing to run a family business; it's another to do so under the microscope of securities laws with thousands of shareholders to appease.

John is not only unique in the industry for being son of the founder, he's also the longest-serving current CEO among S&P 500 energy companies. According to a 2013 Bloomberg ranking, his years in charge at Hess put him just ahead of James Dolan of Cablevision—another man who took over from his father, albeit in charge of a family that holds special preferred shares in the business, giving it a measure of control over the company's stock.[4]

And what made Leon a baron? It's not just the passage of the company reins to the next generation, it's also the size and scope of the business he formed, a business that even now seems to be adhering to a new "shrink to grow" strategy amid dwindling support for a big integrated entity that could do anything across the spectrum of energy services. Would anyone have the initiative, the sheer audacity to think he or she could create a mini-Exxon in the future? If one did, could he or she find backers to fund such a venture?

For investors, the energy industry is being cut into finer and finer slices to appeal to those who no longer see a benefit in a company offering "cradle-to-grave" services in the sector (that is, finding, producing, transporting, refining, and ultimately selling you the fuel you need). Investors who want to chase refining returns can't see the point in a company being in the exploration and production business, and vice versa.

The model of an energy company that could do everything, from drilling to gas station sales, stems from John D. Rockefeller, whose Standard Oil sought to control all portions of the energy process. Like Rockefeller, Leon Hess's first big investments were in refineries and then expanded to production and retail sales. (Both men also shared a fondness for fast horses, although Rockefeller's appreciation for the sport extended into driving his own equine fleet around at speeds through his neighborhood in Cleveland and later in New York.[5])

The so-called integrated model for energy companies—exemplified in the diverse businesses of ExxonMobil and the other big oil companies—has not been very integrated for a long time. Instead, they show what Lord John Browne, the former CEO of BP, calls the "group model." Companies maintain production, pipelines, refineries, and retail outlets because they think they can run them best—and not because there are necessarily any inherent benefits in sending *your* oil along *your* pipelines to *your* refineries to sell in *your* gas station.

In some instances, the integrated model may work—especially for companies that produce heavy oil from Canada, a type of product that requires special handling on pipelines and railroads as well as refineries capable of processing the thicker crude. Elsewhere, the model is to run each business under the same umbrella even if the pieces are no longer as conjoined as they once were.

In the United States, many refineries have been used to handling crude from Canada, Venezuela, and Mexico, a type of oil that doesn't resemble the light, sweet variety being pumped out of the Bakken in North Dakota. Refiners, warily eyeing any moves to allow greater U.S. exports of petroleum (which would erode their price advantage), have begun to invest in expanding capacity at facilities that can process the crude being produced in huge quantities. There have also been some movements toward building new facilities, something that hasn't been seen in the United States, where daily gasoline sales by refiners dropped by more than half between 2002 and 2012.[6]

The shale revolution largely caught the world's biggest oil companies unawares. Smaller, more nimble ventures, like George Mitchell's Mitchell Energy & Development Corp. were able to come up with the magic formula that could crack open dense shale rock and allow oil and natural gas to flow from an area that other companies had drilled through to get to traditional reservoirs. Everyone knew the oil and gas was there, trapped in the shale rock, but no one was able to free it at an economical rate.

Entrepreneurs like Mitchell, unable to compete in the bigger projects, could go back over these prospects the majors had hit and quit, and devote the time and attention to getting the fracking mixture correct and pairing that with a drilling method that involved going horizontally into the shale layer to get the most access (instead of hitting the rock at only one point in a vertical well). Once other companies were able to come up with their own fracking mixes that worked in other places, like the Marcellus Shale of Pennsylvania and the Bakken in North Dakota, and the industry got its hands on new technology that allowed drilling pipes to curve around and drill horizontally through that rich layer of shale, American energy production was forever changed.

Fracking itself isn't new. Exxon CEO Rex Tillerson told *Fortune* magazine[7] that he used to keep himself warm as a 24-year-old engineer by standing between the big diesel engines that powered water pumps for fracking. The process has been in use for years, gaining more traction after the easy-to-find oil in the United States began to be tapped out in the 1970s. At that point, talk of "peak oil" had begun—the concern that production of the resource was on its way down.

The so-called super-major oil companies—those that are big enough to compete with nationally owned producers in Saudi Arabia and Venezuela, for example—faced a lack of easy oil and responded by throwing money at expensive projects in search of big pools of crude, such as in deep ocean waters. They weren't much interested in spending the time and money to figure out how to unlock vast shale formations that had been uneconomic for years. Scale was the key, and having a huge balance sheet (Exxon's market value is more than $400 billion) was the way to go, as a series of mergers in the 1990s consolidated the industry.

But bigger companies didn't always lead to bigger growth. The super-majors faced "the challenge of managing and sustaining growth in these much larger portfolios: finding new prospects, building new projects, and choosing between different multibillion dollar options," Bob Dudley, CEO of BP, told investors in March 2014. Adding to the problem, rising oil prices led to increased costs for the companies, host nations were seeking a greater piece of the pie, and technical problems were mounting with the big, complex projects.

"As a result, it has become less obvious where to deploy scarce resources in the form of capital and capability," according to Dudley. "And investors tell us that they find it harder to see how the industry can continue to deliver the kinds of returns that they seek."

And that was before oil prices began their precipitous drop in the fall of 2014, losing half their value as global demand faltered and shale production kept increasing, pushing the U.S. into the role once again as the world's largest energy producer.

The major oil companies "became excessively bureaucratic and developed tunnel vision," Robert A. Hefner III, head of natural gas producer GHK Companies, wrote in *Foreign Affairs* magazine.[8]

Even as costs for the big projects rose, the super-majors were largely missing the boat on shale in the United States. Chesapeake Energy Corp., an Oklahoma company formed by a mullet-sporting landman named Aubrey McClendon, amassed huge shale resources and for a time became the largest U.S. producer of natural gas. Competitors drilled underneath Exxon's Irving, Texas, headquarters before it awoke to the benefits of shale, deciding in 2009 to buy XTO Energy in a $35 billion deal. The company bought near the top of the market for natural gas—prices would drop from around $13 to less than $2 three years after Exxon's buy. The CEO said in 2012 that companies producing natural gas were "losing our shirts" as output from shale boomed and prices cratered.

Shell, meanwhile, eager to get on the bandwagon in the Eagle Ford shale formation in Texas, managed to get land that failed to produce much oil in an area that's been heralded for prolific output. The company started buying up rights from 2008 to 2011, getting access to drill on more than 250,000 acres. In 2014, it announced plans to sell its acreage because of "disappointing results." Shell had taken a $2 billion writedown—a reduction in the value of its assets—in part because of the bad U.S. shale prospects it was holding. Former CEO Peter Voser told the *Financial Times* the company's bet on shale was the biggest regret he had from his time in charge.[9]

Being bigger doesn't always mean being smarter or even fulfilling the promise to shareholders that bigger inevitably means better returns. During the five years leading up to the most recent oil price crash, the major U.S. oil companies (Exxon, Chevron, ConocoPhillips) have gained from about 45 percent to 125 percent in price. Including dividend payments, the total returns to investors have been 66 percent for Exxon, 113 percent for Chevron, and 176 percent for Conoco. Those are tidy returns.

However, the returns for smaller oil and gas producers, including Pioneer Natural Resources, Cabot Oil & Gas, and EOG Resources, have been far larger—ranging from 262 to 837 percent. Not surprisingly, these are some of the companies that have been active in shale. These independent companies have become the new model for energy investors—so much so that in 2014 BP announced it would operate its U.S. onshore group like an entirely separate entity to help it better compete with "mom-and-pop" shops in shale.

The hierarchies of the big Exxon-like energy companies, their lack of nimbleness, and generally late arrival to the shale boom have led investors and industry observers to wonder—what is the point of being big? Why does one company need to do it all? No one needs to be the biggest guy in the room anymore. No one wants to be Exxon.

But Leon did. And he may be the last man capable of seeing the dream come to fruition. Now, as his son fights to protect his legacy from biographers and from hedge funds keen to force asset sales, it's clear how unique his accomplishment was.

Leon's grave lies in the shadow of the massive Hess building in Woodbridge, New Jersey. You can't miss the former corporate head-quarters from the exit on the New Jersey Turnpike. The building is now for sale, and the gasoline station located at the base of the structure has swapped out its Hess sign for one advertising Marathon's Speedway (see Figure 13.1). (A final irony is that Hess had almost purchased Marathon's gas station and refinery business in 1981, as part of a deal in which Mobil would buy the remainder of the company.) Sixteen years after his death, Leon's legacy is starting to be erased from popular memory. This book is an attempt to capture his life, the company he created, the man he was, and the ways in which his life and industry changed the nation.

Figure 13.1   Hess's former headquarters building in Woodbridge, New Jersey, and the gas station outside of it, now owned by Marathon.
SOURCE: Gerard Trabalka.

Notes

Chapter 1: Hess Family

1. Annual report for the commissioner general of immigration, fiscal year 1905.
2. Annual report for the commissioner general of immigration, fiscal year ended 1906.
3. We use the spelling Ethel, although documents refer to her by other spellings as well, including Etel and Ettel.
4. While some census documents refer to Mr. Hess as Morris, we use the spelling Mores, which was used in his obituary and in documents that the family and company authored.
5. "Mores Hess, 94, Founder of Oil Company Is Dead," *New York Times*. April 12, 1965.
6. "Washington Sees a Bright Outlook," *New York Times*, January 1, 1914.
7. Constance Hess eulogy for Leon Hess.
8. "Asbury Traffic Relief," *New York Times*, July 29, 1928.
9. Asbury Park High School recognizes Leon Hess as a member of its class of 1931, but he identified 1930 as his graduation year in a 1986 deposition.
10. Thomas O'Toole, "Leon Hess: Builder of an Oil Empire," *Washington Post*. March 1, 1976.
11. James R. Norman, "Leon Hess: Can the Bottom-of-the-Barrel Oil Baron Get Back on Top?" *Business Week,* June 29, 1987.
12. Peter Hess Friedland eulogy for Leon Hess; Warren Wilentz eulogy for Leon Hess.

13. "Ex-Democratic Boss Wilentz Dead at 93," *Asbury Park Press*, Thursday, July 7, 1988.

14. "Former Attorney General David Wilentz Dies at 93," *New Jersey Law Journal*, Thursday, July 14, 1988.

15. "Shoeshiner to Senator, They Recall," *News Tribune,* July 8, 1988.

16. "A Legendary Prosecutor Dies at 93," *Record.* July 7, 1988.

17. John Hess eulogy for Leon Hess.

18. O'Toole, "Leon Hess."

19. Bruce Lambert, "Robert Hess, 59, Historian, Dies, Was Brooklyn College President," *New York Times*, January 13, 1992.

20. David Stout, "Robert Wilentz, 69, New Jersey Chief Justice, Dies; Court Aided Women and the Poor," *New York Times,* July 24, 1996.

21. Robert Wilentz eulogy for David Wilentz.

22. John Hess eulogy for Leon Hess.

23. Marlene Hess eulogy for Leon Hess.

24. Marlene Hess eulogy for Leon Hess.

25. Constance Hess eulogy for Leon Hess.

26. Testimonials on Leon Hess.

27. Earl Ganz, "House of Israel: How I Became the Kind of Jew I Am," *Tufts* magazine, Winter 2011.

28. Elizabeth Yancey, "Captain Deerfield and Cheerleaders . . ." *Deerfield Scroll,* undated.

29. Sue Lin and Arianna Markel, "Paris Nets 'Poon Award," *Harvard Crimson,* February 7, 2008.

Chapter 2: Hess at War

1. Dennis Byrd, *Rise and Walk: The Trial and Triumph of Dennis Byrd* (New York: HarperCollins, 1993).

2. Richard C. Biggs and Eric R. Criner, *Spearhead of Logistics: A History of the U.S. Army Transportation Corps* (Fort Eustis, VA: U.S. Army Transportation Center and Washington, DC: Center of Military History, U.S. Army, 1994).

3. H. H. Dunham, *U.S. Army Transportation in the European Theater of Operations 1942–1945.* Historical Unit, Office of Chief of Transportation Army Service Forces. June 1946 (OCROFT Monograph No. 29).

4. Joseph Bykofsky and Harold Larson, *U.S. Army in World War II: The Technical Services; The Transportation Corps: Operations Overseas* (Washington, DC: Office of the Chief of Military History, U.S. Department of the Army, 1957).

5. David P. Colley, *The Road to Victory: The Untold Story of World War II's Red Ball Express* (Dulles, VA: Brassey's, 2000).

6. Hearing of the Subcommittee of the Committee on Interstate and Foreign Commerce, House of Representatives, 79th Congress, 2nd Session, U.S. Government Printing Office, 1946.

7. Testimony of A. P. Frame, director of refining for the Petroleum Administration for War, before the House Subcommittee of the Committee on Interstate and Foreign Commerce, 79th Congress, 2nd Session, April 16, 1946.
8. Statement of Ralph Davies, deputy petroleum administrator, in a hearing before a subcommittee of the Committee on Interstate and Foreign Commerce in the House of Representatives, 79th Congress, 2nd Session. April 17, 1946.

Chapter 3: After the War

1. Transcript of Executive Session, Subcommittee on Multinational Corporations of the Committee on Foreign Relations, January 28, 1974.
2. Thomas O'Toole, "Leon Hess: Builder of an Oil Empire," *Washington Post,* March 1, 1976.
3. Amerada Hess annual report, 1976.
4. Testimony, July 9, 1986, *U.S. Football League v. National Football League.*
5. Testimony of B. A. Hardey, president of the Independent Petroleum Association of America, March 19, 1946, before the Senate Special Committee Investigating Petroleum Resources.
6. Ibid.; testimony of Alfred Jacobsen.
7. Federal Trade Commission report. 1944.
8. U.S. Department of Agriculture, "Farmer Cooperatives in the United States," revised March 1996, www.rd.usda.gov/files/cir1-23.pdf.
9. Amerada annual report, 1959.
10. Amerada Hess annual report, 1971.
11. Daniel Yergin, *The Prize: The Epic Quest for Oil, Money and Power* (New York: Simon & Schuster, 1991).
12. Amerada Hess annual report, 1974.
13. Ibid.
14. Robert Cole, "Gulf Proxy Fight Set by Pickens," *New York Times,* November 1, 1983.

Chapter 4: Amerada

1. Desmond Young, *Member for Mexico: A Biography of Weetman Pearson, First Viscount Cowdray* (London: Cassel, 1966).
2. Lon Tinkle, *Mr. De: A Biography of Everette Lee DeGolyer* (Boston: Little, Brown, 1970).
3. Clyde H. Farnsworth, "A Corporate Profile: Amerada Holds Obstacles to Asset Sale Are Too Great," *New York Times,* December 2, 1962.
4. Transcript of March 27, 1946, testimony before the Special Committee Investigating Petroleum Resources.
5. Testimony before Special Committee Investigating Petroleum Resources.

Chapter 5: Hess Abroad

1. Mike Koehler, "The Story of the Foreign Corrupt Practices Act," *Ohio State Law Journal* 73, no. 5 (December 5, 2012).
2. Paid death notice from Amerada Hess in the *New York Times*, May 9, 1999.
3. Amerada annual report.
4. Frank C. Waddams, *The Libyan Oil Industry* (London: Croom Helm, 1980).
5. Executive Session transcript, hearing on Multinational Petroleum Companies and Foreign Policy, Subcommittee on Multinational Corporations of the Committee on Foreign Relations, October 11, 1973, U.S. Senate, 93rd Congress, 1st and 2nd Sessions.
6. Ibid.
7. J. E. Akins, "The Oil Crisis: This Time the Wolf Is Here," *Foreign Affairs*, April 1973.
8. Transcript of a hearing before the Subcommittee on Multinational Corporations of the Committee on Foreign Relations, January 31, 1974.
9. Chase Manhattan Bank study of capital and exploration expenditures.
10. Pascal Mahvi, *Deadly Secrets of Iranian Princes: Audacity to Act* (Victoria, British Columbia: FriesenPress, 2010).
11. https://www.cia.gov/library/publications/the-world-factbook/geos/ek.html.
12. "Money Laundering and Foreign Corruption: Enforcement and Effectiveness of the Patriot Act Case Study Involving Riggs Bank Report." Prepared by the minority staff of the permanent subcommittee on investigations, July 2004.
13. "Money Laundering and Foreign Corruption: Enforcement and Effectiveness of the Patriot Act." Transcript of July 15, 2004, hearing before the Permanent Subcommittee on Investigations of the Committee on Governmental Affairs, 108th Congress, Second Session.

Chapter 6: Hess in DC

1. "Those Who Gave at Least $100,000 to the GOP," *Washington Post*, January 24, 1989.
2. Hess donation to Jackson in 1972. Disguised by James R. Polk, August 7, 1974.
3. Sworn affidavit, September 14, 1973.
4. Nixon tapes.
5. Memorandum for File Number 500 of John G. Koeltl, February 15, 1974.
6. Morton Mintz and Stephen Isaacs, "CPA May Have Passed Nixon Gift," *Washington Post*, November 25, 1973.
7. Notes from interview of Snyder in Watergate file.
8. September 14, 1973. Sworn affidavit, submitted to the FBI by Roger Oresman.
9. Memorandum of Koeltl, January 8, 1974.

10. Dan Morain, "Oilman Greases Skids for McCain Campaign," *Los Angeles Times*, August 5, 2008.

11. Transcript of March 30, 1976, hearing of the Subcommittee on Merchant Marine of the Senate Commerce Committee.

12. Government Accountability Office report, "Puerto Rico: Characteristics of the Island's Maritime Trade and Potential Effects of Modifying the Jones Act," March 2013, www.gao.gov/assets/660/653046.pdf.

13. March 29, 1976, letter to Senate Commerce Committee Chairman Warren G. Magnuson.

14. Transcript of February 25, 1976, hearing of Subcommittee on Merchant Marine of the Committee on Commerce, U.S. Senate, 94th Congress, 2nd Session.

15. Thomas O'Toole, "Amerada Hess's $400 Million Windfall," *Washington Post*, February 29, 1976.

16. George D. Baker, "The Entitlements Program: Emergency Oil Regulation and Private Proprietary Rights," *Catholic University Law Review* 25, no. 3 (Spring 1976), http://scholarship.law.edu/lawreview/vol25/iss3/7.

17. Transcript of March 30, 1976, hearing.

18. Amerada Hess annual report, 1976.

19. Testimony of Dillard Spriggs, executive vice president of Baker-Weeks & Company, before Senate subcommittee, January 30, 1974.

20. Hearings before the Subcommittee on Multinational Corporations of the Committee on Foreign Relations, U.S. Senate, 93rd Congress, 2nd Session, January 30, 1974.

21. John M. Barry, "2 Firms Listed Outside Carter Price Standard," *Washington Post*, June 15, 1979.

22. Walter Pincus, "Playing Petroleum Robin Hood Proves Difficult for Government," *Washington Post*, February 16, 1981.

Chapter 7: Hess, Refined

1. Thomas O'Toole, Amerada Hess: $400 Million Windfall," *Washington Post*, February 29, 1976.

2. Amerada Hess annual report, 1969.

3. Ralph M. Paiewonsky, *Memoirs of a Governor: A Man for the People* (New York: New York University Press, 1990).

4. *Hovic Islander* newsletter, December 1981.

5. Thomas O'Toole, Amerada Hess: $400 Million Windfall," *Washington Post*, February 29, 1976.

6. Hess Oilgram internal newsletter, December 1979.

7. John Hess eulogy for Leon Hess.

Chapter 8: When You're a Jet

1. Red Smith, "Werblin Reaches Parting of Ways," *Washington Post*, May 25, 1968.
2. "$19 Million Bid Offered for Jets," *United Press International*, June 8, 1978.
3. July 9, 1986, court transcript of testimony in *U.S. Football League v. National Football League*, Southern District of New York.
4. Alex Kroll, "The Last of the Titans," *Sports Illustrated*, September 22, 1969.
5. Bob Addie, "Iselin Races Against Old Taboo," *Washington Post*, November 15, 1972.
6. Joe Namath interview, "Caught in the Draft 1965," *NFL Network*.
7. Addie, "Iselin Races."
8. Austin Murphy, "Down for the Count," *Sports Illustrated*, December 30, 1996/ January 6, 1997.
9. Dave Anderson, "How Hess 'Wouldn't Give Up,'" *New York Times*, February 16, 1997.
10. Bill Parcells and Nunyo Demasio, *Parcells: A Football Life* (New York: Crown Archetype, 2014).
11. Gerald Eskenazi, *Gang Green* (New York: Simon & Schuster, 1998).
12. Mark Cannizzaro, *Tales from the Jets Sideline* (Champaign, IL: Sports Publishing, 2004).
13. *City of New York v. New York Jets Football Club Inc.*, New York Supreme Court.
14. Michael Goodwin, "City Has Lost Jets to Jersey, Koch Declares," *New York Times*, September 29, 1983.
15. Ibid.
16. "Shea in Plea to Jets Owner," *New York Times*, September 19, 1983.
17. Thomas O'Toole, "Leon Hess: Builder of an Oil Empire," *Washington Post*, March 1, 1976.

Chapter 10: Getting and Spending

1. "Forbes 400 List of Wealthiest Americans," Associated Press, October 9, 1989.
2. Hess Foundation Inc. Form 990 for the fiscal year ended November 30, 1971.
3. "Squire N. Bozorth, 67, Adviser to Charities," *New York Times,* November 8, 2002.
4. Elizabeth Myrick, *Hess Foundation: Will This Secretive Foundation Go Beyond Checkbook Philanthropy?* (Washington, DC: National Committee for Responsive Philanthropy, June 2015).
5. "Wind Beneath His Wings," *New York Post*, May 11, 1999.
6. John Hess's eulogy for Leon Hess.
7. Rich Cimini, "The Last Tycoon," *New York Daily News*, May 9, 1999.
8. Marlene Hess's eulogy for Leon Hess.
9. Cimini, "The Last Tycoon."
10. John Hess's eulogy for Leon Hess.
11. Theodore McCarrick's eulogy for Leon Hess.

Chapter 11: A New Hess

1. Suzanne Kapner, "Amerada Hess to Buy Lasmo, British Exploration Concern," *New York Times*, November 7, 2000.
2. Paul Farrelly, "Leon the Gas Guzzler," *Guardian*, November 19, 2000.
3. Ibid.
4. "Amerada Hess Chooses Goldman for $3 Billion New Loans," *Bloomberg News*, November 7, 2000.
5. Mark Lake, "Goldman Concedes to Amerada Hess Request to Keep Credit Line," *Bloomberg*, January 10, 2001.
6. Lisa Margonelli, *Oil on the Brain: Petroleum's Long Strange Trip to Your Tank* (New York: Broadway Books, 2008).
7. Roderick Bruce, "Making Markets," *Energy Risk*, July 2009.
8. Morgan Downey, *Oil 101* (New York: Wooden Table Press, 2009).
9. Louisiana State Museum exhibit on the coffee trade and the port of New Orleans.
10. Lisa Endlich, *Goldman Sachs: The Culture of Success* (New York: Random House, 2013).
11. H. J. Maidenberg, "Goldman, Sachs Buys Big Commodity Dealer," *New York Times*, October 30, 1981.
12. Ann Baldelli, "Hundreds of Hendels Celebrate Their Heritage," *New London Day*, August 22, 1999.
13. James Sterngold, "36 New Goldman Partners Symbolize a Global Outlook," *New York Times,* October 18, 1988.
14. Gina Chon, "Gary Gensler Defends Record as He Leaves CFTC," *Financial Times*, December 30, 2013.
15. Jonathan Leff, "Heat on Hess Raises Specter of Hetco Sale," Reuters, February 19, 2013.
16. "Industry Briefs," *Oil and Gas Journal,* April 13, 1998.
17. John H. Allen, "Treasury Bills Show Rate Drop," *New York Times*, April 1, 1967.
18. Amerada Hess 14A filing with the U.S. Securities and Exchange Commission, March 30, 1998.
19. Gregory Meyer, "Pressure Exposes Hedge Fund within Hess," *Financial Times*, February 18, 2013.
20. "Temporary Tightness, Paradigm Shift, or Speculative Bubble." Paper Delivered at the Annual Energy Policy Conference of the National Capital Area Chapter. U.S. Association for Energy Economics, www.ncac-usaee.org/pdfs/2005Morse.pdf.
21. "Ex-Koch Weather Traders Land at Hess Unit," *Derivatives Week*, May 8, 2000.
22. Paul Lyon, "Hetco Stops Power Trading," *Risk*, December 18, 2002.
23. Amerada Hess Form 10-K, Securities and Exchange Commission, March 29, 1999.
24. Edward L. Morse and Nawaf Obaid, "The $40 a Barrel Mistake," *New York Times*, May 25, 2004.

25. Garry White, "U.S. Trader Hetco Drives Up Oil Price," *Telegraph,* January 19, 2011.
26. In re: *North Sea Brent Crude Oil Futures,* New York Southern District Court, Case 1:13-md-02475-ALC Document 291. Filed November 26, 2014.
27. Chicago Mayor Rahm Emanuel on CNBC, January 15, 2014.
28. Transcript of testimony before the Special Committee Investigating Petroleum Resources, March 21, 1946.
29. www.bp.com/en/global/corporate/sustainability/the-energy-future.html.
30. Tristen Hopper, "Sorry, but Would You Like to Buy Our Oil? Canada Ad Blitz Hits Washington, D.C.," *National Post,* January 23, 2014.
31. Ferriola interview in Bloomberg's "*Oil Buyer's Guide,*" March 20, 2014.
32. Blair interview on MSNBC's "Morning Joe." January 16, 2014.
33. Dave Boyer, "One Word for Oil Fine: Slick," *Philadelphia Inquirer,* November 28, 2005.
34. Scott Gurian, "The List: Top Private Donations Made toward NJ's Hurricane Sandy Recovery," *Spotlight,* November 24, 2014.
35. Matthew Phillips, "Why Hess Stations Recovered Faster from Sandy," *Bloomberg,* November 9, 2012.
36. Tom Fowler, "After Tough Year, Hess CEO Remains Focused," *Wall Street Journal,* February 11, 2014.

Chapter 12: Fight for Control

1. Hess press release, March 4, 2013.
2. Jim Polson and Bradley Olson, "Hess Ends Proxy Fight by Adding Three Elliott Board Nominees," *Bloomberg News,* May 16, 2013.

Chapter 13: The Last

1. Allan Nevins, *John D. Rockefeller: The Heroic Age of American Enterprise* (New York: Charles Scribner's Sons, 1940).
2. Bill Falk, "A Demanding Patriarch," *Newsday,* January 25, 1995.
3. J. Paul Getty, *As I See It: The Autobiography of J. Paul Getty,* reprint (Los Angeles: Getty Publications, 1976).
4. www.bloomberg.com.
5. Ron Chernow, *Titan: The Life of John D. Rockefeller, Sr.* (New York: Random House, 1998).
6. U.S. Energy Information Administration, Petroleum & Other Liquids, U.S. Total Gasoline Retail Sales by Refiners, www.eia.gov/dnav/pet/hist/LeafHandler.ashx?n =PET&s=A103600001&f=A.
7. Brian O'Keefe, "Exxon's Big Bet on Shale," *Fortune,* April 16, 2012, http:// tech.fortune.cnn.com/2012/04/16/exxon-shale-gas-fracking/.

8. Robert A. Hefner III, "The United States of Gas," *Foreign Affairs*, May/June 2014. www.foreignaffairs.com/articles/141203/robert-a-hefner-iii/the-united-states-of-gas#cid=soc-twitter-at-commentary-the_united_states_of_gas-000000.

9. Guy Chazan, "Peter Voser Says He Regrets Shell's Huge Bet on U.S. Shale," *Financial Times*, October 6, 2013, www.ft.com/cms/s/0/e964a8a6-2c38-11e3-8b-0-00144feab7de.html#axzz374wXZNmE.

References

Abramson, Jill. "Return of the Secret Donors." *New York Times*, October 16, 2010.

Addie, Bob. "Iselin Races Against Old Taboo." *Washington Post*, November 15, 1972.

Akins, James. "The Oil Crisis: This Time the Wolf Is Here," *Foreign Affairs*, April 1973.

Allen, John H. "Treasury Bills Show Rate Drop" *New York Times*, April 1, 1967.

Anderson, Dave. "How Hess 'Wouldn't Give Up.'" *New York Times*, February 16, 1997.

Amerada. Annual reports, 1957–1962, 1967.

Amerada Hess. Annual reports 1969–1978, 1980–2014.

Amerada Hess. Paid death notice from Amerada Hess in the *New York Times*, May 9, 1999.

Amerada Hess. Press release, December 29, 2005.

Amerada Hess. Form 10-K. Securities and Exchange Commission. March 29, 1999.

Amerada Hess. Form 14-A. Securities and Exchange Commission. March 30, 1998.

Anderson, Dave. "Leon Hess Deserved More Thrills." *New York Times*, May 8, 1999.

Asbury Park Press. "Ex-Democratic Boss Wilentz Dead at 93." July 7, 1988.

Associated Press. "Amerada Hess Corp. CEO to Retire." January 8, 1986.

Associated Press. "Forbes 400 List of Wealthiest Americans." October 9, 1989.

Baker, George D. "The Entitlements Program: Emergency Oil Regulation and Private Proprietary Rights." *Catholic University Law Review*, Volume 25, Issue 3, Spring 1976. http://scholarship.law.edu/lawreview/vol25/iss3/7.

Baldelli, Ann. "Hundreds of Hendels Celebrate Their Heritage." *New London Day*, August 22, 1999.

Berry, John M. "2 Firms Listed Outside Carter Price Standard." *Washington Post*, June 15, 1979.

Bierman, Stephen, and Joe Carroll. "Hess Agrees to Sell Russian Unit to Lukoil for $2.05 Billion." Bloomberg News, April 1, 2013.

Biggs, Richard C., and Eric R. Criner. *Spearhead of Logistics: A History of the U.S. Army Transportation Corps*. Fort Eustis, VA: U.S. Army Transportation Center and Center of Military History, U.S. Army, Washington, DC, 1994.

Bloomberg News. "Amerada Hess Chooses Goldman for $3 Billion New Loans." November 7, 2000.

Boyer, Dave. "One Word for Oil Fine: Slick." *Philadelphia Inquirer*, November 28, 2005.

Bruce, Roderick. "Making Markets." *Energy Risk Magazine*, July 2009.

Bykofsky, Joseph, and Harold Larson. *U.S. Army in World War II: The Technical Services; The Transportation Corps: Operations Overseas*. Washington, DC: Office of the Chief of Military History, U.S. Department of the Army, 1957.

Byrd, Dennis. *Rise and Walk: The Trial and Triumph of Dennis Byrd*. New York: Harper Collins, 1993.

Cannizzaro, Mark. *Tales from the Jets Sideline*. New York: Sports Publishing, 2004.

Chaban, Matt. "Oil Baron's Slick Move: John Hess Sells Tribeca Digs for $6 Million," *New York Daily News*, December 26, 2013.

Chazan, Guy. "Peter Voser Says He Regrets Shell's Huge Bet on U.S. Shale." *Financial Times*, October 6, 2013. http://www.ft.com/cms/s/0/e964a8a6-2c38-11e3-8b-0-00144feab7de.html#axzz374wXZNmE.

Chernow, Ron. *Titan: The Life of John D. Rockefeller, Sr*. New York: Random House, 1998.

Chon, Gina. "Gary Gensler Defends Record as He leaves CFTC." *Financial Times*, December 30, 2013.

Cimini, Rich. "Carroll's Jets Season Was a Wild Ride." ESPN.com, January 23, 2014.

Cimini, Rich. "The Last Tycoon: Jets Owner Leon Hess Ran His Team the Old-Fashioned Way—with Quiet Dignity." *New York Daily News*, May 9, 1999.

Coffey, Brendan. "Hess CEO Becomes Billionaire Heeding Singer's Call to Sell." Bloomberg News, August 1, 2014.

Colley, David P. *The Road to Victory: The Untold Story of World War II's Red Ball Express*. Dulles, VA: Brassey's, 2000.

D'Amico, Jessica. "Gas Giant's Departure Fuels New Landscape" *New Jersey Sentinel*, June 11, 2015.

De La Merced, Michael. "Dealbook: Elliott Criticizes Hess Chief as Unaccountable." *New York Times*, March 6, 2013.

De La Merced, Michael. "Dealbook: How Elliott and Hess Settled a Bitter Proxy Battle." *New York Times*, May 16, 2013.

Denning, Liam. "Big Oil's Tricky Mix of Shale and Scale—Heard on the Street." *Wall Street Journal*, November 3, 2013.

Derivatives Week. "Ex-Koch Weather Traders Land at Hess Unit." May 8, 2000.

Downey, Morgan. *Oil 101*. New York: Wooden Table Press, 2009.

Dunham, H. H. *U.S. Army Transportation in the European Theater of Operations 1942-1945*. Historical Unit, Office of Chief of Transportation Army Services Forces: June 1946 (OCROFT Monograph No. 29).

Elliott Management Corporation. Press releases, January 29, 2013; March 4, 2013; March 26, 2013; April 4, 2013; April 11, 2014; April 24, 2014; May 1, 2013; May 3, 2013; May 7, 2013; May 13, 2013; May 14, 2013.

Endlich, Lisa. *Goldman Sachs: The Culture of Success*. New York: Random House, 2013.

Eskenazi, Gerald. *Gang Green*. New York: Simon & Schuster, 1998.

Eskenazi, Gerald. "Hess's Address to Jets: You're Full of Wonder." *New York Times*, November 28, 1997.

Eskenazi, Gerald. "Jets Will Remain in New Jersey." *New York Times*, February 7, 1986.

Eskenazi, Gerald. "Leon Hess, Who Built a Major Oil Company and Owned the Jets, Is Dead at 85." *New York Times*, May 8, 1999.

Falk, Bill. "A Demanding Patriarch." *Newsday*, January 25, 1995.

Farnsworth, Clyde H. "A Corporate Profile: Amerada Holds Obstacles to Asset Sale Are Too Great." *New York Times*, December 2, 1962.

Farrelly, Paul. "Leon the Gas Guzzler." *Guardian*, November 19, 2000.

Frankin, Ben A. "Miss Woods's Gift List Links Donors to Corporations." *New York Times*, March 20, 1974.

Fowler, Tom. "After Tough Year, Hess CEO Remains Focused." *Wall Street Journal*, February 11, 2014.

Ganz, Earl. "House of Israel: How I Became the Kind of Jew I Am." *Tufts Magazine*, Winter 2011.

Getty, J. Paul. *As I See It* (reprint). Los Angeles: Getty Publications, 1976.

Gilpin, Kenneth N. "Amerada Chairman Takes Added Title." *New York Times*, January 9, 1986.

Goodwin, Michael. "City Has Lost Jets to Jersey, Koch Declares." *New York Times*, September 29, 1983.

Government Accountability Office. "Puerto Rico: Characteristics of the Island's Maritime Trade and Potential Effects of Modifying the Jones Act." March 2013. http://www.gao.gov/assets/660/653046.pdf.

Gurian, Scott. "The List: Top Private Donations Made Toward NJ's Hurricane Sandy Recovery." *Spotlight*, November 24, 2014.

Hefner, Robert. "The United States of Gas." *Foreign Affairs*, May/June 2014. http://www.foreignaffairs.com/articles/141203/robert-a-hefner-iii/the-united-states-of-gas#cid=soc-twitter-at-commentary-the_united_states_of_gas-000000.

Hess, John B. "United States Energy Policy." Prepared remarks for CERA conference in Houston, March 8, 2011.

Hess Corporation. Press releases, November 2, 2012; March 4, 2013; March 26, 2013; April 4, 2013; April 15, 2013; April 25, 2013; April 25, 2013; April 30, 2013; May 1, 2013; May 3, 2013; May 6, 2013; May 10, 2013; May 13, 2013.

Hess Corporation. 4Q 2012 Earnings Conference Call (transcript), January 30, 2013.

Hess Corporation. Hess Toy Truck Website. "Fun Facts About the Toy Truck."

Hopper, Tristen. "Sorry, But Would You Like to Buy Our Oil? Canada Ad Blitz Hits Washington, D.C.," *National Post*, January 23, 2014.

Janofsky, Michael. "Hess Testifies on Jets' Move." *New York Times*, July 10, 1986.

Janofsky, Michael. "D'Amato Testifies for the U.S.F.L." *New York Times*, May 31, 1986.

Kammerzell, Jaime. "With Hess at the Helm, E&P Shines." *Rigzone*, September 23, 2011.

Kapner, Suzanne. "Amerada Hess to Buy Lasmo, British Exploration Concern." *New York Times*, November 7, 2000.

Koehler, Mike. "The Story of the Foreign Corrupt Practices Act." *Ohio State Law Journal* 73, no. 5 (2012).

Kroll, Alex. "The Last of the Titans." *Sports Illustrated*, September 22, 1969.

Kuperinsky, Amy. "Hess Truck Turns 50 with Mobile Museum (Batteries Included)." NJ.com, November 5, 2014.

Lake, Mark. "Goldman Concedes to Amerada Hess Request to Keep Credit Line." Bloomberg News, January 10, 2001.

Lambert, Bruce. "Robert Hess, 59, Historian, Dies, Was Brooklyn College President." *New York Times*, January 13, 1992.

Leff, Jonathan. "Heat on Hess Raises Specter of Hetco Sale." Reuters, February 19, 2013.

Lin, Sue, and Arianna Markel . "Paris Nets 'Poon Award." *Harvard Crimson*, February 7, 2008.

Lyon, Paul. "Hetco Stops Power Trading." *Risk Magazine*, December 18, 2002.

Mahvi, Pascal. *Deadly Secrets of Iranian Princes: Audacity to Act*. Victoria, British Columbia: FriesenPress, 2010.

Maidenberg, H. J. "Goldman, Sachs Buys Big Commodity Dealer." *New York Times*, October 30, 1981.

Margonelli, Lisa. *Oil on the Brain: Petroleum's Long Strange Trip to Your Tank*. New York: Broadway Books, 2008.

Meyer, Gregory. "Pressure Exposes Hedge Fund within Hess." *Financial Times*, February 18, 2013.

Mintz, Morton. "The Hessians Then and Now." Nieman Watchdog blog, posted August 7, 2008.

Mintz, Morton, and Stephen Isaacs. "CPA May Have Passed Nixon Gift." *Washington Post*, November 25, 1973.

Montville, Leigh. "Off Broadway Joe—Joe Namath, Erstwhile Super Bowl Hero and Playboy and Sometime Actor, Now Has the Best Role of His Life: Family Man." *Sports Illustrated*, July 14, 1997.

Morain, Dan. "Oilman Greases Skids for McCain Campaign." *Los Angeles Times*, August 5, 2008.

Morse, Edward L. "Temporary Tightness, Paradigm Shift, or Speculative Bubble." Paper presented at the Annual Energy Policy Conference of the National Capital Area Chapter, U.S. Association for Energy Economics, April 26, 2005. http://www.ncac-usaee.org/pdfs/2005Morse.pdf.

Morse, Edward L., and Nawaf Obaid. "The $40 a Barrel Mistake." *New York Times*, May 25, 2004.

Murphy, Austin. "Down for the Count." *Sports Illustrated*, December 30, 1996/ January 6, 1997.

Myrick, Elizabeth. "Hess Foundation: Will This Secretive Foundation Go Beyond Checkbook Philanthropy?" National Committee for Responsive Philanthropy, June 2015.

NFL Network. Joe Namath interview. *Caught in the Draft: 1965*, aired April 29, 2015.

Nevins, Allan. *John D. Rockefeller: The Heroic Age of American Enterprise*. New York: Charles Scribner's Sons, 1940.

New Jersey Law Journal. "Former Attorney General David Wilentz Dies at 93." July 14, 1988.

New York Daily News. "The Last Tycoon." May 9, 1999.

New York Post. "Wind Beneath His Wings." May 11, 1999.

New York Southern District Court. "North Sea Brent Crude Oil Futures Litigation." Document 291. November 26, 2014.

New York Supreme Court. *City of New York v. New York Jets Football Club Inc.*, May 11, 1977.

New York Times. "Amerada Merger with Hess Is Set." December 23, 1968.

New York Times. "Asbury Traffic Relief." July 29, 1928.

New York Times. "Hess Buys Up Rest of Jets." February 9, 1984.

New York Times. "Mores Hess, 94, Founder of Oil Company, Is Dead." April 12, 1965.

New York Times. "Shea in Plea to Jet Owner." September 19, 1983.

New York Times. "Susan E. Kessler Exchanges Vows with John Hess." December 16, 1984.

New York Times. "Washington Sees a Bright Outlook." January 1, 1914.

New York Times. "Squire N. Bozorth, 67, Adviser to Charities." November 8, 2002.

News Tribune. "Shoeshiner to Senator, They Recall." July 8, 1988.

Norman, James R. "Leon Hess: Can the Bottom-of-the-Barrel Oil Baron Get Back on Top?" *Business Week*, June 29, 1987.

O'Keefe, Brian. "Exxon's Big Bet on Shale." *Fortune*, April 16, 2012. http://tech.fortune.cnn.com/2012/04/16/exxon-shale-gas-fracking.

O'Toole, Thomas. "Amerada Hess' $400 Million Windfall." *Washington Post*, February 29, 1976.

O'Toole, Thomas. "Leon Hess: Builder of an Oil Empire." *Washington Post*, March 1, 1976.

Oil and Gas Journal. "Industry Briefs." April 13, 1989.

Paiewonsky, Ralph M. *Memoirs of a Governor: A Man for the People*. New York: New York University Press, 1990.

Parcells, Bill, and Nunyo Demasio. *Parcells: A Football Life*. New York: Crown Archetype, 2014.

Petrie, Thomas A. *Following Oil: Four Decades of Cycle-Testing Experiences and What They Foretell About U.S. Energy Independence*. Norman: University of Oklahoma Press, 2014.

Phalon, Richard. "Standard Oil Secondary Issues Stir Guesses on British Portfolio." *New York Times*, August 30, 1965.

Phillips, Matthew. "Why Hess Stations Recovered Faster from Sandy." Bloomberg News, November 9, 2012.

Pincus, Walter. "Playing Petroleum Robin Hood Proves Difficult for Government." *Washington Post*, February 16, 1981.

Polk, James R. "Hess Donation to Jackson in 1972 Disguised." *Washington Star-News*, August 7, 1974.

Pollak, Michael. "Holiday Toys Are Now Prize Collectibles." *New York Times*, November 15, 2004.

Polson, Jim. "Hess Says Singer's Elliott Paying Board to Liquidate Company." Bloomberg News, March 26, 2013.

Polson, Jim. "Elliott Management Increases Hess Stake, Sees Higher Value." Bloomberg News, March 13, 2013.

Polson, Jim. "Hess Shareholder Response Falls Short, Relational Says." Bloomberg News, March 5, 2013.

Polson, Jim. "Hess Tangled Family Ties Targeted in Shareholder Revolt: Energy." Bloomberg News, February 27, 2013.

Polson, Jim, and Bradley Olson. "Hess Ends Proxy Fight by Adding Three Elliott Board Nominees." Bloomberg News, May 16, 2013.

Polson, Jim, Bradley Olson, and David Wethe. "Hess Should Consider Bakken Spin-off, Billionaire Singer Says." Bloomberg News, January 29, 2013.

Polson, Jim, and Jessica Resnick-Ault. "Hess CEO Says Unit Sales 'Not Response' to Activist Shareholders." Bloomberg News, March 4, 2013.

Record. "A Legendary Prosecutor Dies at 93." July 7, 1988.

Resnick-Ault, Jessica, and Jim Polson. "Hess CEO Wants to Keep Assets, Despite Shareholders' Calls." Bloomberg News, January 30, 2013.

Robinson, Matt. "Icahn to Singer Roil Energy Debt Chasing Returns: Credit Markets." Bloomberg News, February 1, 2013.

Rudnitksy, Howard. "It's Not Over Until It's Over." *Forbes*, September 16, 1991.

Russo, Camila. "Evading Singer's Dragnet Means $880,000 Flight: Argentina Credit." Bloomberg News, January 10, 2013.

Sandomir, Richard. "For Hess's Estate, It's a Jets.com." *New York Times*, January 14, 2000.

Sandomir, Richard. "Fan Group Hoping NFL Will Accept Its Bid for Jets." *New York Times*, September 21, 1999.

Sandomir, Richard. "The Jets Fill One Opening: New Owner at $635 Million." *New York Times*, January 12, 2000.

Santora, Marc. "Big Ticket: Sold for $17.25 Million." *New York Times*, June 8, 2012.

Smith, Red. "Werblin Reaches Parting of Ways." *Washington Post*, May 25, 1968.

Star-Ledger. "Norma Wilentz Hess Obituary." April 24, 2010.

Sterngold, James. "36 New Goldman Partners Symbolize a Global Outlook." *New York Times*, October 18, 1988.

Stout, David. "Robert Wilentz, 69, New Jersey Chief Justice, Dies; Court Aided Women and the Poor." *New York Times*, July 24, 1996.

Tinkle, Lon. *Mr. De: A Biography of Everette Lee DeGolyer.* Boston: Little Brown, 1970.

Time Magazine. "Mr. De." December 24, 1956.

Time Magazine. "Scoop Jackson: Running Hard Uphill." February 17, 1975.

U.S. Congress. "Money Laundering and Foreign Corruption: Enforcement and Effectiveness of the Patriot Act Case Study Involving Riggs Bank Report," prepared by the minority staff of the permanent subcommittee on investigations, July 2004.

U.S. Congress. "Money Laundering and Foreign Corruption: Enforcement and Effectiveness of the Patriot Act" (transcript of July 15, 2004, hearing before the Permanent Subcommittee on Investigations of the Committee on Governmental Affairs), 108th Congress, Second Session.

U.S. Congress. Subcommittee of the Committee on Interstate and Foreign Commerce hearing (transcript), House of Representatives, 79th Congress, 2nd Session, U.S. Government Printing Office, April 17, 1946.

U.S. Congress. Subcommittee on Merchant Marine of the Committee on Commerce (transcript), U.S. Senate, 94th Congress, 2nd Session. February 25, 1976.

U.S. Congress. Subcommittee on Multinational Corporations of the Committee on Foreign Relations hearing, Executive Session (transcript). U.S. Senate, 93rd Congress, 1st and 2nd Sessions. October 11, 1973.

U.S. Congress. Subcommittee on Multinational Corporations of the Committee on Foreign Relations hearing, Executive Session (transcript), January 28–31, 1974.

U.S. Court of Appeals, 4th Circuit. *U.S. Football League v. National Football League.* Testimony, July 9, 1986.

U.S. Department of Agriculture, "Farmer Cooperatives in the United States." Revised March 1996. http://www.rd.usda.gov/files/cir1-23.pdf.

U.S. Department of Labor. *Annual Report for the Commissioner-General of Immigration, Fiscal Year Ended 1905.*

U.S. Department of Labor. *Annual Report for the Commissioner-General of Immigration, Fiscal Year Ended 1906.*

U.S. District Court, Southern District of New York. Court transcript of testimony in *U.S. Football League v. National Football League*, July 9, 1986.

U.S. Football League et al. v. National Football League et al., U.S. Court of Appeals for the Second Circuit, decision March 10, 1988.

U.S. Football League et al. v. National Football League et al., U.S. District Court for the Southern District of New York, decision October 2, 1986.

U.S. Senate. The Role of Futures Markets in Oil Pricing, Hearing of the U.S. Senate Committee on Governmental Affairs, November 1, 1990.

U.S. Senate. Testimony of B. A. Hardey, president of the Independent Petroleum Association of America, March 19, 1946, before the Senate Special Committee Investigating Petroleum Resources.

United Press International. "$19 Million Bid Offered for Jets." June 8, 1978.

Van Voris, Bob. "Argentina Asks U.S. Supreme Court to Hear Bond-Default Case." Bloomberg News, June 26, 2013.

Velsey, Kim. "Co-op of Former New York Jets Owner, Oil Baron Leon Hess Scores $17M." *New York Observer*, June 4, 2012.

Waddams, Frank C. *The Libyan Oil Industry*. London: Croom Helm, 1980.

Washington Post. "Those Who Gave at Least $100,000 to the GOP." January 24, 1989.

Washington Star-News. "Secret Panel Data Show Donor Hid Gifts to Jackson's '72 Race." August 8, 1974.

Wethe, David, and Bradley Olson. "Hess Exits Refining as Billionaire Singer Seeks Directors." Bloomberg News, January 28, 2013.

White, Garry. "U.S. Trader Hetco Drives Up Oil Price." *Telegraph*, January 19, 2011.

Wirthman, Lisa. "Handing It Down: The Changing Dynamics of Family Businesses." *Forbes*, September 25, 2013.

Yancey, Elizabeth. "Captain Deerfield and Cheerleaders ..." *Deerfield Scroll*. Undated.

Yergin, Daniel. *The Prize: The Epic Quest for Oil, Money and Power*. New York: Simon & Schuster, 1991.

Young, Desmond. *Member for Mexico: A Biography of Weetman Pearson, First Viscount Cowdray*. London: Cassel, 1966.

Acknowledgments

The authors would like to thank everyone who had to listen to us enthuse about all things Hess for the past few years, especially those poor souls stuck next to us at dinner parties who made the mistake of asking us what we were working on. We would also like to thank our employers for the time and space to do this work and our agent, Andrew Wylie, for supporting the idea in its infancy.

Tina wishes to extend special appreciation to family and friends, including Rachel Horwood, Peter Riley, Dawn Kopecki, Margalit Edelman, Shara Arnofsky, and James Tracey. Thanks to colleagues who covered for me, encouraged me, or just listened politely while I moaned, including Tim Coulter, Ed Greenspon, Reg Gale, Reto Gregori, John Micklethwait, Matt Winkler, Laurie Hays, Susan Warren, Simon Casey, Carlos Caminada, Stephen Cunningham, Jim Efstathiou, Steven Frank, Jasmina Kelemen, Robin Saponar, and Will Wade. For research help, thanks to historian Richard Killblane of the U.S. Army Transportation Museum and Kevin Reilly of the National Archives in New York City as well as staff of New York's Science, Industry and Business Library, the National Archives in Maryland and the Library of Congress. I would dedicate this book to Toby, but I'm trying to avoid becoming a crazy dog lady.

Jessica wishes to thank her family and friends, including Stephen Ault, who read early drafts, Daniel Resnick-Ault, a lifelong Hess Truck enthusiast, and especially Margery Resnick for endless support allowing me to work on the book. Thanks to all of the colleagues at both Bloomberg and Reuters who allowed me time to work on the book, and listened to me discussing it endlessly, especially to Jonathan Leff and Josephine Mason, the New York energy team, Terry Wade, and the Houston Bureau. Special thanks to my husband, Peter Gimbel, and daughter, Helen, who allowed me to slip away many weekends to dedicate time to this effort.

About the Authors

Tina Davis is an editor for *Bloomberg News* and has been writing about energy issues for almost two decades. She previously worked for the *Economist*, the *Sunday Times of London*, and the *Energy Daily*.

Jessica Resnick-Ault is an editor for Reuters and has been writing about energy for more than a decade. She previously worked for *Bloomberg News*, *Dow Jones Newswires*, and the *Providence Journal*.

Index